HONEY FROM THE ROCK

HONEY FROM THE ROCK

*Sixteen Jews Find
the Sweetness of Christ*

COMPILED BY
ROY SCHOEMAN

IGNATIUS PRESS   SAN FRANCISCO

Unless otherwise noted, Scripture quotations (except those within
citations) have been taken from the Revised Standard Version
of the Holy Bible, Catholic Edition. The Revised Standard Version
of the Holy Bible: the Old Testament, © 1952; the Apocrypha,
© 1957; the New Testament, © 1946; the Catholic Edition of the
Old Testament, incorporating the Apocrypha, © 1966;
the Catholic Edition of the New Testament, © 1965, by the
Division of Christian Education of the National Council
of the Churches of Christ in the United States of America.
All rights reserved.

Cover art:
Moses Striking the Rock and the Fall of Manna, 1543–1545.
(Detail, left panel)
Agnolo Bronzino (1503–1572)
Chapel of Eleonora of Toledo, Palazzo Vecchio, Florence, Italy
© Scala / Art Resource, New York

and

Christ the Redeemer
Rio di Janeiro
©iStockphoto

Cover design by Roxanne Mei Lum

© 2007 by Ignatius Press, San Francisco
All rights reserved
ISBN 978-1-58617-115-5
Library of Congress Control Number 2006924091
Printed in the United States of America ∞

CONTENTS

PREFACE

Honey from the Rock. The image is a rich one, particularly so from a Jewish-Catholic perspective. The phrase comes from Psalm 81, in which the Jewish people are promised that if they turn to God with their whole hearts, they will receive honey from the rock:

Sing aloud to God our strength;
    shout for joy to the God of Jacob!
Raise a song, sound the timbrel,
    the sweet lyre with the harp. . . .
He made it a decree in Joseph,
    when he went out over the land of Egypt.
I hear a voice I had not known:
"I relieved your shoulder of the burden;
    your hands were freed from the basket.
In distress you called, and I delivered you;
    I answered you in the secret place of thunder;
    I tested you at the waters of Meribah. . . .
    O Israel, if you would but listen to me! . . .
I am the LORD your God,
    who brought you up out of the land of Egypt.
    Open your mouth wide, and I will fill it. . . .
O that my people would listen to me,
    that Israel would walk in my ways! . . .
I would feed you with the finest of the wheat,
    and with honey from the rock I would satisfy you."

               (Ps 81:1–2, 5–7, 8b, 10, 13, 16)

The psalm reveals God's tender love for His people, the Jewish people. He reminds them of the protective love He showed for them in rescuing them from the land of Egypt, and then immediately reminds them of Meribah. For Meribah was where, shortly after the Jews had fled Egypt and entered the desert, they lost confidence in God and were convinced that they had been abandoned to die of thirst in the desert. It was there that they challenged Moses, "Why did you bring us up out of Egypt, to kill us and our children and our cattle with thirst?" (Ex 17:3), at which point God told Moses to "take in your hand the rod ... [and] strike the rock, and water shall come out of it, that the people may drink" (Ex 17:5–6).

At Meribah God gave them water to drink, which was enough to sustain life. But in this psalm God promises ever so much more: that when Jews turn to Him with their whole hearts, He will give them honey—sweetness itself—rather than water to drink.

And this was precisely the experience of the Jews whose stories fill this book. They recount lives in which, before they found Christ, something essential—*the* essential—was missing from their lives, making them feel like the Jews of the exodus, crossing the desert, dying of thirst. Like the Jews of the exodus, they too gave up believing that God knew them and loved them, or, in most cases, even existed. They were figuratively, and in several cases literally, dying from their desperate "thirst" to know the real meaning in life—to know God, to love Him, to serve Him. And then, when through an unmerited gift of grace, God Himself— our God, our Lord, our Savior, our Messiah, our born-Jewish Jesus—revealed Himself to them, He not only gave them *water* to drink, to sustain them in their crossing of this desert of exile on earth on the way to the Promised

Land, Heaven, He did ever so much more than that. In the overflowing richness of the intimacy with Him that He made available through the sacraments of the Catholic Church, it was not just *water*, but *honey*, a river of pure sweetness, that He gave them to drink, truly honey from the rock.

It is no coincidence that the phrase immediately preceding "honey from the rock" is one that, in a currently popular Communion hymn, is used to refer to the Blessed Sacrament—"the gift of finest wheat".[1] For it is precisely the "gift of finest wheat", the most Holy Eucharist, which is ultimate honey from the rock: pure distilled consolation, distilled joy, distilled love, the Body, Blood, soul, and divinity of our Messiah Himself. Before becoming Catholic, it was as though trying to *know* God was like trying to suck water from a rock, maybe at times getting enough to moisten one's lips; but after becoming Catholic, once participating in the sacramental life of the Church, those few sparse drops became a geyser, a gusher, a tidal wave of grace sweeping one away in a flood of consolation, of intimacy with God Himself. Honey from the rock indeed—a raging river of honey, flooding one away into a sea of divine intimacy.

Some of the "converts"[2] in this book came from secularized, liberal, or even atheistic Jewish backgrounds, while others came from Orthodoxy[3] or even Hasidism. Some were

[1] It is, of course, only wheat prior to the Consecration, after which "there takes place a change of the whole substance of the bread into the substance of the body of Christ our Lord and of the whole substance of the wine into the substance of his blood." Council of Trent (1551), Denzinger 1642.

[2] "Converts" is, of course, the usual term, but most of those in this book consider(ed) themselves "fulfilled Jews" rather than converts, since they did not "turn away" from Judaism, but rather they entered Judaism's completed or fulfilled form, the Catholic Church, i.e. "post-messianic" Judaism.

[3] Judaism in the United States is divided into three principle groups: Orthodox Jews, the most observant of traditional Jewish practices and laws;

unschooled in Judaism, while others were among the most highly trained Jews of their day. Some were rich and wildly successful, others down and out. But one thing they all had in common was a profound (dare I say, archetypically Jewish?) longing for God that gave them no peace until they found God Himself, peace Himself in the Catholic Church. They were all dying of thirst in the desert—some actually at the point of suicide in their frustrated despair at failing to find God. And it was at that point they found so much more than they had suspected even existed. Longing for a sip of water in the parched desert, they found a river of honey, honey from the rock.

But I will let them tell their own stories.[4] They are all unique. Alphonse Ratisbonne, a wealthy aristocratic Jewish French banker, was converted on the eve of his marriage by an unexpected, unsought, and most unwelcome (before the fact; most welcome after the fact!) apparition of the Blessed Mother herself and proceeded to call off his wedding to become a priest in the Holy Land. Hermann Cohen, one of the foremost musicians of his day, lived a wild life of fame and sensual indulgence until he was converted by an overpowering experience of the Blessed Sacrament. Rabbi Zolli, the Chief Rabbi of Rome, had an experience of Jesus while he was celebrating the Yom Kippur liturgy in the synagogue there, and he knew on the spot that was his last time officiating as Rabbi. Charlie Rich, a profoundly devout

---

Conservative Jews, who are somewhat less so; and Reform Jews, the least traditionally observant of the three groups. In addition there are the Hasidim, the "ultra-Orthodox", who are by far the strictest in their practices and usually live in separate communities.

[4] All of the accounts in this book are based on the converts' own words, except that of Sister Katzmann, which is an account written by her religious community.

Hasidic Jew from Hungary, lost his faith on the streets of New York City and was converted by an extraordinary experience in front of a stained glass window of Jesus in an otherwise empty church. And on and on and on—sixteen such stories, as different as the individuals involved, but at the same time with haunting similarities.

In today's world of soft drinks, sugar, and ice cream, we may not appreciate honey the same way as did the Jews of three thousand years ago, who knew nothing else as sweet. Perhaps those born Catholic, in a somewhat analogous way, have a harder time fully appreciating the unique gift of the Catholic Church than do those who, like the Jews in this book, went through much of their lives wishing and hoping, but not really believing, that they could have intimacy with God. May the deep appreciation of the Jews in this book for the "honey from the rock" they eventually found sharpen the taste buds of those who always have lived with the taste of it, so to speak, in their mouths; and may it inspire those still wandering in the desert to strike the rock, receive the rivers of milk and honey waiting for them, and "taste and see the sweetness of the Lord" (Ps 34:8).[5]

[5] This wording is Charlie Rich's translation. Having grown up as a Hasidic Jew, he read the Psalms in the original Hebrew.—ED.

"Remember, O Most Gracious
Virgin Mary . . ."

Alphonse Ratisbonne

*Alphonse Ratisbonne was born in 1814 into a wealthy and aristo-
cratic Jewish family in Alsace, France. Endowed with exceptional intelligence and charm, he seemed destined for a brilliant career in the
family's bank. Then, at the age of twenty-seven, shortly before his marriage, the Blessed Virgin Mary appeared to him, and everything
changed. He immediately entered the Catholic Church, became a priest,
and spent the remainder of his life in the Holy Land, establishing
religious communities and charitable works, and working and praying for the conversion of the Jews. Fortunately, he left a lengthy letter
describing his conversion—one of the most dramatic of modern times—
from which the following is drawn. It is followed by an extract from
another account written by his friend Theodore de Bussières, who was
an eyewitness to many of the events.*

I began my schooling on the benches of the grammar school
of Strasbourg, where I made more progress in the corrup-
tion of the heart, than in the training of intelligence. Then,

From Marie Théodore Renouard Bussières, *Conversion de M. Marie-
Alphonse Ratisbonne: Relation Authentique* (Paris: A. Bray, 1859). The original
letter was addressed to M. Dufriche-Desgenettes, director of the Archconfraternity of Our Lady of Victories.

I

around 1825 (I was born on May 1, 1814), my brother Theodore, on whom great hopes were laid, declared himself a
Christian; and, soon after, in spite of the most fervent pleas
and the great sadness which he caused, he went even further: he became a priest and exercised his ministry in the
same city before the inconsolable eyes of my family. As young
as I was, this behavior of my brother revolted me and I
began to hate his cassock and his character. Raised among
young Christians who were as indifferent as I was, I had till
then neither sympathy nor antipathy for Christianity, but
the conversion of my brother, which I saw as inexplicable
madness, made me to believe in the fanaticism of the Catholics, and I was horrified by it.

I was withdrawn from the college in order to be placed
in a Protestant institution, where the sons of the best Protestant families went to be trained for the fashionable life of
Paris and to give themselves over to pleasure far more than
to science. More by luck than by merit, I nonetheless managed to attain a Bachelor of Arts degree.

I was the master of my family inheritance, because I lost
my mother in infancy, and a few years later, my father. I
was left with a kindhearted uncle, the patriarch of my family, who being childless, lavished all his affection on the
children of his brother and became a second father to me.

This uncle, extremely well known in the financial world
for his integrity and exceptional talent, wanted me to join
the bank of which he was the director, but I first got my
law degree in Paris, and then, with my lawyer's diploma
and gown, was called back to Strasbourg by my uncle who
tried everything to keep me by his side. I could not number all the signs of his prodigality: horses, carriages, voyages, a thousand generosities were shown me, and he would
not refuse me any caprice. To these signs of his affection

my uncle added a more positive proof of his confidence: he gave me power of attorney over his firm and promised me, in addition, a partnership—a promise that he fulfilled on January 1, 1842. It was in Rome that I received the news.

My uncle reproached me only one thing—my frequent trips to Paris. "You are too fond of the Champs-Élysées", he would say kindly. He was right. I loved only pleasures; business irritated me, the atmosphere of offices suffocated me; I thought that we are in the world to enjoy it; and, even though a certain prudishness kept me away from the basest pleasures and company, I nonetheless dreamed only of parties and enjoyments, which I indulged in with passion.

Happily, at this time a good work presented itself to me, which I took warmly to heart. It was the "regeneration" of poor Jews, as it was inappropriately called, since I now understand that something more than money is needed to regenerate a people without faith. But at the time I believed in this form of regeneration, and I became one of the most zealous members of the Society to Find Work for Young Jews, a society that my brother the priest had founded in Strasbourg fifteen years earlier, and which had survived despite a shortage of resources.

So I worked hard on behalf of my poor coreligionists, even though I had no religion. I was a Jew in name only; I did not even believe in God. I never opened a religious book, and neither in my uncle's house nor at my brothers' and sisters', was the least prescription of Judaism observed.

A great void was in my heart, and I was not in the least happy, in the midst of an abundance of riches. Something was missing, but this, too, was given to me—or at least so I thought.

I had a niece, the daughter of my older brother, who was destined for me since we were both children. She grew in grace under my eyes, and in her I saw my whole future, and the hope of all the happiness that was to be mine. This is not the place to sing the praises of the one who was my fiancée. It would be useless for those who do not know her, but those who do, know that it would be difficult to imagine a sweeter, more lovable or gracious girl. She seemed to me an entirely special creature, made uniquely to complete my existence, and when the wishes of my entire family, as well as our own mutual feelings, finally set the date for this so-long-desired marriage, I thought that finally nothing more was lacking for my happiness.

In fact, after the celebration of my engagement, I saw my entire family overflowing with joy. My sisters were so happy! They had only one reproach, that I loved my fiancée too much, and they claimed to be jealous, for I must say here that there are few families more loving than mine. The most intimate union, the tenderest love, reigns and will always reign between my brothers and sisters, a love that almost amounts to idolatry. Oh, my sisters are so good, so loving! Why are they not Christian?

There was only one member of my family that I hated: my brother Theodore. But nonetheless he too loved us; his religious habit repelled me; his presence offended me; his somber and serious words made me angry. One year before my engagement, I could no longer restrain my feelings, and I expressed them in a letter to him that should have severed forever any relations between us. This was the occasion: a baby being at the point of death, my brother Theodore was not afraid openly to ask the parents for permission to baptize him, and may have been about to do so, when I found out about it. I saw the undertaking as shameful and despicable; I wrote to the priest that he should go after adults and not infants, and I accompanied the words with so many invectives and threats that still today I am amazed that my brother did not say one word in return. He continued relations with the rest of the family, but, as for me, I no longer wanted to see him. I nourished a bitter hatred against priests, churches, monasteries, and above all against the Jesuits. The mere name provoked my fury.

After this incident, I had no more contact with Theodore, I thought no more of him, I forgot him . . . all the while that he, he was praying for me!

I must note here a certain revolution in my religious ideas during the period of my engagement. As I said, I believed in nothing, and in this total nothingness, in this negation of all faith, I found myself in perfect accord with my friends, Catholic or Protestant, but the sight of my fiancée awoke in me a mysterious sense of the dignity of man; I began to believe in the immortality of the soul; even more, I instinctively began to pray to God. I thanked Him for my happiness, yet I was not really happy. I could not account for my own feelings; I saw my fiancée as my good angel, and often told her so; and, in effect, the thought of her raised my heart toward a God that I did not know, and to whom I had never prayed.

It seemed appropriate, given that my fiancée was only sixteen years old, to delay the wedding, so it was decided that I would take an extended tour while awaiting the hour of our union. I did not know in what direction to head; one of my sisters, who lived in Paris, wanted me close to her; a very good friend invited me to Spain. I resisted the entreaties of several others, who presented me seductive offers, and finally settled on the idea of going first to Naples, then to spend the winter in Malta to build up my delicate heath, and to then return via the Orient. I even took with me some letters of introduction for Constantinople, and I left near the end of November 1841. I was to return at the start of the following summer.

Oh, how sad was my departure! I left behind a beloved fiancée, an uncle who lived for me, sisters, brothers, nieces, and nephews whose company was my greatest delight. I left behind the trade schools run by the Society to Find Work for Young Jews, and the poor Israelites with whom I was so actively involved. Finally, I left behind so many friends who loved me, childhood friends I could never leave without shedding tears, because I loved them, and I still love them!

Leaving alone on a long voyage! The idea threw me into a deep melancholy. "But", I said to myself, "perhaps God will send me a friend along the way".

I remember two peculiar events that marked the last days before my departure, the memories of which strike me strongly today. I wanted, before embarking on my voyage, to sign a large stack of receipts for the Society to Find Work. I dated them ahead, to January 15, and exhausted from writing this date so many times, I said in putting down my pen, "God knows where I will be on January 15; it might be the day of my death!" That day found me in Rome, and that day was for me the dawn of a new life!

The other notable occurrence was a meeting of important Jews who got together to discuss ways to reform Judaism and adapt it to the spirit of the times. I attended this gathering, at which each gave his opinion on the proposed improvements. There were as many opinions as participants and much discussion. They considered what suited man, the requirements of the age, the dictates of public opinion, the ideas of civilization; all sorts of things were taken into account. One thing alone was forgotten, the law of God. That was not even an issue; the very name of God was not spoken a single time, nor was the name of Moses or the name of the Bible.

My own opinion was to abandon all forms of the religion, relying neither on books or on men, and to let each practice his faith however he understood it. This seemed to me the highest wisdom with respect to religion; I was very progressive, you see! We dispersed, having accomplished nothing.

One Jew, more sensible than I, made this remarkable statement that I recount exactly: "We must hurry out of this old temple, which is falling apart all around us, if we don't want soon to be buried under its ruins!" Words full of truth, that every Jew today repeats under his breath. But, alas! It has been eighteen centuries since they left their own temple, yet they do not enter the new temple whose doors are open before them.

Finally I left. Leaving Strasbourg, I wept a great deal; I was troubled by a host of fears, a thousand strange forebodings. Arriving at the first stop, cries of joy mixed with music in the open air pulled me from my reveries. It was a village wedding, joyously and noisily exiting from the church to the sound of flutes and country violins. The wedding party surrounded my car, as though to invite me to take part in their joy. "Soon it will be my turn!" I cried. And this thought reawoke all my gaiety.

I stopped a few days in Marseille, where my relatives and friends festively celebrated my arrival. I could barely pull myself away from their gracious hospitality.

The boat, before arriving in Naples, made a stop at Città Vecchia. As we were entering the port, the fort's cannon thundered forcefully. I asked with malicious curiosity the reason for this sound of war in the peaceful lands of the Pope. I was told, "It's the Feast of the Immaculate

Conception!" I shrugged my shoulders, not wanting to go ashore.

The next day, with the smoke of Vesuvius sparkling in the light of a magnificent sun, we docked at Naples. Never has a scene from nature dazzled me more than the glorious images of Heaven that the artists and poets presented me there, and I contemplated them avidly. I spent a month in Naples seeing, and writing about, everything. Most of all I wrote against the religion and the priests who, in this happy country, seemed to me entirely out of place. Oh! the blasphemies in my diary! If I speak of them here, it is to reveal the baseness of my spirit. I wrote to Strasbourg that on Vesuvius I drank the *lacryma christi* to the health of Father Ratisbonne and that those tears did me good. I dare not retell here the horrible pun that I allowed myself at the time. My fiancée asked me if I shared the opinion of those who say, "See Naples and die." I replied, "No, but see Naples and live; live to see it again." Such was my state of mind.

I had no desire to go to Rome, even though two friends of my family, whom I often saw, eagerly pressed me. These were M. Coulmann, a Protestant and the former Deputy of Strasbourg, and Baron de Rothschild, whose family in Naples showered me with hospitality. I could not yield to their advice. My fiancée wanted me to go straight to Malta, and sent me an order from my doctor telling me to pass the winter there, and strictly forbidding me to go to Rome on account of the malignant diseases that my doctor said were rife there.

Thus I had more than enough reasons to avoid Rome even if it had been on my itinerary. I thought of going there on my return, and I got on board the *Mongibello*, that was to take me to Sicily. A friend came onboard with me and promised to return at the time of departure to say good-bye. He came, but did not find me at the rendez-vous. If ever M. de Rechecourt learns the reason that he missed me, my rudeness will be explained, and he will undoubtedly forgive me.

M. Coulmann put me in touch with a likeable and worthy man who was, like me, to make the journey to Malta; I was happy to meet him, and he told me, "Ah! There's the friend that Heaven sent me!"

But by the first of the year, the boat had not yet left. That day dawned for me under the saddest conditions. I was alone in Naples without receiving the felicitations of anyone, without having anyone to hug in celebration. I thought of my family, of the good wishes and parties that surrounded at such a time my good uncle. I shed tears, the gaiety of the Neapolitans only adding to my sadness. I went out to distract myself, mechanically following the flow of the crowd. I arrived at the central square and found myself, I do not know how, at the door of a church. I entered. A Mass was being said, I believe. Whatever it was, I stayed standing, leaning against a column, and my heart seemed to dilate and breathe in an unknown atmosphere; I prayed in my own way, without paying attention to what was going on around me. I prayed for my fiancée, for my uncle, for my dead father, for the good mother whom I lost so young, for all those who were dear to me, and I asked God for guidance in my projects to better the condition of the Jews, a thought that ceaselessly pursued me.

My sadness left me like a dark cloud that the wind breaks up and chases far away; and my entire interior, flooded with an inexpressible peace, felt a consolation like that which I would have experienced if a voice had said to me, "Your prayer has been answered!" Oh! yes, it was answered a hundredfold and beyond anything I dreamt, because the last

day of that very month, I was to solemnly receive baptism
in a church in Rome!

But how did I end up in Rome? I cannot explain it, I do
not understand it myself. I think I took the wrong street,
because instead of arriving at the reservation office for Palermo, where I was going, I ended up at the stagecoach
office for Rome. I entered and bought a seat. I sent word
to M. Vigne, the friend who was to accompany me to Malta,
that I could not resist taking a short excursion to Rome,
and that I would positively return to Naples in time to leave
again on *January 20.* I was wrong to promise, because
although man proposes, God disposes, and the date of January 20 was to be marked in a different way in my life.

Rome was not at all, at first, what I hoped. I had in any
case so few days to devote to this impromptu excursion,
that I hurried to devour somehow all of the ancient and
modern attractions that the city offers to a tourist's greed. I
piled them up helter-skelter in my memory and my diary.
I visited with a monotonous admiration the museums, the
circuses, the churches, the catacombs, the uncountable mar-
vels of Rome. . . .

On January 8, I heard a voice call my name on the
street—it was a childhood friend, Gustave de Bussières. I
was happy to see him, because my loneliness weighed on
me. We went to eat at his father's house, and in this sweet
company, I felt some of the joy that one feels when, in a
foreign country, you rediscover vivid memories of your
homeland.

As I was entering the room, M. Theodore de Bussières,
the eldest son of this honorable family, was just leaving. I
did not personally know Baron Theodore, but I knew that
he was a friend of my brother, his namesake; I knew that
he had left Protestantism to become Catholic. That was

enough to inspire in me a profound antipathy. It seemed to me that he held toward me the same feeling. Nevertheless, as M. Theodore de Bussières was known for his travels in the Orient and in Sicily, which he had published, it would be advisable for me, before undertaking the same routes, to ask him for some pointers. Whether for that reason, or mere politeness, I expressed my intention to pay him a visit. He replied kindly and added that he had just received a letter from Father Ratisbonne, and he gave me the new address of my brother. "I thank you for it," I told him, "even if I have no intention to use it."

We stood there, and in leaving, I complained to myself that now I would have to pay a useless visit and waste some precious time, which I did not have to spare. I continued running around Rome all day, except for two hours that I spent in the morning with Gustave, and evening relaxation at the theater or a ball. My conversation with Gustave was animated, because, as we had been in the same boarding school, the smallest memories furnished inexhaustible motives for laughter and chatter.

But he was a zealous and enthusiastic Protestant, as the Pietists[1] from Alsace tend to be. He boasted of the superiority of his sect over all other Christian sects, and tried to convert me, which amused me greatly, because I thought that it was only the Catholics who had the mania of proselytism. Most often I responded with jokes, but one time, to humor his vain attempts, I promised that if I ever felt like converting, it would be to Pietism. His pleas that I remain in Rome were useless.

[1] Pietism originated in Alsace in the early seventeenth century as a movement within Lutheranism that reacted against a perceived over-emphasis on dogma and Church hierarchy in favor of personal devotional life and a lay-run Church.

Some other friends in Rome tried to get me to decide to stay in Rome for the Carnival, but I feared to displease my fiancée, and M. Vigne was waiting for me in Naples, from where we were to part on January 20.

So I set out to profit from the last hours of my stay by finishing my program. I went to the Campidoglio and visited the church of Aracoeli. The imposing build of the church, the solemn chants that echoed in its vast interior, and the history that awoke in me from the very ground underfoot, all produced in me a profound impression. I was moved, penetrated, transported, and my guide, perceiving my agitation, looked at me coldly and said that more than once he has noticed this reaction in foreigners who visit the Aracoeli.

Descending from the Campidoglio my guide had me cross the Jewish Ghetto. There I felt an entirely different emotion, one of pity and indignation. What! I said to myself at the sight of this spectacle of poverty, is this then that famous charity which Rome proclaims so loudly! I shuddered with horror, and I asked whether, for having killed one man eighteen centuries ago, an entire people deserved such barbarous treatment and such endless discrimination. Alas! I did not know then this one man! And I did not know of the bloody cry that this people had shouted, a cry that I dare not repeat here, and that I wish never repeated. I prefer to recall that other cry, exhaled from the Cross, "Forgive them, my God, for they know not what they do!"

I let my family know what I had seen and felt. I remember having written that I would prefer to be among the oppressed than in the camp of the oppressors. I returned to the Campidoglio, where there was a lot of commotion at the Aracoeli, for a ceremony to be held the next day. I asked what was the purpose for all of the preparations, and was told that they were preparing for the baptism of two Jews. I was unable to express the indignation that seized me at these words, and when my guide asked if I wanted to attend, I cried, "Me! Me! Attend such an infamy! No, never; I would be unable to restrain myself from throwing myself at the baptizers and the baptizees!"

I can say, without fear of exaggeration, that never in my life was I more embittered against Christianity than after my sight of the ghetto. I could not stop blaspheming. I still had some good-bye visits to make, and the one to Baron de Bussières kept coming to mind, as an unwelcome obligation that I had needlessly imposed on myself. Happily I had not asked his address, and having such a fine excuse delighted me.

It was January 15, and I was on my way to buy my seat in the coach for Naples; my departure was to be on the 17th, at three in the morning. I had two days left, and I would use them on new excursions and errands. But in leaving a bookstore where I had been looking at some works on Constantinople, I ran into a servant of the father of Theodore de Bussières, who greeted me and stopped me. I then asked him for the address of Theodore de Bussières; he answered in an Alsatian accent, "Piazza Nicosia, number 38".

So then I had to, whether I wanted to or not, make the visit. Nevertheless I resisted twenty times more. Finally I scribbled a note on my visiting card and set out. I looked for Piazza Nicosia, and after a lot of detours and circles, I finally arrived at number 38. It was the door exactly next to the coach office where I had bought my seat earlier in the day. I had taken a long route to arrive from where I had just left; the path of more than one man's life! But from this same spot where I again found myself, I was to depart again on an entirely different path!

My entry into the house of de Bussières made me laugh, because the servant, instead of just taking the visiting card I held in my hand, announced my entry and brought me into the parlor. I hid my annoyance, and for good or ill, put on a smile and seated myself beside the Baroness de Bussières, who was surrounded by her little girls, as graceful and sweet as Raphael's angels. The conversation, at first vague and superficial, quickly took on the colors of all the passion with which I recounted my impressions of Rome.

I imagined Baron de Bussières to be devout in the pejorative sense that one can give to this word, and I was greatly relieved to have the chance to beat my drum about the state of the Jews in Rome. This was a relief for me, but these complaints put the conversation on religious ground. De Bussières spoke about the grandeur of Catholicism; I responded with the ironies and accusations that I had so often read or heard; yet I put a brake on my impious verve out of respect for Mme. de Bussières and the faith of the children who were playing at our feet. Finally M. de Bussières said to me, "So, since you detest such superstition, and you profess such liberal doctrines, since you are such a strong and enlightened spirit, would you have the courage to submit yourself to an entirely innocent test?"

"What test?"

"To wear an object that I will give you.... Here! It is a medal of the Blessed Virgin Mary. This seems quite ridiculous to you, no? But as to me, I attach a great value to this medal."

The proposition, I confess, stunned me with its childishness. My first reaction was to laugh, shrugging my shoulders, but the thought came to me that this scene would provide a delicious chapter to my travel journal, so I consented to take the medal, as a memento to offer to my fiancée. No sooner said than done. The medal was put around my neck, not without difficulty, because the cord was too short. Finally, by pulling, I got the medal on my chest, and I burst out laughing: "Ah! Ah! Look at me, Catholic, Apostolic, Roman!" It was the demon prophesying through my mouth.

De Bussières was innocently triumphant in his victory and wanted to reap all the benefits. "And now," he said, "you must complete the test. You must every morning and evening recite the Memorare, a very short but very efficacious prayer that Saint Bernard composed to the Virgin Mary."

"What's with this Memorare of yours?" I exclaimed. "Enough of this idiocy!" For at this moment I felt all my animosity boil up again within me. The name of Saint Bernard reminded me of my brother who wrote a biography of that saint, a work I never wanted to read; and this memory in turn reawoke all my resentment toward proselytism, Jesuitism, and what I called hypocrites and apostates.

So I begged de Bussières to stop there, and, all the while making fun of him, I regretted not having, myself, a Hebrew prayer to offer him so that we would be even; but I had none and knew none.

Nevertheless my interlocutor insisted: he said that in refusing to recite this short prayer I was rendering the test invalid, and that I proved, in that very way, the truth of the willful obstinacy that the Jews are accused of. I didn't want to attach too much importance to these things, so I said, "Okay! I promise to recite this prayer. If it does me no good, at least it can do me no harm!" So M. de Bussières went to get it and asked me to copy it. "I will consent on the condition," I answered him, "that I give you my copy and keep your original." I was thinking to enrich my notes with this new trophy.

Thus we were both entirely satisfied with each other; our exchange, in fact, seemed bizarre and amusing to me. We parted, and I went to spend the evening at the theater, where I forgot all about the medal and the Memorare. But returning home, I found a note from M. de Bussières, who had come to return my visit and invited me to see him again before my departure. I had to give him the copy I made of his Memorare, and before leaving the next day, I packed my bags and made my preparations, then I sat down to copy the prayer, which went as follows:

> Remember, O most gracious Virgin Mary, that never was it known that anyone who fled to thy protection, implored thy help or sought thy intercession, was left unaided. Inspired by this confidence, I fly unto thee, O Virgin of virgins and Mother; to thee do I come, before thee I stand, sinful and sorrowful. O Mother of the Word Incarnate, despise not my petitions, but in thy mercy hear and answer me. Amen.

I copied these words of Saint Bernard mechanically, not even paying attention. I was tired, it was late, and I needed to get to sleep.

The following day, January 16, I collected my passport and completed the formalities of my departure; but while doing all these things, I was repeating continually the words of the Memorare. How, O God, were these words so strongly, so vividly impressed on my mind? I could not defend myself; they returned continually, like those musical tunes that pursue and irritate you, and that you hum despite yourself, however hard you try to free yourself.

Around eleven o'clock I went to the de Bussières', to return to him his inextricable prayer. We spoke about my voyage to the Orient, and he gave me some excellent information. "But," he cried out all of a sudden, "it is strange that you are leaving Rome just when the whole world is arriving to be present at the celebration at Saint Peter's! Maybe you will never return, and will regret having missed an occasion that so many others have come for so eagerly!"

I answered that I had reserved and paid for my seat, that I had already informed my family, that mail was waiting for me at Palermo, and, finally, that it was too late to change my plans and that, no matter what, I was leaving.

This conversation was interrupted by the arrival of the postman, who brought M. de Bussières a letter from Father Ratisbonne. He brought it to my attention, and I read it without interest, since it was only about a religious work that M. de Bussières was having printed in Paris. Besides, my brother did not even know I was in Rome. This unexpected event should have served to shorten my stay, because I would normally flee at the mere memory of my brother.

Yet nevertheless, as a result of some incomprehensible influence, I decided to prolong my time in Rome. I gave in to the insistence of a man I scarcely knew, that which I had stubbornly refused to my most intimate friends.

What then, O God, was this irresistible impulse that made me do that which I did not want to do? Was it not the same that, in Strasbourg, had pushed me to go to Italy, despite the invitations from friends in Valence and Paris? The same that, in Naples, made me go to Rome, despite my determination to go straight to Sicily? The same that, in Rome, at the hour of my departure, forced me to make the visit that I found repugnant, meaning that I would not even have the time to do what I wanted? O guiding hand of Providence! Is there thus a mysterious influence that accompanies man on his road of life? At birth I received the name of Tobias along with that of Alphonse. I had forgotten my first name, but the invisible angel did not forget at all. He was the true friend sent to me by Heaven, but I did not know him. Alas! There are so many Tobiases in the world who are oblivious to this celestial guide and who resist his voice!

I did not plan to spend Carnival in Rome, but I did want to see the Pope, and M. de Bussières assured me that I would see him at Saint Peter's on the first day. So we went around together. Our conversation was about what we were seeing; at times a monument, at times a painting, at times the customs of the country, and all these different subjects would lead to the topic of religion. M. de Bussières was so naïvely insistent, with such a lively passion, that more than once in the secret of my thoughts I said that if there was one thing that could drive a man away from religion it was this sort of insistence on conversion. My natural gaiety led me to laugh at the most serious things, and the sparks of my jokes ignited an infernal bonfire of blasphemies that I dare not even think of today, they are so scandalous.

Yet meanwhile M. de Bussières, even while expressing his sorrow, remained calm and indulgent. He even said to me at one point, "Despite your carrying on, I'm convinced that one day you will be Christian, because there is in you a depth of honesty that reassures and persuades me that you will be enlightened, even if the Lord has to send you an angel from Heaven."

"At the right moment," I replied, "or else it will be tough."

Passing the Holy Stairs,[2] M. de Bussières became enthu-siastic. He stood up in the carriage, and uncovering his head, he cried with passion, "Hail, holy stairs! Here is a sinner who one day will climb you on his knees!"

It would be impossible for me to express the effect that this unexpected gesture, this extraordinary honor paid to a *staircase* produced in me. I laughed as at an entirely insane act, and when we were later walking the grounds of the lovely villa Wolkonski, whose ever-flowering gardens are divided by Nero's aqueduct, I in turn raised my voice and, parodying his earlier exclamation, cried out "Hail, true mar-vels of God! It is before you that one should bow down, and not before a staircase!"

These excursions of an hour or two were repeated over the next two days. On Wednesday the 19th I again saw M. de Bussières, but he seemed sad and depressed. I withdrew, discreetly refraining from asking the cause of his sorrow. I only found out the next day, in the Church of San Andrea delle Fratte.

Having again reserved a seat for Naples, I was to leave on the 22nd. M. de Bussières' preoccupation diminished his proselytizing fervor, and I thought that he had forgot-ten his miraculous medal, while I, inconceivably annoyed, continued to murmur the perpetual invocation of Saint Bernard.

So, in the middle of the night of January 19, I woke up with a start—I saw right in front of my eyes a huge black cross of a strange shape, without Christ. I tried to chase away the image, but I could not; it remained before my

---

[2] A white marble staircase brought to Rome from Jerusalem by Saint Hel-ena, and venerated as the stairs from in front of Pilate's praetorium and up which Jesus was taken during His Passion (see Mt 27, Mk 15, Lk 23, Jn 18).

eyes, whichever way I tossed. I cannot tell how long this struggle lasted. I eventually fell back asleep, and the next day when I woke up I did not think any more of it.

I had several letters to write, and I remember that in one of them, addressed to the young sister of my fiancée, I ended with these words, "May God watch over you!" Later I received a letter from my fiancée, also dated January 20, and, by a strange coincidence, that letter too ended with the same words, "May God watch over you!" That day, indeed, was watched over by God.

Nevertheless, had someone said to me on the morning of that day, "You got up a Jew and you will go to bed a Christian", I would have thought him the craziest person in the world.

Thursday, January 20, after breakfast, I visited my friend Gustave, the Pietist, who was very surprised to find me still in Rome. I told him that it was because I wanted to see the Pope. "But I will leave without seeing him," I said, "because he wasn't at the ceremony where I had hoped to see him." He ironically consoled me by telling me about another very curious ceremony that was soon to take place, I believe it was in Santa Maria Maggiore, the blessing of the animals. You can imagine the mocking puns and jeers we, a Protestant and a Jew, exchanged on the subject.

I left Gustave, and around noon was reading the papers at a café on the Piazza di Spagne. If anyone had approached me and said, "Alphonse, in fifteen minutes you will be adoring Jesus Christ, your God and your Savior; you will be prostrate in a poor church; and you will throw yourself at the feet of a priest in a Jesuit convent where you will be spending Carnival preparing for baptism, ready to be a holocaust for the Catholic faith; you will renounce the world with its pomps and its pleasures; you will renounce your riches, your hopes, and your own future; and, if necessary, you will further renounce your fiancée, the love of your family, the esteem of your friends, your association with other Jews, and you will wish for no more than to follow Jesus Christ and to carry His cross until death!" I say that if some prophet had made such a prediction, I would have thought that the only man in the world crazier than he was would be the one who believed such an insanity!

Yet it is precisely this insanity that today is my wisdom and my happiness.

Leaving the café, I saw the carriage of M. Theodore de Bussières. It stopped, and I was invited to climb aboard for a drive. The weather was superb, and I accepted with pleasure. Then M. de Bussières asked me if he could stop for a few minutes at the Church of San Andrea delle Fratte, which was nearby, for an errand he had to do. He suggested that I wait in the carriage, but I preferred to get out to see the church. Preparations for a funeral were underway, and I asked the name of the deceased who was to receive the final honors. M. de Bussières replied, "It is a friend of mine, Count de Laferronays; his sudden death is the cause of the sadness that you've noticed in me the last two days."

I did not know, had not even ever seen, M. de Laferronays, and I had no reaction other than the vague discomfort one always feels at the news of a sudden death. M. de Bussières went into the cloister to make some arrangements, telling me, "Be patient; it will only take two minutes."

The Church of San Andrea delle Fratte was small, poor, and deserted; I think I was pretty much alone. No piece of art attracted my attention. I walked, mechanically, looking around, without stopping at any particular thought. I remember only a black dog that ran and jumped around my feet. . . . Then the dog disappeared, the whole church disappeared, I no longer saw anything ... or, rather, O my God! I saw only one thing!!!

How could I ever even speak of it? Oh! no, human words are totally incapable of expressing that which is inexpressible; any description, however sublime, would only be a profanation of the ineffable truth. I was there, prostrate, bathed in my tears, my heart beating out of my chest, when M. de Bussières recalled me to life.

I was unable to reply to his sudden questions, but finally I grabbed the medal that I had left around my neck, I bathed with kisses the image of the Virgin pouring forth rays of grace. "Oh! It was really she!"

I didn't know where I was, I didn't know whether I was Alphonse, or someone else; I felt so entirely changed that I thought I was another self. I tried to find myself, and couldn't. The most intense joy burst in the depths of my soul; I was unable to speak; I wanted to reveal nothing; I felt something solemn and sacred in me that made me ask to see a priest. I was taken to one, and it was only after receiving a direct order that I spoke to the extent possible, on my knees and with trembling heart.

My first words were acknowledgment for M. de Laferronays and for the Archconfraternity of Our Lady of Victories. I somehow knew for certain that M. de Laferronays had prayed for me, but I did not know how I knew it, nor could I account for the faith and the knowledge that I had acquired. All that I can say is that in a moment the blindfold dropped from my eyes; not only a single blindfold, but a whole slew of blindfolds that had enveloped me disappeared rapidly one after the other, as snow and fog and ice disappear under the influence of the burning sun.

I climbed out of a tomb, an abyss of shadows, and I was alive, perfectly alive. But I wept! I saw at the bottom of the abyss the extreme misery from which I had been pulled by an infinite mercy; I shuddered at the sight of all my iniquities, and I was stupefied, moved to compassion, crushed with admiration and gratitude. I thought of my brother with a indescribable joy, but tears of pity mingled with my tears of love. Alas! So many men went calmly down into that pit, blinded by pride or indifference! They descended there to be swallowed alive in the horrible shadows! And my family, my fiancée, my poor sisters!!! Oh! I was torn apart with anxiety! It was of you that I was thinking, O you that I love! It was for you that I offered my first prayers! Will you not raise your eyes to the Savior of the world, whose blood erased the stain of original sin? Oh, how hideous is the imprint of that stain! It renders completely unrecognizable the creature made in the image of God.

I have been asked how I learned these truths, since I swear that I never opened a religious book, never read a single page of the Bible, and that the dogma of original sin, totally forgotten or denied by the Jews of today, had not for an instant occupied my thoughts; I do not think I even knew the name. How then did I arrive at this knowledge? I cannot explain it. All that I know is, that I entered the church knowing nothing, and I left it seeing clearly. I cannot explain the change except by comparing it to a man who awakens suddenly from a deep sleep, or to a man born blind who all of a sudden sees the light of day; he sees, but he is unable to explain the light that illumines the objects he is seeing. If physical light cannot be explained, how can one explain the light that is, in essence, nothing but Truth itself? I believe that I am telling the truth when I say that, without having had any book learning, I glimpsed the meaning and the spirit of the dogmas of the Catholic Faith. I felt these things more than I saw them, by the inexpressable effects that they produced in me. Everything was happening within me, impressions a thousand times faster than the speed of thought, a thousand times deeper than contemplation, not only moving my soul, but turning it around in another direction, toward a new goal and a new life. I am explaining myself badly, but how can I enclose in narrow, dry words feelings that even the heart cannot contain?

However incomplete and inexact the language, the certain fact is that I found myself a new being, a blank tablet. The world suddenly meant nothing to me; my bias against Christianity no longer existed; the prejudices of my childhood did not leave the slightest trace. So much did the love of God take the place of all other love, that my fiancée herself appeared in a new light. I now loved her as one loves something that God holds in His hands, as a precious gift that makes one love the giver even more.

I begged my confessor, Father de Villefort, and M. de Bussières to keep what had happened to me completely secret. I wanted to bury myself in a Trappist monastery to occupy myself only with eternal things. And also, I confess, I was thinking that my family and many of my friends would think me crazy, would ridicule me, and so I thought it best to escape entirely from the world, its affairs, and its judgments.

However, my ecclesiastical superiors showed me how ridicule, insults, false judgments were part of the chalice of a true Christian; they invited me to drink this chalice and reminded me that Jesus Christ had forewarned his disciples of suffering, torments, and torture. These grave words, far from discouraging me, inflamed my interior joy; I felt ready for anything, and I eagerly sought baptism. They wanted me to wait. "What!" I cried. "The Jews who heard the preaching of the Apostles were baptized on the spot, and you want me to wait, after I heard the Queen of Apostles?"

My emotions, my violent desire, my supplications touched the hearts of these kind men who had welcomed me, and they promised me, to my everlasting joy, baptism!

I could barely wait for the day fixed for the realization of this promise, so deformed did I see myself to be in the eyes of God. And yet what goodness, what charity I witnessed during the days of my preparation! I entered the convent of the Jesuit fathers[3] for a retreat under the direction of Father de Villefort, who nourished my soul with all that is sweetest in the word of God. This man of God is not a man at all; he is a heart, he is the personification of heavenly charity! Scarcely had I my eyes opened than I discovered around me many other men of the same sort, of whom the world has no idea. My God, what goodness, what delicacy and grace in the hearts of these true Christians! Every evening during my retreat, the venerable Father General, Superior of the Jesuits, himself came to me, and poured into my soul the balm of Heaven. He said a few words to me, and these words seemed to open up and grow in me as I heard them, filling me with joy, with light, with life.

This priest, so humble and yet so powerful, could even not have spoken to me at all, because the sight of him alone produced in me the same effect as his words; the thought of him still today is enough to bring me into the presence of God and to enkindle the liveliest gratitude. I have no words to express this gratitude; I would need a heart far more vast, and a hundred mouths to express the love that I feel for these men of God; for Theodore de Bussières, who was the angel of Mary; for the family of Laferronays, for whom I hold a veneration and attachment beyond words.

---

[3] Located at the Gesù, the principal Jesuit church in Rome.—ED.

January 31 finally arrived, and it was not just a few souls, but a whole multitude of pious and charitable souls who enveloped me with such tenderness and love! How I would like to know them and thank them. May they always pray for me as I pray for them! . . .

I will not recount what happened at my baptism, my confirmation, and my First Communion, ineffable graces that I received, all in the same day, at the hands of His Eminence Cardinal Patrizzi, Vicar of the Holy Father. . . .

One final consolation was saved for me. You will remember that my desire was to see the Holy Father, a desire, or rather curiosity, that had kept me in Rome. But I was far from suspecting under what circumstances this desire would be realized. It was as a newborn child of the Church that I was presented to the Father of all the faithful. It seems to me that from the moment of my baptism I felt for the Holy Father the respect and love of a son. I was therefore very happy when I was told that I would be presented to the Holy Father by the Father General of the Jesuits, but nevertheless I trembled, because I had never before appeared before the great of the world, and those greats are very small in comparison to this true greatness. I confess that all the royalty of the world seemed to me concentrated on him who here below possesses the power of God, on the Pontiff who, by an unbroken succession going back to Saint Peter and to the High Priest Aaron; the successor of Jesus Christ Himself, from whom he holds his unshakeable throne.

I will never forget my fear and the beating of my heart as I entered the Vatican, and crossed so many vast courts, so many imposing halls, on the way to the sanctuary of the Pontiff. But all my anxiety fell away, and was replaced by my surprise and astonishment, when I actually saw him; so simple, so humble, so paternal. This was not in the least a monarch, but a father of the greatest goodness who treated me as a much loved son.

So ends Ratisbonne's account. Theodore de Bussières also wrote a narrative of Ratisbonne's conversion, an account which sheds further light on the grace that was at work. The following extract from de Bussières' account begins as Ratisbonne leaves de Bussière's house, having just agreed to wear the miraculous medal and recite the Memorare.[4]

After he had gone, my wife and I looked at each other for some time without saying a word. Then, still upset by the blasphemies to which we had been obliged to listen, we implored God to pardon our visitor, asking our little daughters to say the Hail Mary each night for his conversion. That evening, it was my turn to watch before the Blessed Sacrament, in company with a certain prince and some friends. I begged them to join with me in praying for the conversion of a Jew.

The following day, January 16, 1842, I dined at the Borghese palace with the Count de Laferronays. After dinner I told him what was on my mind, earnestly commending my young Jewish friend to his prayers. In the course of our intimate conversation, he told me of the confidence he always had in our Lady's protection even in the days when a busy political life had not allowed him much time for prayer. "Have no fear," he said. "If he says the Memorare he is yours, and many more too."

Ratisbonne came to my house about one o'clock, and we embarked on some more sightseeing. I was really grieved to

---

[4] The source for de Bussières' account is also Marie Théodore Renouard Bussières, *Conversion de M. Marie-Alphonse Ratisbonne: Relation Authentique* (Paris: A. Bray, 1859). Once again the translation is by Roy Schoeman.—ED.

notice how little impression I was making on him. He was still in the same frame of mind, still hating Catholicism intensely and constantly making disparaging remarks about it.

That night M. de Laferronays died suddenly at eleven o'clock, leaving to those who mourned him the memory of a life of exemplary virtue. Having loved him a long time as though he were my father, I shared not only the sorrow felt by family, but the sad duties that devolved upon them in making funeral arrangements. Yet, the thought of Ratisbonne followed me everywhere, even as I knelt beside my dead friend's coffin. I spent part of the night with the sorrowing family. I did not wish to leave my friend's remains, but I could not banish from my mind the thought of the soul I was anxious to win for the Faith. When I mentioned my predicament to Father Gerbet, he urged me by all means to carry on the work I had begun. In doing so, he said, I would best fulfill the wishes of my departed friend, who had prayed so fervently for the conversion of the young Jew.

And so there I was running after Ratisbonne and dragging him by the hand, showing him more of the city's religious antiquities, in an endeavor to impress the great truths of Catholicism upon his mind. At Saint John Lateran I showed him the bas-reliefs above the statues of the Twelve Apostles. On one side the Old Testament figures, on the other their fulfillment in the person of the Messiah. He found the parallel rather clever. However, he remarked that he was more of a Jew than ever. I replied that I had perfect confidence in God's promises and was convinced that, being an honest and sincere man, he would one day be a Catholic, even if it required an angel from Heaven to enlighten him.

At about one o'clock I had to go and make some arrangements at the Church of San Andrea delle Fratte for the funeral ceremony fixed for the next day. Seeing Ratisbonne coming down the Via Condotti, I invited him to accompany me and wait a few minutes while I attended to my business, and then continue on with me. We entered the church. Noticing the funeral preparations, he asked for whom they were being made. "For a friend I have lost," I replied, "whom I loved very much, M. de Laferronays." He then began to walk up and down the nave, his cold, indifferent gaze seeming to say, "What a frightful church!" I left him and went off to the sacristy to make some arrangements for the funeral. I could not have been away much more than ten minutes.

When I returned I saw nothing of Ratisbonne at first. Then I caught sight of him on his knees, in the Chapel of Saint Michael the Archangel.[5] I went up to him and touched him. I had to do this three or four times before he became aware of my presence. Finally he turned toward me, face bathed in tears, clasped his hands together, and said with an expression that no words can describe, "How that friend of yours must have prayed for me!"

I was petrified with astonishment. I felt what people must feel in the presence of a miracle. I helped Ratisbonne to his feet and led him, almost carrying him, out of the church. Then I asked him what was the matter, and where he wanted to go. "Take me wherever you like," he cried, "after what I have seen, I shall obey." I urged him to explain his meaning, but he was unable to do so—his emotion was too strong. Instead he took hold of his miraculous medal and kissed it with passionate emotion. He broke into tears at the thought of all the heretics and unbelievers. Finally, he asked me if I

[5] Interestingly, St. Michael the Archangel is, according to the Bible, the patron saint of the Jewish nation (Dan 12:1).—ED.

thought him mad. "Of course I am not mad;" he went on, before I had a chance to speak, "I am in my right mind. O God, of course I am not mad! Everyone knows that I am not mad!"

Gradually this delirious emotion subsided, and he grew calmer, and now his face was radiant, almost transfigured. He begged me to take him to a priest, and he asked me when he could receive holy baptism, for now he was sure he could not live without it. I took him at once to the Gesù to see Father de Villefort, who invited him to explain what had happened. Ratisbonne drew out his medal, kissed it, and showed it to us, saying, "I saw her! I saw her!" and again emotion choked his words, but soon he grew calmer and spoke. I shall give his own words:

> I had only been in the church a moment when I was sud-
> denly seized with an indescribable agitation of mind. I looked
> up and found that the rest of the building had disappeared.
> One single chapel seemed to have gathered all the light and
> concentrated it in itself. In the midst of this radiance I saw
> someone standing on the altar, a lofty shining figure, all
> majesty and sweetness, the Virgin Mary just as she looks on
> this medal. Some irresistible force drew me toward her. She
> motioned to me to kneel down and when I did so, she
> seemed to approve. Though she never said a word, I under-
> stood her perfectly.

Brief as his account was, Ratisbonne could not utter it without frequently pausing for breath, and to subdue the overwhelming emotion he felt. We listened to him, awe mingled with joy and gratitude. One phrase struck us espe-cially, so deep and mysterious was it: "She never said a word, but I understood her perfectly." From this moment on, it was enough to hear him speak; faith exhaled from his heart like a precious perfume from a casket, that holds but cannot imprison. He spoke of the Real Presence, like a man who believed in it with all his being—like a man who had experienced it.

Upon leaving Father de Villefort, we went to give thanks to God, first at Saint Mary Major, the basilica beloved of Our Lady, and then at Saint Peter's. He prayed with great fervor at the tombs of the Holy Apostles. When I told him the account of the conversion of Saint Paul all his former emotion returned.

At the altar of the Blessed Sacrament, the Real Presence of Jesus so overwhelmed him that he was on the verge of fainting, and I was obliged to take him away, so terrible did it seem to him to remain before the living God stained as he was with original sin. He hastened to take refuge in the Lady Chapel. "Here", he said, "I have no fear, for I feel protected by some boundless mercy." I asked him for more details of the miraculous vision. At first he had been able to see clearly the Queen of Heaven, appearing in all the splendor of her immaculate beauty, but he had not been able to bear the radiance of that divine light for long. Three times he had tried to look up to her, and three times he had found himself unable to raise his eyes higher than her hands, from which blessings and graces seemed to fall like so many shining rays.

"O God," he cried, "only half an hour before I was blaspheming and felt a deadly hatred for the Catholic religion! All my acquaintances know that humanly speaking I had the strongest reasons for remaining a Jew. My family is Jewish, my bride to be is a Jewess, my uncle is a Jew. By becoming a Catholic, I am sacrificing all my earthly hopes and interests; and yet I am not mad. So they must believe me." Surely the sincerity and good faith of such a man are beyond question—one who, at the age of twenty-eight, could sacrifice all his joys and all his hopes for the sake of his conscience. The news of this striking miracle began to spread throughout Rome. I was with him at Father de Villefort's when General Chlapouski came up to him. "So you have seen a vision of Our Lady!" he said. "Tell me ..."

"A vision!" cried Ratisbonne, interrupting him. "I saw her herself, as she really is, in person, just as I can see you standing before me now."

Such are the facts which I submit for the consideration of all serious-minded people. I myself once wandered long— too long in the gloom and confusion of Protestantism, and I shall be happy if this simple narrative may rouse some soul to cry, like the blind man in the Gospel, "Lord, that I may see!" For if a man but pray, God will not fail to open his eyes to the light of Catholic truth.

Alphonse Ratisbonne immediately entered the Catholic Church and soon after joined the Jesuits and began studies for the priesthood. After ordination he requested, and was granted, permission to leave the Jesuits in order to move to the Holy Land and work for the conversion of the Jews. With his brother Theodore, he founded a congregation there—the Sisters of Our Lady of Sion—specifically to pray for the conversion of the Jews. Their convent was built on the site of Pilate's palace, the very spot where Pilate showed the beaten and bloody Jesus to the crowd suggesting that he be released, to which the crowd of Jews cried back, "Crucify him! His blood be on us and on our children!" (see Mt 27:11–26, Mk 15:1–15, Lk 23, and Jn 19). Alphonse Ratisbonne died in 1884 at Ein Karem, John the Baptist's birthplace near Jerusalem. His heartfelt prayer that New Year's Day in Naples, that God lead him to fulfill his cherished goal to work to improve the lot of the Jews, had been granted, as he said, "beyond all expectation."

Apostle of the Blessed Sacrament

Hermann Cohen

On November 10, 1821, Hermann Cohen was born into a wealthy Jewish family in Hamburg, Germany, a city that at the time was one of that country's foremost centers of economic, intellectual, and artistic activity. His father, a successful banker, was a leader of the liberal segment of the local Jewish community, which embraced a modern, "enlightened" form of Judaism eschewing many of the traditional Jewish beliefs and practices.

Both the young boy's intellectual brilliance and his extraordinary musical talent became apparent at a very young age, and while he was still a child, his performances on the piano made him the darling of Europe's cultural and artistic elite. Once in that glittering world of fame, parties, and loose morals, he fell into a panoply of vices, into which he descended deeper and deeper. Rescued from that darkness by a miraculous grace received in the presence of the Blessed Sacrament, Hermann rededicated his life, this time to God, and embraced a life of prayer, contemplation, penance, and apostolic activity. He became a Carmelite priest and monk and was instrumental in reestablishing the Carmelite order in France, England, Ireland, and Scotland. He traveled throughout Europe, preaching and founding houses for the order. He died in 1871 from smallpox contracted while administering extreme unction to soldiers dying of the disease. Father Hermann's cause for beatification is being promoted.

Paris.

The following account was written by Roy Schoeman for the present volume.

As a young child Hermann had a pious, devout nature and was much drawn to prayer. He loved going to synagogue and chanting prayers and psalms at home, an activity into which he would frequently draw his siblings. Yet even at that early age, he felt a certain dissatisfaction with Jewish observance:

> When I saw the Rabbi mount the steps of the sanctuary, draw the curtain and open the door [of the tabernacle], I waited expectantly.... My expectation was not satisfied when I saw the Levites solemnly take out from a magnificent container a large roll of parchment studded with Hebrew letters and surmounted by a royal crown. The roll of parchment was then carried with great ceremony to a lectern ... and the Hebrew Scriptures were read aloud. I was full of anxiety during the whole of this ceremony.[1]

Hermann's extraordinary talents soon pulled him away, in any case, from his religiosity. His intellectual gifts were such that he soon far surpassed his older siblings in his knowledge of Latin, French, and other school subjects, and made him always first in his class. Yet even this intellectual brilliance paled beside his musical genius. At the age of four he begged to be taught to play the piano; by six he was playing all of the then-popular opera tunes, to which he would add improvisations of his own. By twelve his professional recitals were the talk of the town. Unfortunately,

---

[1] Hermann Cohen wrote a spiritual autobiography, his *Confessions*, which has since been lost, but not before extracts from it were incorporated into other works. This passage from Cohen's *Confessions* is quoted in Tadgh Tierney O.C.D., *The Story of Hermann Cohen* (Oxford: Teresian Press, 1980), p. 10. © 1980 and used by permission.

his mother had entrusted him to a professor of piano of great talent but low morals; the example of this revered teacher, combined with the intoxication of his own success, had a corrosive effect on the young Hermann's morals. As he later wrote:

> [The teacher's great genius] was enough to justify, in the eyes of the public, all of his whims and adventures, however irresponsible and scandalous. . . . Since I admired him above anyone, I soon began to imitate his wild behavior. He loved gambling; I, alas, early on acquired the taste for it. He loved the horses and all the pleasures, and since he found the purses of his admirers always open to satisfy all his caprices, I began to think that there could be no existence on earth happier than that of an artist.[2]

When Hermann was twelve his mother took him to Paris, the home of the finest musicians in Europe, to continue his musical education. When she was finally able to convince the great pianist Franz Liszt to hear the child play, he was immediately won over, and took the prodigy under his wing. Soon they were inseparable. Unfortunately, Liszt's morals were every bit as disordered as those of Hermann's previous teacher, and the boy was soon following his master in the paths of vice. Having grown up amidst constant attention and praise, with every whim indulged, Hermann already was terribly spoiled, arrogant, and self-centered, which only exacerbated the situation. The constant adulation he received as the darling of the concert halls and salons of Paris only made things worse.

[2] From Cohen's *Confessions*, quoted in Dom Jean-Marie Beaurin, *Flèche de Feu* (Paris: Editions France-Empire, 1981), p. 23. This and all other quotes from Cohen's writings taken from *Flèche de Feu* have been translated by Roy Schoeman.

The depravity of the circles to which Liszt introduced his protégé can barely be exaggerated. Members of the circle with whom Hermann became good friends included Mikhail Bakunin, the Russian anarchist and revolutionary, and the notoriously free-thinking (and cross-dressing) novelist George Sand, with whom Hermann became particularly close. As he later wrote of his friendship with the writer: "It enhanced my own reputation that I was known to be a friend of the author of *Lelia*. My name was constantly linked with hers, imagination supplying the answer as to what took place in her garret. She sometimes entertained me for days on end, and as she wrote I used to prepare cigarettes for her. I wish now I had never read [any of her books] and remained satisfied with her acquaintance—then I might have retained the few principles I had." [3]

These friendships soon took their toll on the impressionable young boy. As Cohen later wrote to Father Alphonse Ratisbonne:

> I was spoilt in the salons, and most of all in so much impious company. Soon, they were making me the scapegoat of all of their disgusting doctrines—atheism, pantheism, socialism, anarchism, terrorism, the massacre of the rich, the abolition of marriage, expropriation of all property, and the common enjoyment of all pleasures. Before long there was plenty of room for all this in the head of a fourteen-year-old (evil is quickly learned).... I soon became one of the most zealous propagandists for all these groups, who had sworn to renew the face of the earth. [4]

[3] From Cohen's *Confessions*, cited in Tierney, *Story of Hermann Cohen*, p. 17.
[4] From a letter from Cohen to Fr. Alphonse Ratisbonne recorded in Cohen's *Confessions* and quoted in Beaurin, *Flèche de Feu*, p. 29.

The young musician's adventures over the next decade were a continual chain of ups and downs, artistic and popular successes and failures, romantic alliances with other musicians and singers, young married women, and even a circus performer. His self-centered hedonism and irresponsibility caused Cohen to alienate friends and burn out friendships; his gambling resulted in repeated financial catastrophes that also took a toll on his relationships. He lived only for the pleasures of the moment; as he later wrote: "I am not exaggerating, all the young people I knew lived like me, seeking pleasure wherever it was to be found, passionately wanting wealth in order to be able to indulge all their inclinations, satisfy all their desires. The thought of God never occurred to them; . . . their morals were limited to those necessary to stay out of trouble with the law." [5]

Yet even during this extended period of self-indulgence and depravity, the Lord was working to draw the young Cohen to Him. He would later write of one such incident, listening to Liszt play the organ in the cathedral of Fribourg:

> Liszt touched the keys of this colossal harp of David, whose majestic sounds give a vague idea of Your grandeur, O my God. Was I not penetrated with a sense of the holy? Did You not make the first stirrings of a religious sense vibrate in my soul? What then was that deep emotion which I experienced each time that, since my youth, I touched or heard touched the keys of an organ, an emotion so strong that it threatened to harm my health, so much so that it was strongly forbidden to me? O Jesus my beloved, You were knocking at the door of my heart and I would not open to You. [6]

[5] Ibid., p. 53.
[6] From Cohen's *Confessions*, quoted in Beaurin, *Flèche de Feu*, p. 38.

The decisive moment of Cohen's conversion came when, at the age of twenty-six, he was asked to fill in directing the choir at a church service. In his own words:

It happened during May 1847. Mary's month was celebrated with great pomp at the Church of Sainte Valère. Some amateur choirs were formed and would sing there, drawing a lot of people. Prince Moskowa, who led these pious concerts, and whom I already had the honor of knowing, asked me one evening if I would take his place directing the choirs. I agreed and went, solely from my love of music and the desire to do a friend a favor. During the ceremony I felt nothing special, but at the moment of Benediction, even though I had no intention to prostrate myself like the rest of the congregation, I felt an indefinable agitation; my soul, deafened and distracted by the discord of the world, re-found itself, a bit like the prodigal son coming to his senses, and sensed that something previously entirely unknown was taking place. I felt for the first time a very powerful, but indefinable emotion. Without any participation of my will, I was forced, despite myself, to bow down. When I returned the following Friday, the same emotion came over me, even more powerfully, and I felt a great weight that descended over my whole body, forcing me to bow, even to prostrate myself, despite myself, and I was struck with the sudden thought of becoming Catholic.

A few days later I was passing near the same Church of Sainte Valère; the bells were ringing for Mass. I went in and was present at the Holy Sacrifice, remaining motionless and attentive throughout. I stayed for one, two, three Masses without a thought of leaving, although I had no idea what was keeping me there. After having returned home, involuntarily I was led to go out again that evening and go back to the same place; the bells made me enter once again. The Blessed Sacrament was exposed and as soon as I saw it I was drawn to the altar rail and fell to my knees. This time, at the moment of Benediction it was easy for me to bow down, and getting up again I felt a very sweet peace in my whole being. I returned to my room and went to bed, but throughout the entire night, my mind was, whether in dream or awake, occupied with the thought of the Blessed Sacrament. I burned with impatience to be at more Masses. In the following days, I attended many at Sainte Valère, always with an inner joy that absorbed all my faculties.[7]

I wanted to see a priest, to settle down the agitation that was incessantly troubling my spirit since this extraordinary event. Until now priests had been, for me, monsters to flee, and I do not know how I was led by an irresistible force to find one. Eventually I was introduced to Father Legrand. I told him what had happened to me. He listened with interest and exhorted me to be calm, to persevere in my current disposition, and to have wholehearted confidence in the paths that Divine Providence would not fail to point out to me.

This cleric's benevolent and kind welcome made a strong impression on me, and in an instant made fall one of the deepest prejudices I held. I had been afraid of priests! I only knew them from novels in which they were portrayed as the most intolerant of men, ceaselessly hurling threats of excommunication and hell-fire. Yet I found myself in the presence of a learned man, humble, kind and open-hearted, looking entirely to God, not himself.[8]

Later that summer Cohen found himself in Ems, Germany, to give a concert. As he described the experience:

---

[7] This description combines two accounts that Cohen wrote of the experience, one from a letter to a former teacher of his and the other to Fr. Alphonse Ratisbonne, both quoted in Beaurin, *Flèche de Feu*, pp. 58–59.

[8] From a letter from Cohen to Fr. Ratisbonne, cited in Beaurin, *Flèche de Feu*, pp. 59–60.

The day after my arrival was a Sunday, the eighth of August, and not caring about human respect, that is, despite the presence of my friends, I went to Mass. There, bit by bit, the prayers, the presence—invisible, and yet felt by me—of a supernatural power began to act on me, agitate me, make me start trembling; in a word, *divine grace deigned to descend on me with all its force*. At the moment of elevation, all of a sudden I felt burst forth, behind my eyelids, a flood of tears that did not cease to flow with voluptuous abundance down my inflamed cheeks. O moment forever memorable for the salvation of my soul! I had You there, present, in my spirit, with all the celestial sensations that You brought down to me from on high! With passion I invoked the all-powerful and all-merciful God, that the exquisite memory of His beauty remain eternally engraved in my heart, along with the ineradicable stigmata of an unassailable faith, and gratitude for the enormity of the blessings that He was flooding me with.

I undoubtedly felt then what Saint Augustine must have felt in his garden at Cassiacum, at the moment when he heard the famous words "take and read", what you, my dear Father, must have experienced in San Andrea's Church in Rome on January 20, 1842, when the Most Holy Virgin deigned to appear to you.[9]

I remember having cried a few times as a child, but never, no, never did I know such tears. While they were drowning me, I felt surge up from the depths of my chest, split open by my conscience, the most tearing remorse over my entire past life. All of a sudden, and spontaneously, as though by intuition, I offered God a general confession, interior and rapid, of all of my enormous sins since childhood. I saw them there, piled up before me by the thousands,

[9] See the account of Fr. Alphonse Ratisbonne's conversion on pp. 1–32 above.

hideous, repulsive, revolting, deserving all of the anger of a
sovereign Judge.... And yet, I also felt an unknown peace
that soon spread over my entire soul like a soothing balm,
that the God of mercy would forgive me these, that He
would turn His gaze away from my crimes, that He would
take pity on my sincere contrition, on my bitter sorrow.
Yes, I felt that He would give me grace, and that He would
accept in expiation my firm resolution to love Him above
all else and to turn to Him from then on.

When I left the church, I was already a Christian, as much
a Christian as it is possible to be before baptism.[10]

The next day, eager to tell Father Legrand what had happened, Cohen left Ems to return to Paris. Transformed by
grace, he was virtually unrecognizable. He shut himself up
in his room to study Christian doctrine and immediately
began to follow all the practices of the Christian life: morning and evening prayer, the Mass, Vespers and Holy Hours
at the church, abstinences, chastity; all these he observed
easily and readily. His greatest sorrow was his inability, as of
yet, to receive Holy Communion. "Not yet having had the
joy of making my First Communion, I could not be present
at that supreme moment without weeping from that priva-
tion that was killing me."[11]

Each evening Father Legrand received Cohen for instruction. On August 15, Father Theodore Ratisbonne[12] baptized four Jewish converts in the Chapel of Our Lady of

[10] From an account Cohen wrote a few days after his baptism and quoted
in Canon Charles Sylvain, *Vie du R.P. Hermann, en religion Augustin-Marie du
T.S. Sacrement* (Paris: Oudin, 1883), pp. 44–45. This and all subsequently quoted
passages from the book have been translated by Roy Schoeman.

[11] Ibid., p. 46.

[12] See the conversion story of Alphonse Ratisbonne, Theodore's brother,
on pp. 1–32.

Sion, with Cohen in attendance. Father Ratisbonne was himself, of course, a Jewish convert, as were all of the young girls in the choir. The service included a litany written by Father Ratisbonne:

> ... Jesus of Nazareth, king of the Jews, have pity
> on the children of Israel!
> Jesus, divine Messiah expected by the Jews, have pity
> on the children of Israel!
> Jesus, desire of the nations, Jesus of the tribe of Judah,
> Jesus who healed the deaf, the dumb, and the blind,
> have pity on the children of Israel!
> Lamb of God, who takes away the sins of the world,
> forgive them, for they know not what they do![13]

It was all that Cohen could do to restrain himself from throwing himself at the priest's feet, begging to be baptized himself.

Cohen was baptized just thirteen days later, on August 28, the Feast of Saint Augustine, in the very same chapel. The night before his baptism, as Cohen recounted, the evil spirit "sent a dream full of seductions, and reawoke in me burning images that I thought I had banished for good from my memory. Stumbling, I threw myself beside my bed, falling at the feet of my crucifix, and there, eyes full of tears, I begged the merciful aid of the All-Powerful, and the assistance of the most holy and most pure Virgin Mary, and the temptation fled."[14] The next day, in Cohen's words:

> On Saturday, August 28, at three o'clock, the chapel of Our Lady of Sion shone with an unusual brilliance; the freshest and most beautiful flowers adorned the altar, resplendent

---

[13] Sylvain, *Vie du R.P. Hermann*, p. 47.

[14] From a letter from Cohen to Fr. Alphonse Ratisbonne and quoted in ibid., pp. 49–50.

with a thousand candles. The convent bells were ringing out the most joyful carillons, a pious crowd filled the nave, a choir of young girls, covered with long white veils, sang beseechingly the litany for the conversion of the Jews; the organ mixed its harmonies with this beautiful singing ... and never did an infant come into the world more tenderly surrounded by his sisters and brothers than did I when, a simple catechumen, I approached the altar.

"Do you wish to be baptized?"

"Yes, I wish to!" (Yes, You know, Lord, with what ardor I wish it, and how impatient I am to be Yours!)

"Then kneel down ..."

The earth disappeared; the priest holding the shell with holy water was no longer a man. God had promised to descend Himself in that moment and take possession.... [When the holy water touched my forehead] all of a sudden my body shook, and I felt such a violent, powerful movement, that I can only compare it to an electric shock. The eyes of my body were closed, but at the very moment the eyes of my soul opened to a supernatural and divine light. This light expanded in my whole being; God the Holy Spirit, as though to seal His promise, descended from the heights of Heaven to me, taking me by the hand and showing to me in ecstasy that which a finite being could never comprehend—the Infinite. Yes, I saw (the eyes of my body closed, but those of my soul wide open with joy) an immense brilliance, without end, better to say without space itself, because the sight soared, plunged ever further—ever further!—never meeting an obstacle. Everywhere myriads of angels sang with an indescribable beauty, ever more beautiful, ever more ravishing, such that no human ear ever heard, and the heavenly scents! And a soft warmth penetrated me ... and my sight, despite the dazzling light that shone everywhere, never stopped plunging into the rays ... and, in the center, reigned a light even more brilliant in its whiteness. There, sitting on a glorious throne, with on His right His glorious, well-beloved mother, was Our Lord Jesus Christ, beautiful with an eternal youthfulness, and at His feet, all around Him, the army of saints, clothed in the most brilliant colors of the rainbow.

These saints were prostrate at the foot of the throne adoring Him and yet, at the same time, they turned and looked at me with sweet smiles of welcome. . . . All of Heaven and its inhabitants seemed to be rejoicing at my baptism, as though the poor small soul of a redeemed sinner could hold real weight in the scales of Eternity. . . .

Yes, I saw the paradise of the Church triumphant. No, it was not a vision, it was real. God permitted that I, miserable worm of earth, be admitted, by a grace for which I could never find a name, to experience for an instant that which I scarcely dare remember!

I was plunged into an ecstasy of love, my heart connected to the indescribable joys of paradise and drinking at the torrent of delights with which the Lord drowns His elect in the land of the living. I was so moved that still today I can only imperfectly recall the ceremonies that followed. I do remember, though, that I was clothed with the white robe of innocence and a lit candle was placed in my hands, as a symbol of the truth that had just appeared so brilliantly before my eyes, and I swore in my heart to live and die to protect and defend that truth.[15]

The Blessed Sacrament, which was the source of Hermann Cohen's initial conversion, ever remained at the center of his spirituality:

[15] From a letter by Cohen to Fr. Ratisbonne, cited in Sylvain, *Vie du R.P. Hermann*, pp. 49–51, and in Beaurin, *Flèche de Feu*, pp. 65–66.

O Jesus! Eucharist! In the desert of this life, You appeared one day! You revealed to me Your light, Your grandeur, Your beauty! You changed my entire being; You in an instant vanquished all my enemies. Then, attracting me with an irresistible pull, You excited in my soul an all-consuming hunger for this Bread of Life, You lit in my heart a burning thirst for Your divine Blood. Then the day came when You gave Yourself to me. Even today when I remember it my heart skips a beat and I dare not breathe.[16]

Describing one of the first eucharistic processions at which he was present, Cohen wrote: "When the Holy Eucharist passed by, I felt terrified, a torrent of tears came to my eyes. I felt a profound respect, I directly felt the Real Presence; an indescribable sensation. As long as the procession lasted, each time the Blessed Sacrament approached, my respectful terror and my humble love increased."[17]

In 1848, just a year after his initial conversion experience, he started the Association of Nocturnal Adorers, a group of men dedicated to adoring our Lord in the Blessed Sacrament throughout the night.[18] He started the group because

to contemplate You [i.e., Jesus in the Blessed Sacrament] enough, the hours of the day fly by too quickly. I will call together other Christians burning with the same fire, and we will pass the nights in Your churches. In the evening You will be exposed on the altar, and the dawn will find us

[16] From Cohen's journal entry of Sept. 3, 1847, five days before his first communion, quoted in Sylvain, *Vie du R.P. Hermann*, pp. 313–14 and Beaurin, *Flèche de Feu*, p. 73.

[17] From Cohen's journal quoted in Beaurin, *Flèche de Feu*, pp. 81–82.

[18] The group initially met at the Church of Our Lady of Victories in Paris, a church that also played a special role in the life of St. Thérèse of Lisieux.

still kneeling before Your splendor. Nights beyond words! "Let my right hand wither! Let my tongue cleave to the roof of my mouth, if I ever forget you!" (Cf. Ps 137:5–6).

In these heavenly nights, O my Jesus, You draw me to Yourself by a charm so sweet and tender, so loveable, that the final thread tying me to this world is broken, and I run far from these cities to throw myself in Your arms, to live entirely for You, undividedly, forever.[19]

What did nocturnal adoration mean to Cohen? "Stripped of all that ties me to the earth, I can pierce the mysterious clouds that envelop Your tabernacle, and expose myself to the penetrating rays of this beautiful sun of grace, and dive into this ocean of light to be consumed in the flames of this blazing furnace.... Then, in the refreshing shade of this Tree of Life, I breathe the scent of the flowers, I savor the fruits ..."[20] Later, when he was a Carmelite priest, Father Cohen took a vow never to preach without extolling the Blessed Sacrament, and as he traveled throughout Europe preaching, he founded cells of the Association of Nocturnal Adorers wherever he went.

Hermann Cohen did not abandon his love for his own Jewish people when he entered the Church—quite the opposite. Upon his entry into the Church he took a vow "to do everything in the world for the conversion of the Jewish people".[21] When in 1849 he joined the Carmelite Order, it was in part its roots in the Old Testament that attracted him. As he wrote in a letter to his mother:

---

[19] From Cohen's dedication to a collection of his canticles, *Love of Jesus Christ*, quoted in Beaurin, *Flèche de Feu*, p. 91.

[20] Beaurin, *Flèche de Feu*, p. 96.

[21] From his *Confessions*, cited in Sylvain, *Vie du R.P. Hermann*, p. 58.

I find myself in the novitiate of a religious order that is famous for its austerities, its penances, and its love of God. This order was born among the Jews, 930 years before Jesus Christ; it was the prophet Elijah of the Old Testament who founded it on Mount Carmel, in Palestine. It is an order of true Jews, of children of the Prophets who waited for the Messiah, who believed in Him when He came, and who continue to our time, living always in the same manner, with the same bodily deprivations and the same spiritual joys, as they lived on Mount Carmel in Judea, about 2,800 years ago. They still bear today the name of the Order of Mount Carmel.... Why follow this life? To draw down the mercy of the All-Powerful onto the earth, and turn away His just anger, ready to strike those who offend Him; to love God as He loved us, in imitating the life Jesus led when He came on earth to save men, through suffering, self-denial, sacrifice, obedience, submission, humiliation, poverty, and death. This is the life I have chosen.[22]

He saw in the Catholic Church the fulfillment of the promises of the Old Testament: "[Once] I decided to believe in Jesus Christ, all that I read, felt, saw, and heard appeared to me in a new light, a dazzling, luminous light, and I tumbled from one joy to the next, as with this faith I saw the magnificent tableau of our Holy Scriptures unfold; I touched on each page this Messiah promised in the Old Testament." [23]

He found nothing but joy in his new religious life:

In the world during my life as an artist, I never had a childhood, because I was introduced to the life of the salons at the age of twelve. God, in his great goodness has amply made up to me for that during my novitiate, where I rejoice

[22] From a letter to his mother quoted in Sylvain, *Vie du R.P. Hermann*, pp. 84–86.

[23] From a sermon Cohen quoted in Sylvain, *Vie du R.P. Hermann*, p. 106.

in the joys of spiritual childhood. I am bathed in the milk
of consolation and want nothing else but to see God's will
alone in me and in everyone. Holy Communion occupies
me totally—either in thanksgiving or in preparation. I prolong these in such a way that my life is a continual communion. This I think is like the joy of heaven. Here we are
always in the real presence of the Eucharist.[24]

To express to you the happiness that I experience here without interruption since I took my habit would be impossible; it would take the pen of an angel to describe the delights
of the interior life that one leads here in the novitiate. Being
continually in the presence of the Blessed Sacrament and
having nothing to distract the soul from the exercises of the
religious life, one forgets the earth and one lives with the
seraphim and cherubim prostrating themselves eternally before
the Lamb. It is a perpetual communion. The most extraordinary thing is that one barely notices the austerities of our
life.[25]

It was not that he did not suffer in the religious life,
especially later on, but that suffering itself, accepted out of
love of Jesus, became his joy:

At the beginning I was constantly on Tabor, drowning in
consolations, but something was missing, I had not yet drunk
from the chalice of bitterness of our Jesus, and I was thirsty
for it . . . thirsty to suffer in love with my Jesus! But for the
past two years, I did not go a single day without this divine
gall, and I love it with a passion.

    May I remain until my final breath on Calvary with my
Savior. I ask nothing else, and I dare say that I sometimes

[24] From a letter to Mother Marie-Thérèse, foundress of the Congregation
of Adoration Reparatrice cited in Tierney, *Story of Hermann Cohen*, p. 48.

[25] From a letter to Visitation Sister Marie-Pauline, cited in Beaurin, *Flèche
de Feu*, pp. 137–38.

enjoy the suffering more than I ever, in past days, enjoyed the divine consolations![26]

He took his first religious vows in 1850, taking the religious name Augustine-Mary of the Most Blessed Sacrament. He was ordained to the priesthood in 1851 and spent most of the rest of his life traveling around Europe preaching and helping to establish new Carmelite foundations—this despite the fact that his deepest longing was for an eremitical, contemplative life. Wherever he went he preached to huge, enthusiastic crowds, frequently drawing many to a conversion of their way of life on the spot. Usually his theme was the joy to be found in loving Jesus, as it was in the first homily he preached in Paris, at the Church of Saint Sulpice, on April 24, 1854. Many acquaintances from his former life were in attendance. So too was a young Jewish man, Bernard Bauer, who had mingled with the crowd out of mere curiosity; by the end of the homily he had made his decision and within two months had taken the Carmelite habit.[27] An extract from that homily follows:

My first thought as I appear in this Christian pulpit is to make amends for the bad example that I unhappily gave in this city in the past. You might well ask me, "what right have you to preach to me, to exhort me to virtue and goodness, to teach me the truths of the faith, to speak to us of Jesus and Mary whom we love? You have so often dishonored them in our sight, you who have kept bad company and behaved outrageously, you who we know to have

[26] From a letter to an unidentified friend, dated June 6, 1853, cited in Beaurin, *Flèche de Feu*, pp. 195–96.

[27] By the designs of Providence, Bauer was assigned to the same cell in the monastery that Cohen had previously occupied; they later became close friends.

swallowed every false theory and so often insulted us with your conduct." Yes, my brethren, I confess that I have sinned against heaven and against you. I admit that I have deserved to be unpopular with you and that I have forfeited your goodwill. I come to you brethren, clothed in a robe of penance and committed to a strict order, barefooted and wearing a tonsure. Mary obtained for me, from the God of the Eucharist, a cure infinitely more important to me than that of my bodily eyes, that of freeing me from my spiritual blindness.[28] It was the month of Mary and they were singing hymns. Mary, the mother of Jesus revealed the Eucharist to me. I knew Jesus, I knew God. Soon I became a Christian. I asked for baptism and before long the holy water was flowing over me. At that moment all the many sins of my twenty-five years were wiped out. Brethren, God pardoned me, Mary pardoned me, will you not pardon me too?

I have traveled throughout the world, I have loved the world. I have learnt one thing about the world—you don't find happiness there. And you, brethren, have you found it? Can you say you are happy, that you do not want anything? It seems to me I can hear a sad chorus of sighs all around. I seem to hear the unanimous cry of suffering humanity: "Happiness where are you? Tell me where you are hidden and I will search for you, hold you and possess you."

I have looked for happiness. I have searched in cities and crossed the seas to find it. I have searched for happiness among the beauties of nature. I have sought it in the elegant life of salons, in the deafening din of balls and parties. I have sought it through the accumulation of gold, in the excitement of gambling, in the hazards of adventure and in trying to satisfy a boundless ambition. I have looked for it in the glory of the artist, in the friendships of famous

[28] Interestingly, fourteen years later Cohen, going blind, received a miraculous, total healing of his bodily eyes at Lourdes.

people, and in all the pleasures of sense and spirit. Dear God, was there anywhere I failed to seek happiness? How can one explain this mystery? For human beings are made for happiness. The mystery is that most people don't know in what happiness consists. They look for it where it doesn't exist. Well then, listen. I have found happiness, I possess it, I enjoy it so fully that I am able to say with the great apostle, "I am overflowing with joy." My heart brims over with happiness, so that I cannot contain it within me. I wanted to leave my solitude in order to come and find you and tell you, I am overflowing with joy. Yes, I am so happy that I come to offer it to you. I come to entreat you to share with me this overflowing happiness. "But", you object, "I don't believe in Jesus Christ."

I too, I did not believe, and that is precisely why I was unhappy. Faith brings us to happiness in God and in Jesus Christ his son. It is a mystery which pride cannot grasp. But to find Jesus Christ one must watch and pray. Scripture says, "Happy is the man who watches at the doors day and night", that is to say who watches at the door of his heart to find Jesus Christ.

So, pray, ask, and you will receive this intoxicating wine of immortality which flows from the winepress of prayer. Prayer imparts faith, sheds light through prayer which, united to faith, imparts peace, love, wisdom, light, freedom—all of which are contained in Jesus Christ. It is not possible for someone who does not love Jesus Christ to be happy.[29]

Father Cohen spent the rest of his life trying to bring others to the happiness that he had found. His constant theme was that happiness can only be found in Jesus Christ, particularly Jesus in the Blessed Sacrament, as in the following

[29] From a homily Fr. Cohen preached at St. Sulpice, Paris, on April 24, 1854, cited in Tierney, *Story of Hermann Cohen*, pp. 103–6, and in Beaurin, *Flèche de Feu*, pp. 226–28.

extract from a homily preached on the occasion of the baptism of another Jewish convert:

> Do you believe, my brothers, that God converted us just
> for our own benefit? No, a thousand times no. It is for
> others as much as for ourselves, that they may avoid the
> reefs against which we have shipwrecked. Yes, He has nailed
> us as signposts before the gates of Hell to say, "Don't go
> this way."...[30]

The happiness to be found in Jesus was the theme of
many, if not most, of his homilies, as the following extracts
show:

> Not finding the happiness I sought, I was continually flee-
> ing He who was pursuing me, up until that day I entered a
> church, and the priest at the altar was holding in his hands
> something white.... I looked at the little host and heard
> the words, "I am the way, the truth, and the life."...
>
> My God, is it possible to have lived without thinking of
> Jesus, without loving Jesus, without living for Jesus and in
> Jesus? And now that Your grace has awoken me, my eyes
> have seen, my hands have touched, my ears have heard, my
> heart has tasted.... Yes, I love Jesus Christ and no longer
> want to hide myself; I take it to be an honor to proclaim it
> to the whole universe. I love Jesus Christ: that's the secret
> of my immense happiness, which has only increased since I
> began to love Him. I love Jesus Christ, I want to shout it
> to all the corners of the earth, I would like if the walls of
> this temple could expand and enclose all the millions of
> men who cover the globe, and that my voice could reach
> and penetrate all the fibers of their hearts and make them
> vibrate in unison with mine, and that all, in a single voice,

[30] From a homily Cohen preached on the occasion of the profession of
Bernard Bauer, quoted in Beaurin, *Flèche de Feu*, p. 219.

would reply in an immense song of jubilation and triumph, reaching from earth to Heaven, "We too, we love Jesus Christ!"

It is not possible for someone who does not love Jesus Christ to be happy. We love being happy, and Jesus Christ, the only possible happiness, is not loved; we love pleasures, splendor; but Jesus Christ, the most exquisite pleasure, the splendor of eternal glory, is not loved.[31]

On another occasion Cohen addressed his former friends, exhorting them to partake of the same happiness that he had found:

O Jesus my love, how I want to set my former friends on fire with the passion that inflames me! How I want to show them the happiness You give me. No, I dare say it, if the Faith didn't teach me that contemplating You in Heaven is a yet greater joy, I would never believe it possible that a greater happiness existed than that which I experience in loving You in the Eucharist, and in receiving You in my poor heart, so rich because of You. What delicious peace, what happiness! What holy joy!

If you no longer see me killing myself to get applause, scheming for empty honors, it is because I've found my glory in the humble tabernacle of Jesus-Host, Jesus-God.

If you no longer see me betting on a single card the wealth of an entire family, or breathlessly running after gold, it is because I've found the true wealth, the inexhaustible treasure in the ciborium of love that encloses Jesus-Host.

If I no longer deafen myself at your frivolous parties, it is because there is a wedding feast where I dine with the angels of Heaven; it is because I have found the supreme happiness. Yes, I've found it, the good that I love is mine, I possess it.

[31] Beaurin, *Flèche de Feu*, pp. 218–20.

Poor riches, sad pleasures, humiliating honors, which I chased after with you! But now that my eyes have seen, my hands have touched, my heart has beat upon the Heart of a God, oh! how I pity your blind pursuit of pleasures that are incapable of filling your hearts!

Come then to this celestial banquet prepared for you by Eternal Wisdom. Come, approach, leave behind your little toys, your chimeras; throw far from you those lying rags that cover you. Ask Jesus for the white robe of pardon, and with a new heart, a pure heart, drink at the clear fountain of His love.[32]

In 1851 Father Cohen published a collection of motets entitled *Love of Jesus Christ*; its introduction is an unbroken hymn of praise to the Blessed Sacrament:

O Adorable Sacrament, intoxicating spring from which my parched lips drink in long draughts the first fruits of eternal life, my heart overflows with joy. I must bless You and sing Your praises in songs of joy and thanksgiving. . . . It was from behind the Eucharistic veil that You unveiled the eternal truths to me, and the first mystery You revealed to my heart was that of Your Real Presence in the Most Holy Sacrament. Did I not want even then, still a Jew, to throw myself at the holy table, to bring You into my erring heart? If I shouted for baptism, was it not to unite myself to You? Impatient, sighing after this beautiful day of my life, I wept with jealousy in seeing others receive. I devoured with my eyes the little Host, where Your love for man has imprisoned the infinite God. . . .

And when at last I was admitted to the heavenly banquet, I drew an unknown strength with which to conquer myself. This divine Flesh transformed me into a new man; this treasure detached me from all that previously held me captive.

[32] Beaurin, *Flèche de Feu*, p. 93.

An ever more burning thirst drew me to this source of living water; I was consumed with the hunger of a starving
man for this wheat of the elect. Must I not now sing You
songs of joy?

Is it not Your Sacrament that did all this, that made me
renounce seductive pleasures for a saving penitence, splendor and ostentation for a coarse habit, the bright lights of
fame for the obscurity of a monastery? [33]

Virtually all of his writings and sermons are permeated
with praises of the Blessed Sacrament:

The Holy Eucharist is the only thanksgiving offering worthy
of God.... God ordered the Israelites to keep in the tabernacle a container filled with manna, as a perpetual memory of the benefits He showered on them in feeding them
in the desert; thus, manna has always been seen as an image
of the Eucharist. But even the name of the true manna, of
the "Eucharist", this name so sweet, which expresses in a
single word all the treasures of God's goodness, means literally in Greek, "thanksgiving". And since man's thanksgiving is inadequate, this treasure is called "the divine
Eucharist"—the divine thanksgiving, and so an infinite, inexhaustible, incessant thanksgiving adequate for the immense
goodness of God.

Oh, yes, I hear, O my God, when I offer You this host of
praise and love, the Father's voice from the heights of Heaven
again descend on Jesus in the waters of the Jordan, saying,
"this is my beloved Son in whom I am well pleased." If
then we offer Him this well-beloved Son, become our portion in the divine Eucharist, we present to the Eternal Father
an infinitely pleasing thanksgiving, a thanksgiving worthy
of Him, equal to Him, and so superabundant.... This is

[33] From the dedication to a collection of motets by Cohen, Carmelite
Priory, Agen, March 1851, cited in Beaurin, *Flèche de Feu*, pp. 161–62.

how, my brothers, we can give full thanks to God, through
our divine Mediator, Jesus, in the Eucharist, at the sacrifice
of the altar, through Jesus Christ, without which we could
never give God a glory, a praise, appropriate to the infinite
greatness of His blessings.[34]

I would like you to live totally by the Eucharist. May He be
the source of your thoughts, feelings, words, and deeds. May
He be the light that guides you, your inspiration, your model
and your constant preoccupation. As Magdalene shed tears
and poured perfume over the feet of Jesus, may you never tire
of offering your prayers, aspirations, and gifts before the tabernacle. I wish the Eucharist to be for you a fire of love, a
burning fire into which you can throw yourself so as to emerge
as a flame with love and generosity. May the altar where Jesus
sacrifices Himself also receive your sacrifices, so that with Him
you may become a victim of love, whose odor of sweetness
rises before the throne of the eternal.[35]

The one dark spot on Father Cohen's happiness was his
concern for his mother's soul, who did not follow him into
the Catholic Faith. On the Feast of the Immaculate Conception 1852, he went on pilgrimage to a Marian shrine to
pray for her salvation:

Mother of Heaven, for your Divine Son, I have abandoned a mother on earth. Will you return her to me one
day? As her son was once, she still is sitting in the shadow
of death; she is looking for the coming of the Messiah in
the future. She does not know that the bright Star of Jacob
has appeared for us, and that its brilliance has shone for
eighteen centuries, without eclipse, in the skies of the
Church. She does not know that you were its dawn, and

[34] Sylvain, *Vie du R.P. Hermann*, pp. 89–91.
[35] From a letter of Fr. Cohen's, cited in Tierney, *Story of Hermann Cohen*,
p. 85.

that your sweet light never ceases to direct the steps of the weakest mortals towards this Sun of Justice that God has given us to enlighten all the nations and to be the Glory of His people Israel.

O Mary! Daughter of Israel, she belongs to your family, turn then upon her a look of pity and of love.

O Mary! You have saved the son; let him not then be forever separated from his mother. She is your image for me, and her memory never enters my heart alone. She gave me birth in suffering, and you also, to give me a second life, adopted me as your child at a price as high as all the sufferings of Calvary! O Mother of Jesus, O my Mother! If the thoughts of earth are not transformed on high, could I see you without her in Heaven with full joy, would not her eternal loss be a cloud upon my happiness?[36]

When his mother passed away in late 1854, still not having embraced the Catholic Faith, Father Cohen was deeply distressed. In his anguish he spoke with his friend the Curé of Ars, who reassured him with a mysterious prophecy: "Hope, hope! You will receive one day, on the Feast of the Immaculate Conception, a letter which will bring you great joy." Seven years later, on December 8, 1861—the Feast of the Immaculate Conception—a Jesuit priest brought Father Cohen a letter written by a woman well known for her sanctity and interior life, who had herself written a number of well-regarded books on Catholic spirituality. The letter contained an account of a revelation that she had received a few months earlier:

My Jesus showed me in a ray of His divine light [that] the moment that Father Hermann's mother was on the point of

[36] Prayer made by Cohen at the Shrine of Our Lady of Peyraqude, Dec. 8, 1952, and quoted in Sylvain, *Vie du R.P. Hermann*, p. 122.

dying, when she seemed already unconscious, almost dead,
Mary, our Blessed Mother, presented herself before her divine
Son and, prostrating herself at His feet, she said, "Grace, pity,
O my Son, for this soul about to perish. In an instant she will
be lost, lost for eternity. Do, I beg You, for the mother of Your
servant Hermann that which You would want him to do for
Yours, if she were in her place and You were in his. He has
consecrated her to me; can I allow her to perish? No, this soul
is my prize, I want it, I claim it, as the price of Your Blood,
of my sorrows at the foot of Your Cross."

Scarcely had the supplicant to God stopped speaking than
a strong, powerful grace came out of the source of all graces,
the adorable heart of our Jesus, and illumined the soul of
the poor dying Jewish woman and instantly vanquished her
stubbornness and resistance. This soul immediately turned
with a loving confidence toward Him whose Mercy had
pursued her into the arms of death and said to Him, "O
my Jesus, God of the Christians, God whom my son adores,
I believe in You, I hope in You; have pity on me." [37]

When the Franco-Prussian War broke out in 1870, Father
Cohen decided to leave France for neutral Switzerland, in
order to protect his community from potential harassment
on the basis of his German nationality. After a few months
ministering outside Geneva, the local Bishop summoned
him with a special request. The many thousands of French
prisoners of war being held in German prisoner-of-war camps
were being deprived of the sacraments, because the German government would not allow any French priests to
enter. Father Cohen, as a German national, would probably be allowed in. Was he willing to go? He immediately
agreed. He had a premonition of the outcome. On leaving
Switzerland, he was heard to say, "Germany will be my

[37] Beaurin, *Flèche de Feu*, pp. 259–60.

tomb",[38] but, as he said to his sister in a letter, "I did not feel that I could decline, since Jesus said to those he reproved, 'I was a prisoner, and you did not visit me.' " [39]

Father Cohen left for the prisoner-of-war camp in Spandau, outside Berlin, on November 24, 1870—the Feast of the consummate Carmelite Saint John of the Cross. When he arrived, he found over five thousand underfed and underclothed prisoners, many deathly ill in the freezing Prussian winter. He ministered to all of their needs—celebrating Mass daily, hearing their confessions, visiting the sick, consoling the despairing, administering last rites to the dying, as well taking care of temporal needs such as obtaining additional clothing for them. Father Cohen held nothing back, working in the freezing cold from before dawn to late at night, and soon the brutal conditions took their toll. A fellow priest who saw him at the time recounted, "I found him aged and pale, his expression exhausted but joyful. I saw, on his forehead, something like a halo ready to shine soon." [40]

On January 9, 1871, Father Cohen was called to administer the last rites to two prisoners dying of smallpox. Unable to find the spatula usually used for the anointing oil, and aware of the urgency of the moment, he did not hesitate to use his finger, despite a scratch on it that exposed him to the deadly infection. He contracted the disease and died of it just eleven days later, on January 20, 1871—the exact anniversary of the apparition of the Blessed Virgin Mary to his fellow Jewish convert and friend, Alphonse Ratisbonne. His last words were "And now, O my God, into your hands I commend my spirit."

[38] Ibid., p. 367.
[39] Letter dated Nov. 21, 1870, cited in ibid.
[40] Ibid., p. 372.

From Socialism to the Church

David Goldstein

David Goldstein was born in 1870 to Dutch Jews who immigrated to the United States. After years as a zealous Socialist organizer, soap-box proselytizer, and politician, he realized that the ideals and the truth that he had sought in Socialism were only truly found in the Catholic Church. He then spent the rest of his life defending the Catholic Faith: in books, in weekly newspaper columns, and by criss-crossing the country, speaking and debating all comers, night after night for years. His full-length autobiography, Autobiography of a Campaigner for Christ, *was recently republished by Roman Catholic Books.*

"Why I am a Catholic" is a theme as old as the Church itself, yet it is as new to the convert as though he were the first man to discuss it. Many of the ablest and most eloquent men throughout the Christian centuries have made it their theme, each treating it in his own way. First and foremost stands St. Paul, setting for all time the ground of right reason with which to view our past and the confidence with which to go forward to a fuller understanding of the glories of the Faith.

Reprinted with permission from Rosalie Marie Levy, *Why Jews Become Catholics* (New York: Rosalie Marie Levy, 1924), pp. 12–25.

My conversion to the Church was by way of the Social-ist movement. A man's honest enthusiasm for a cause which is false may set him on his way to find the right path. The active propaganda of Socialism through which I passed was at first so seductive in its appeal for the brotherhood of man as to exclude a fair view of the natural constitution of things human, and to make it utterly impossible to look upon the Church save as an ally of Capitalism, under which name Socialists include all those forces which oppress the wage-earners. Consequently, one of the reasons why I have selected "From Socialism to the Church—Why I am a Cath-olic," as my title is first to warn those who would enter the Socialist movement in search of brotherhood that it is not there to be found, but just the contrary; for every man's hand is necessarily turned against every other man when acting under Socialist principles. Secondly, I seek to induce those in search of the brotherhood of man to look to the Catholic Church for its fulfillment, for there is the Father-hood of God, without which all search for the brother-hood of man is in vain. Within the keeping of the Church may be found the perfect plan laid down by our dear Lord Himself for us all to work out in the everyday life of Chris-tian civilization. There alone is the heaven on earth the idealist believes in and works for. If I could lead but one person who is looking the wrong way for the light of truth to turn to the "Light of the World," the Catholic Church, I should feel amply rewarded for my work.

Another reason for selecting "From Socialism to the Church—Why I am a Catholic," as my topic is the burn-ing desire to be an instrument to stir the hearts of my own race—the Jewish people—to an unbiased investigation of the claims of the Catholic Church. For there they shall find that its Founder is Christ, the Son of God. He is the

Anointed, the Word made Flesh, for whom our forefathers waited for forty long centuries before He came upon earth, and for whom pious Jews still look forward with longing. Indeed, I have the still greater hope that I may help to enlighten those irreligious Jews who have abandoned belief in the very existence of God, and are wandering over the earth like Ishmael, with their hand turned against everything born of the spirit. Having left the wholesome restraints of their old faith, they are at once a disaster to themselves and a menace to whatsoever state they inhabit. Under the spur of a false zeal they are being engulfed in the maelstrom of Socialism. Nothing but the acceptance of Christian doctrine can avail them, for the fulfillment of the Old Law is the foundation of the Catholic Church.

Perhaps another reason for having selected "From Socialism to the Church" as my subject is, after all, the hope that I may help to strengthen weak-kneed Catholics; that I may encourage timid Catholics to stand up as defenders of the glorious Faith they have inherited. To have been born a Catholic! To have been endowed, by God's grace, with the greatest of all inheritances! What other gift of fame, of honor, of riches, can compare with the gift of the true Faith? What nation is there so good or so great as the Catholic Church? Look at her organization, her history, her dogmas, her priesthood, her sacraments, her sisterhoods! The work she has done for the halt, the lame and the blind, is too great for human speech to declare. We should ever cherish our Catholic inheritance and proudly and fearlessly proclaim to all the world, "I am a Catholic!"

A word or two may not be out of place as to how I got into the Socialist movement. Of course, as an abstract proposition, it was simple enough. Having given up the practice of my Jewish religion and having no correct standards of intellectual judgment, with a boundless enthusiasm for the material betterment of the people, it was but natural that I should be lured by the promises of Socialism into its camp. As a boy, surrounded on all sides by poverty, my heart yearned to do something in the world to make the conditions of life happier. . . .

[Later] I had the good fortune to come into contact with some truly able minds, and, just as bad company, intellectual and otherwise, endangers the moral character, so does good association tend to lift the heart and mind to a recognition of eternal truth and to encourage its application.

From these friends I learned a few basic principles which progressively brought to my mind the knowledge that the ground floor of Socialism is utterly without support in right reason, and with this conviction came an understanding of the barrenness of the hope which Socialists hold out to the poor. Oh, the pity of it!

Hammering away at these principles, I was led to see that man is, as the Church has always said, a special creation. Of course, this is exactly contrary to the Socialist doctrine, which makes out men to be the product of mere evolution from the lower animals. But the argument from the ground of right reason was so plain that I must perforce accept that dogma of the Church, though, at that time, I did not relate it to Christian Faith, but accepted it rather as the truth. . . .

Animals do what they do by mere instinct, for the verdict of science is that animals do not think. Consequently, they are neither moral beings nor immoral slugs, but merely nonmoral beings. But with men, how different! Man is endowed with the positive art principle. He is endowed not only with instinct, but also with intelligence. He creates his own designs by which he superadds civilization to his natural habitation. God made man in His own image, to have dominion over all things. He is endowed with the power to use and to discover the substances, the forces and the laws of nature, and to shape them to the satisfaction of his own wants.

Man changes his art designs in accordance with his added knowledge and his attained capacity. His primitive habitation differs widely from that of civilized life. He is able to preserve his life in almost any environment, be it at the temperate zones, the poles, or the tropics, be the place barren or fertile, hot or cold, wet or dry. Man extends the use of his natural gifts by the use of this art, his hearing with the telephone, his arm with the derrick, his locomotion by the steamship and airship. [This] principle, which is never bridged over by the instinctive working of the animal, places man in a class of creation by himself on the economic field. And it is the economic field which socialists pretend to know all about.

I began to reason: If animals do what they do by instinct alone, if they do what they do because they can act in no other way in sustaining themselves within the limits of their environment, they must be merely expressing the design according to which they were created. So it was that I was taken back to the old and simple, yet ever up-to-date, argument of original design. This theory drove accidental creation, or a preponderance of force in a given direction, as an explanation of creation, from off the field. For, the universal experience of mankind testified to these facts—facts which are so simple, and at once so mysterious, as that if you plant an acorn in a given soil it will evolve into a full-grown oak tree, not an apple tree or a blueberry bush. It is simply that there is implanted within the acorn a design which, when it unfolds itself, is shown to be an oak tree, and nothing but an oak tree. What we see at its completed stage of development is just what existed in the acorn potentially. Why? At least, I could say, willy-nilly, it is so. So it is with the created universe, man included. What man, by taking thought, can add one cubit to his stature? In the process of evolution, the universe, as such, is unfolding its design, manifesting the phenomena implanted within it by its Designer. Though we behold but an infinitesimal part of the immensity of the created universe, seeing the order of its multitudinous parts, our reason points irresistibly to a Perfect Designer, and so compels the rational mind to conclude that, while the Infinite Designer is seen within His creation, He is at once known as distinct and separate from His creation. As the cause is necessarily greater than the effect, so must God be greater, and other, than His creation.

All that this argument suggests to the open-minded man is as a sealed book to the Socialist, for he is bent, not upon finding out the nature of God, but rather upon disproving the very existence of God. The materialistic philosopher neither sees nor hears. He cannot see the sublime lessons nature spreads out for his instruction, nor does he listen to the chosen ones of God.

So it was that, after years of mere naturalism, I came to the realization of the existence of God, and simultaneously, I began to get some appreciation of the dignity of man, and of the responsibility of the individual to the will of God, who is the cause of man's being. Then, too, I began to appreciate the intelligence with which we are endowed and our power of creating our own designs, by which we may work out this, that or another purpose. Yet best of all, with the realization of the existence of God came the positive belief in free choice—free will—one of our greatest gifts which makes us like unto God Himself. For, when I got a grip on the real meaning of self-direction, upon our power to go to the right or to the left, to go up or to go down, to do good or to do evil, it was a vision that opened up a new world to me. It showed me the infinite possibilities of man in attaining to the greatest heights of happiness here and hereafter, and too, the possibility of falling to the lowest depths. Then was God's goodness and power made known to my own consciousness, as it is laid down in the 30th Chapter of Deuteronomy, in which God says: "I call Heaven and earth to witness this day, that I have set before you life and death, blessing and cursing. Choose, therefore, life, that both thou and thy seed may live."

Surely I had seen the light, and I must obey the knowledge I had gained. I must depart from the Socialist camp to do them battle.

It was hard indeed to throw over an ideal which I had cherished so long. Suffice it to say I resigned from the Socialist movement on May 23, 1903. I was absolutely convinced that the Socialist authorities, from Marx and Engels to Herron, are in favor of the Darwinistic evolution, atheism, personal irresponsibility, and free love, and these doctrines are bone of the Socialist movement's bone, and flesh of its flesh.

When I left the Socialist party I did not have the remotest idea that I should ever enter the Catholic Church, though I was greatly impressed with its attitude towards the family. Its utterance was straightforward, while the speech of others was more or less wavering. [I became] aware of the fact that the Catholic Church is the strongest factor in the world in protecting the family.

I am sure that the dear Lord was leading me by the hand, for I attended the conferences at the Immaculate Conception Church of Boston, where I heard such reasonable and convincing addresses from the Jesuit Fathers that I fell in love with the soundness of Catholic doctrine. I found, at every point, the Catholic Church to be the direct opposite of what its enemies had declared it to be.

Not satisfied with mere admiration of Catholic doctrine, I began attending the daily Mass at the Carmelite convent. This I kept up for a year or more. No doubt it was the prayers of the nuns, as well as the instruction and patient example of my teacher, also a convert to the Church, that opened up to me the road from Socialism to the Church—so that one more man might be privileged to say "I am a Catholic." She had impressed upon me the necessity of going to fundamental principles and to original sources. From this instruction, I could see that an examination of the doctrines of the hundreds of sects, all claiming to be Christian, would lead only to confusion, without giving a root knowledge of the Christian Church. Just as I realized that the discussion of the Talmud might be interminable though not enlightening, as one can get no nearer to the Mosaic Law save by study of the Law itself.

On walking through the Jewish quarter of Boston one evening on my way home from work, I chanced to look into a store window of a Protestant Mission. My eyes lighted upon a pamphlet—"Israel's Messiah"—just the subject I wanted to know something about. Fortune favored me, for, although the only copy was in the window, yet the attendant insisted upon giving it to me.

The pamphlet told, in simple and eloquent language, the story of our Lord. It brought out the fact that both Joseph and Mary were of the house of David, from which it was foretold the Messiah would come. It told of the strictness with which the Jews kept, protected and cherished their genealogical tables; that all the people of Israel "were reckoned by genealogies." Thus it was that the Jews were able to trace the ten tribes—to know who was a true son of the house of Levi, from whom their priests were selected, and the records would show who was a true son of the house of David, in which the Messiah was to be born. The pamphlet made clear that at the time of the birth of the Christ Child no one had ever disputed that both Mary and Joseph belonged to the house of David—nor was it disputed during the life of our Lord Himself that He was a son of the house of David. But, since all the records were destroyed by Titus when Jerusalem was destroyed, how desolate must be the hearts of those Jews who still look for the coming of their Messiah! From reading this pamphlet, I turned to the prophecies in the Bible. The more I read, the more I believed in the Messiah-ship of the Child of Bethlehem.

Especially was I impressed with the prophecy of Daniel, in which he foretold the exact time when the vision and the prophecy would be fulfilled; when the Saint of Saints would be anointed; when the Messiah would be here, in accordance with God's promise, for in the fullness of that time Christ our Lord was born.

Just two years after I resigned from the Socialist movement, by God's grace, the waters of regeneration were poured over me in Baptism by Rev. Joseph H. Rockwell, S.J.

This is, in brief, the story of my journey from Socialism to the Church. A few moments in the telling, but what a world of difference between the one state and the other! For once again, our Lord's promise has been fulfilled, "Seek, and ye shall find; knock, and it shall be opened unto you."

My experience was the story of the Holy Grail over again. "Wanderers search afar for the truth, battling against our ignorance and the temptations to indulge our passions, only to find that the Lord God loves us so that He has planted His Church with the Sacred Vessel at our very door, the place from which we set out."

Before the Dawn

Rabbi Israel Zolli

Israel Zolli was born in 1881 into a wealthy Jewish family in Brody, a town in Poland just a few miles from the Russian border. His father owned a silk factory across the border in Russia. In 1888 the Russian government confiscated the factory without compensation, and the family was thrown into poverty. Only with great difficulty and sacrifice was the family able to enable Israel, a brilliant student, to complete his schooling and go on to higher studies. He eventually completed the necessary studies both to become a Rabbi and to obtain a doctorate in philosophy. At the unprecedented young age of thirty-seven he was named Chief Rabbi of Trieste, at the time one of the most important Jewish communities in Europe. After twenty years in that post, during which time he also taught at the University of Padua and wrote several well-received scholarly works, he was named Chief Rabbi of Rome. During the Nazi occupation of Rome, Rabbi Zolli worked heroically to help save the Jewish community. With the help of Pope Pius XII, he raised fifty kilos of gold to give the Nazis as a ransom to spare Rome's Jews. In entering the Church in 1945, Rabbi Zolli took Pius XII's baptismal name, Eugenio, as his own,

Extracted from Rabbi Israel Zolli, *Before the Dawn* (New York: Sheed and Ward, 1954), with permission of Roman Catholic Books, New York, which has reprinted the book as *Why I Became a Catholic* (n.d.).

in homage for all that the Pope had done to save Jews during the war. After becoming Catholic, Zolli was ostracized and calumniated by the Jewish community and thrown once again into poverty. He spent the remainder of his life teaching and writing, and he started a religious congregation dedicated to aiding Jews after their entry into the Catholic Church. He died in 1956 in Rome. The following account of his life and conversion is extracted from his autobiography, Before the Dawn.

I was born in 1881 in Brody, which had become a part of Austria after the partition of Poland in 1795. I was the youngest in the family; there were three brothers and a sister older than myself. When I was very small my father owned a large silk factory in Lodz, in ex-Polish Russia; he was an upright man, well known and respected. By the time I was seven, this was only a memory. Russia [had forced] every foreign-owned industry on Russian soil to be shut down, but the owner was not permitted to convert his property into cash. Thus our family was plunged into straitened circumstances.

My mother belonged to a family of learned rabbis; this family could boast of two centuries of intellectualism. My mother wished me to become a rabbi.

It was from my father that I learned the great art of praying with tears. During the Nazi persecution, long years afterward, I lived near the center of Rome in a small room. There, in the dark, in hunger and cold, I would pray, weeping: "O thou keeper of Israel, protect the remnants of Israel: do not allow this remnant of Israel to perish!"

When I was eight years of age, I attended a Hebrew school. There, on Sunday, Monday, and Tuesday, the teacher expounded to us the Hebrew texts, which first he made us read and translate. These texts were the Torah, the Psalms, and others. On Wednesday and all day Thursday, with the exception of two hours, and again on Friday until two o'clock in the afternoon, there was a repetition of what we were learning. This continual reading and translating helped me to memorize everything, so that I knew my Hebrew texts by heart. On Saturdays the teacher took me to the house of the Chief Rabbi of the Synagogue, who gave me a kind of examination. As a reward I would receive a sweet red apple.

At this same time I was attending an elementary school in addition to the religious school. The class was a large one, composed of about thirty Christians and six Israelites. Stanislaus, a widow's son, was my companion. He and his mother lived on the ground floor of a house in the suburbs. Once or twice a week I would go to spend the afternoon with Stanislaus. The modest home had something in it very attractive for me. I was happy there. There was only a large square room and a small kitchen, that was all. In the middle of one wall hung a crucifix of plain wood, with the branch of an olive tree over it. We boys never became boisterous or disorderly during our study or in the intervals. It seemed that in that white room, and in the presence of the crucifix, one could not help being serene, gentle, and good. Sometimes—I did not know why—I would raise my eyes to that crucifix and gaze for a long time at the figure hanging there. This contemplation, if I may call it that without exaggeration, was not done without a stirring of my spirit.

Why was this man crucified? I asked myself. Was he a bad man? Are all the wicked crucified? Why did so many people follow him if he was so wicked? Why are those who follow this "crucified one" so good? How is it that Stanislaus and his mother are so good, and they adore this crucified one? Why do we boys become so different in the presence of this crucifix? It was thoughts like these that would pass through my mind as I gazed at the crucifix.

This crucified one, moreover, awakened in me a sense of great compassion. I had the same strong impression of his innocence as of his pain ... he agonized.

This man on the cross bows his head, he is very tired, a sweet sleep is about to envelop him. He does not cry out in his pain, he does not lament, he does not curse. On his face is no expression of hatred or resentment. The olive branch above his head seems to whisper softly of peace.

No, He, Jesus, that man—now he was "He" for me, with a capital "H"—He was not bad; He could not have been in any way wicked. Perhaps He was, or perhaps He was not, the "Servant of God" whose canticles we read at school. Perhaps He was, or perhaps He was not, that sufferer of whom the master told us. . . . I did not know. But of one thing I was certain: He was good.

But then, why did they crucify Him? In the book of Isaiah there are four canticles—42:1–7, 49:1–5, 50:4–9, and 52:13–53:12—which present to us an innocent man, purer than any other in the world. He is stricken and humiliated, exhausted by so much suffering; He dies in silence as in silence He suffered. Then the crowd seems to recover from its fury: "Why have we tormented and put to death Him who bore our sins?"

Why did I so often think of the crucifix in Stanislaus' home, affirming to myself, with a lively feeling of sympathy, He was good, He could not have been bad? More than once I saw again in spirit that thorn-crowned head, the blood-stained face—gentle, exhausted, the eyes half-closed—and I would ask myself: But *why*? . . .

I was about twelve years old. An invisible Someone had begun to knock on the door of my soul. I felt a great void. My soul was wounded. I yearned for a kindred spirit. Then I remembered once more the "Servant of God" of whom the prophet Isaiah speaks. I wanted to read and reread those canticles. . . . There is Job, but more beautiful, because more mysterious, is the silence of the Servant of God. It is a fertile silence; it speaks to the heart as God does, without the sound of voice. It leaves a void in my soul, enlarges the wounds and deepens them and causes them to bleed. We must listen to the silence of God and of His Servant. Who was this Servant of God? The answer brought to my mind the thought of Stanislaus, his white room and of Him hanging on the wall.

He, the crucified in Stanislaus' big white room, and He whose voice called me, calls everybody. He speaks, He calls— only He. His voice reaches me from afar. I am listening like the beloved in the mystical Canticle of Canticles, and hear Him come from on high, in the air as on the wings of a gentle wind. I do not see Him but I feel Him near, always nearer. Then I wait, and wait still longer, and my waiting becomes prayer: it is invocation. I invoke Him, the One whom I know, and yet do not know.

My high school education completed, I had as my objective the University of Florence. In the city of flowers, Florence, I lived gray and cold years in the midst of privations of both body and spirit. Here I received degrees in Philosophy at the University (Ph.D., with psychology as a specialty) and at the Rabbinical College, institutions a short distance from each other. All this work was done in Florence. Afterwards, in 1913, I was nominated Vice Rabbi at Trieste, and became Chief Rabbi in 1918.

I think it was towards the end of 1917. One afternoon I was alone in the house, writing one of my regular articles. I was feeling wholly detached from myself, absorbed in my work. Suddenly, without knowing why I did so, I put my pen down on the table and, as if in a trance, began to invoke the name of Jesus. I found no peace until I saw Him, as if in a large picture without a frame, in the dark corner of the room.

I gazed on Him for a long time without feeling any excitement, rather in a perfect serenity of spirit. Neither then, nor now after thirty years, could I say what happened in my soul to produce such a phenomenon. I do not seek to penetrate the mystery. What did it all mean? To me now, as then, the nearness of Jesus is sufficient. Was this experience objectively real or only subjective? I do not know; nor am I competent to analyze it. It was like other experiences, under different forms, that I have had since—in 1937–1938, and again in 1945. I had no desire to speak of it to anyone, neither did I think of it as a conversion. What had happened concerned me, and only me. My intense love for Jesus and the experiences I had concerned no one else; nor did they seem to me at the time to involve a change of religion. Jesus had entered into my interior life as a guest, invoked and welcomed.

No denial or acceptance of a formal character entered into my mind. The Israelite Community and the Church represented religious life for me, each in itself. I felt myself to be a Hebrew because I was naturally Hebrew, and I loved Jesus Christ. Neither Hebraism nor Christianity seemed to interfere in my love for Jesus. Jesus was present in me, and I in Jesus.

Rabbi Zolli remained the Chief Rabbi of Trieste from 1918 to 1938. During this period he distinguished himself as an academic and a scholar, writing several important scholarly works and becoming Professor of Semitic languages at the University of Padua, where many of his students were priests; as Zolli notes in his autobiography, "Even at that time they were remembering me in their holy Masses, asking God (as they told me years later) for my conversion." One of the books he wrote during this period was a study of Jesus of Nazareth entitled The Nazarene, *which although written from a Jewish perspective was so consistent with the Catholic view that an Archbishop told Zolli that he would be able to give the book an* imprimatur.

In 1939 Zolli left Trieste to become the Chief Rabbi and spiritual leader of the Jewish community in Rome. Zolli's final conversion experience took place in 1944, while he was celebrating the Yom Kippur services—the most solemn holiday of the Jewish liturgical year—as Chief Rabbi of Rome. Continuing in his words:

It was the Day of Atonement in the fall of 1944, and I was presiding over the religious service in the Temple. The day was nearing its end, and I was all alone in the midst of a great number of persons. I began to feel as though a fog were creeping into my soul; it became denser, and I wholly lost touch with the men and things around me. And just then I saw with my mind's eye a meadow sweeping upward, with bright grass. In this meadow I saw Jesus Christ clad in a white mantle, and beyond His head the blue sky. I experienced the greatest interior peace. If I were to give an image of the state of my soul at that moment I should say a crystal-clear lake amid high mountains. Within my heart I found the words: "You are here for the last time." I considered them with the greatest serenity of soul. The reply of my heart was: So it is, so it shall be, so it must be.

Later my wife, my daughter, and I went home for supper after the fast. After supper my wife went to her room, and so did my daughter. When I was tired I went to the bedroom. The door of my daughter's room was shut. Suddenly my wife said to me: "Today while you were before the Ark of the Torah, it seemed to me as if the white figure of Jesus put His hands on your head as if He were blessing you." I was amazed but still very calm. At this very moment we heard our younger daughter, Miriam, call from afar, "Papaaa!" I went to her room. "What is the matter?" I asked. "You know, Papa, tonight I have been dreaming that I saw a very tall, white Jesus, but I don't remember what came next."

It was a few days later that I resigned my post in the Israelite Community and went to a quite unknown priest in order to receive instruction. An interval of some weeks elapsed, until the 13th of February, when I received the Sacrament of Baptism and was incorporated into the Catholic Church, the Mystical Body of Jesus Christ.

Some of Rabbi Zolli's comments on his conversion follow.

The convert, like someone who is miraculously healed, is the object and not the subject of the prodigy. It is false to say of someone that he himself converted, as if it were a matter of personal initiative. One does not say of someone who was miraculously healed that he healed himself, but that he *was* healed. One must say the same of the convert.

Is conversion an infidelity, an infidelity towards the faith previously professed? ... Faith is an adherence, not to a tradition or family or tribe, or even nation, it is an adherence of our life and our works to the Will of God as it is revealed to each in the intimacy of conscience.

Conversion consists in responding to a call from God. A man is not converted at the time he chooses, but in the hour when he receives God's call. When the call is heard, he who receives it has only one thing to do: *obey*.

Paul is "converted". Did he abandon the God of Israel? Did he cease to love Israel? It would be absurd to think so. But then? The convert is one who feels impelled by an irresistible force to leave a pre-established order and seek his own proper way. It would be easier to continue along the road he was on.

Conversion is light renewed, love of God renewed. The convert is a man who has died and has risen again. But the

Spirit of God breathes where it wills and how it wills. . . . Unconsciously, quite unconsciously, I was beginning to find in Christianity a springtime of the spirit, full of the expectation of new life made eternal; Christianity represented for me the object of a longing for a love which should temper my soul's winter, an incomparable beauty which should quench my desire for beauty. . . . In the words of the Canticle of Canticles: "Winter is now past, the rain is over and gone. The flowers have appeared in our land: the time of pruning is come; the voice of the turtle-dove is heard."

The slow preparation for spiritual rebirth is much like the preparation which takes place in nature: all is accomplished in silence, and no sign appears of the wondrous event to come. All of a sudden, it seems, the earth is covered with green and the trees are decked with red and white blossom. Like snow-crystals petals float in the air, and there is promise of fruit. One great biological process has reached completion, and a fresh cycle of life is taking on concrete reality, becoming crystallized. The dying we saw was only apparent; it meant the transformation of the life lived into a new life, a life to be lived. . . . What seemed to die in me had left in my soul the germs of a new life, the life of Jesus Christ.

When asked why he had given up the synagogue for the Church, Zolli replied:

But I have not given it up. Christianity is the integration, completion or crown of the Synagogue. For the Synagogue was a promise, and Christianity is the fulfillment of that promise. The Synagogue pointed to Christianity: Christianity presupposes the Synagogue. So you see, one cannot exist without the other. What I converted to was the living Christianity.

Taste and See the Sweetness
of the Lord

Charlie Rich

*Charlie Rich was born in 1899 to a devout Hasidic family in a
small village in Hungary. As a child his schooling was entirely
religious, and he had a prayerful, pious nature, spending many
hours alone in the woods around his home in loving contemplation of God. However, after his family immigrated to the United
States and settled in a Jewish ghetto in New York City, Charlie
lost his faith and became an atheist. Desperate to find the meaning of life, and unable to afford formal education, he spent most
of his twenties in the public library, studying philosophy and
religion. When he was unable to find the answer there, he fell
into despair and twice tried to commit suicide. Then, at the age
of thirty-three, he found all the meaning he had been hoping
for, and more, in Jesus Christ and the Catholic Church. He
spent the rest of his long life as a Catholic lay contemplative,
most of it with a Jesuit community in New York City. He died
in 1998. The following is taken from his own words, minimally
edited.*

These excerpts are from Charles Rich, *Autobiography* (Petersham, Mass.:
St. Bede's Publications, 1990), and Charles Rich, *Reflections* (Petersham, Mass.:
St. Bede's Publications, 1986), slightly modified and used with permission.

I was born in 1899 in the beautiful Hungarian country, as beautiful a country as I was ever in. My mother came from a strong Hasidic background and was one of the most spiritual human beings I ever met. Her Hasidic father, she told me, was noted for his charity to the poor, and kept open house for Jewish travelers who were too poor for any other kind of lodging. He was also famous for his deep Hasidic piety. I once asked my mother where she got all her beautiful spiritual qualities, and she said she derived them from her holy father. My own father lived in the United States, so I saw him only once during the first ten years of my life. In the meantime, my mother arranged for me to be with holy Jewish men who remained unmarried in order to be able to devote themselves completely to the study of the holy Scripture and the commentaries made on them by the different rabbinical schools.

There were no public schools where I lived for the first eight years, so an arrangement was made for individual Jewish men to teach the boys to read and write in Yiddish, the reading consisting in this study of the first five books of the Old Testament known as the holy Torah. My spiritual life during those early years consisted in attending the morning prayers which took place in the synagogue, which began before daybreak. Each morning I found myself walking to the synagogue to attend these early-morning prayers, so my getting up for Mass now around three or four o'clock is no problem. As far back as I can remember, I found going to the synagogue a form of intense delight and prayer, a form of recreation to me and a source of deep joy, making me feel surrounded by supernatural forces. From as far back as I can remember, I never felt myself alone in the world and this even though I only had one friend. I felt spiritual forces making themselves my companions and felt them with me wherever I found myself, especially in the beautiful Hungarian forests in which I used to spend hours without any other boys.

When he was ten years old, Charlie's father had saved up enough money to bring his family to join him in New York City. Once in his new, secular environment, and falling under the influence of a kindly but agnostic teacher who had taken him under his wing, Charlie lost the faith of his childhood and became an atheist. He retained, however, an intense thirst for philosophical and religious truth, and during his twenties spent hours a day, day after day and month after month, in the public library studying philosophy and religion. Continuing in his own words:

At the age of thirty-three I had read every important literary work held famous in the eyes of men, and yet there was something keenly ill at ease in my spiritual and intellectual outlook. I had even read the writings of the great Christian writers like Saint Augustine, Saint Thomas Aquinas, Saint Bernard, Saint Catherine of Siena, and Saint Teresa of Avila. At one time I decided to read everything Shakespeare had written and I did. I also read the sermons of the great Anglican writers like Cardinal Newman. And yet, there was so much distress in my spiritual and intellectual make-up that I thought of suicide as a way out of the spiritual and intellectual misery I was in. I felt like a famished person who had not eaten for days and my soul was hungry for the truths of the Christian religion, that I did not know how to attain. I felt that without supernatural faith I could not go on living and this in the same way as anyone would soon die if he was not given food to eat. So despairing of ever arriving at the truths of religion, I actually went to the Bronx Park with the intention of hanging myself. I had picked out a tree and had a rope in my hand, when someone passed by and courage failed me. I made another attempt to take my life and this also failed. Anyway, I one day passed a Catholic church—it was a hot summer day, and I felt weary and exhausted. So I thought if I went inside I could cool off. But I was afraid that not being a Catholic, I would be unwelcome, all the more as I was shabbily dressed and unkempt. But overcoming my fears I went inside and found myself completely alone. I went into this church because I was weary of my existence, so weary of it, that I even tried to bring it to an unlawful end. I went into that church to find what I had so far been unable to find, something unknown and ineffable, something which would enable me to go on living and not die out of sheer despair.

There, seated in the shadows in the empty church, he looked up to a stained glass window depicting Jesus stilling the waters during the storm (Lk 8:22–25) and said to himself:

If only I could believe with the same assurance as those who come to worship here believe! If only I could believe that the words in the Gospels are really true, that Christ really existed, and that these words are exactly those that came from His own mouth, were uttered from His own human lips, and that they are literally true. Oh, if this were only a fact, if I could only believe that this were a fact, how glorious and wonderful that would be, how consoled, happy and comforted I would be, to know that Christ was really divine, that He was God's own Son come down from another world to this earth to save us all! Could it be possible, I felt, that that which seemed too wonderful to be true actually was true, that it was no deception, no fraud, no lie? All of a sudden something flashed though my mind and I heard these words spoken in it. "Of course it is true, Christ is God, is God come down to make Himself visible in the flesh. The words in the Gospels are true, literally true."

The next thing I remember was that I found myself on my knees in fervent prayer and thanksgiving. From then on, the story takes on a delicacy which can hardly be expressed in the words of earth, for it has to do with the remarkable experience that took place in my whole spiritual and intellectual make-up during the few moments I kept kneeling in thanksgiving for a favor from Heaven I never thought would ever be granted me in the present life, the favor from Heaven which enabled me to believe in the divinity of Christ. God Himself came to my rescue that day, and He Himself spoke to me with His own voice saying to me that Christ is God. Those few minutes brought such a profound change in me spiritually and intellectually that I have since that time been unable to recognize the self I had been prior to that experience, an experience the full nature of which will only be able to be known after this life is over.

I felt a deep gratitude in my heart for something which made me feel very happy, but what it was I could not say. All that I know is that, from that day on the name of our Lord Jesus Christ took on a significance which it never before had. There was an ineffable fragrance about the words "Jesus Christ," a sweetness with which nothing can be compared. The sound of these words to this day fills me with a strange inexpressible joy, a joy which I feel does not come from this world.

I have, since my Baptism and First Communion, acquired a happiness which I would not exchange for anything in all the world. It has given to me a peace of mind and a serenity of outlook which I did not think was possible on this earth. I suppose the Buddhist would characterize this sort of peace by the word "Nirvana," but I would much prefer to call it by the familiar language of Paul: "The peace of God that surpasses all understanding."

Later Charlie Rich wrote:

It would in my case have been in vain to have been born had God not been good enough to extend me the grace to become a member of the Mystical Body of Christ the Church of Rome is. Without the Life Christ is, there is no life at all. It is for Heaven we have been made and for no other earthly good thing. It is to Heaven every good and beautiful experience points and has in view.

I became a Catholic so that I may in that way be happy, not just for a few years, but forever and ever. I became a Catholic that I may in that way get the grace to one day participate in the joys of the angels and saints in the life to come. It is to that life the grace of conversion is meant to lead. It is meant to lead to a happiness we cannot now imagine or conceive.

No, it is not for this life alone we are Catholics. We are Catholics that by being so we may get the grace to live the life Christ Himself is and which can never have a limit to it. It is for the boundlessness of Heaven that we have been born. Does not St. Paul say that "if for this life only we have hoped in Christ, we are of all men most to be pitied" (1 Cor 15:19)? We have not been born to be happy on earth. I did not become a Catholic to be happy in the present life but in the one to come, my holy Catholic faith being the way that leads to the eternal and everlasting kind of joys they experience in Heaven. It is the Heaven of unimagined bliss my becoming a Catholic has in view. It is not of the earth my holy Catholic faith speaks to me. It does so of the transcendent Good Jesus can alone be for a human being.

One can write and write and write about the story of one's conversion and never come to an end. He can never come to an end of enumerating the blessings conferred upon him by the grace of becoming a Catholic. "The mercy of the Lord I will sing forever"[1] (Ps 89:1). What "mercy of the Lord" can exceed the mercy of God that enables me to believe in all the Catholic Church teaches? Can the mercy of God be made more manifest than in the grace extended to us to become members of the only true Church? It is becoming a Catholic that matters and not in any other thing the world has to offer, be this good and beautiful as it may. The Church of Rome gives us God Himself. It does so in all His fullness—a greater gift than God is, a human being cannot hope to receive. We receive the gift God Himself is, when we receive Holy Communion. Can Protestantism and Judaism endow the soul with such a sublime gift? It is to the Church we must go to have God in the fullness He may be experienced by us this side of Heaven. To become more intimately united with God than the Church enables us to be by means of the Holy Sacraments, we must take leave of this life. It is Christ the Church gives us as He may be had under the conditions of the present life. To have God in all His fullness we have to have the grace of membership in His Mystical Body. It is the Voice of Christ the Church makes use of when He says, "I came that they might have life, and have it abundantly" (Jn 10:10).

There is the beauty in the Church, and it is made manifest in the writings of the fathers and doctors of the Church

[1] Charlie Rich prayed the psalms in Hebrew. This is his own translation. —Ed.

as well as all the saints who have ever lived. Christ lives in the saints; they exemplify Him in their daily lives and with this exemplification there is the beauty to be found like in the angels and saints in Heaven. The saints bring down this beauty on this earth for in them we get a living experience of what the beauty of the God man was like. Do we wish to become beautiful with Christ's own beauty? If we do, it is to the Church of Rome we must go for that kind of beauty, and beauty to be found in everything she promulgates by way of her liturgy, her chants, her statues and her paintings. It is to the Church of Rome we have to go to get a living experience of the beauty of Christ's being, seeing that that beauty of His is enshrined and interwoven with everything she does and is. There is the beauty from Heaven to be had in the Church of Rome and is found in the doctrines she promulgates.

And so, one can go on and on writing of all that the Church of Rome is and never come to an end in praising all her divine qualities. Is she not the heavenly Jerusalem which has descended on this earth?

There is a need in the soul for the presence of God in His naked essence. And, though some people like to speak of the "historical Christ", it is Christ on the altar that matters so much for a member of the household of the true faith. For a member of the household of the faith, it is Christ in His Eucharistic Presence that the saints go to for warmth of heart and mind and the consolations they stand in need of all the time they find themselves away from the home of the soul that Christ is in the state of glory.

How joyous, how tremendously peaceful the hours have been that as a Jewish convert I have spent in prayer before the Blessed Sacrament! How sorry I feel for my fellow Jews who failed to have their God in that way in their own synagogues! Who is there who would want to go to a synagogue for the warmth of Heaven's joys to be had in a Catholic church? And, one may ask, what is a church without Christ's Sacramental Presence in her? Is not that place nothing else but just another building? In ancient times God dwelt in the "ark". He does so today in the tabernacle on the altar, in front of which a light burns to tell us that the Lord and Creator of the universe is there present in the Sacramental Presence of His Divine Son. Is this not enough to make a Jewish person dissatisfied with his synagogical form of worship? Is there not a craving in the heart of a Jewish person for Christ the Lord as He may be had on this earth by means of the Holy Eucharist? What can any religion have to offer which cannot give us Christ in His Eucharistic Presence? So that when we go to the place where He is there present, we get the feeling that we will have when we shall be with Christ in the state of Glory, the state of Glory which has its beginning right here on this earth so as to enable us to "taste and see how sweet the Lord is" [2] (Ps 34:8).

Christ is sweet to the souls of those who have the grace to have the thought of His Being deeply rooted in that part of themselves made in the image of His Father in Heaven. There is a sweetness of Christ to be experienced in the Church of Rome in which He has deigned to take up His Blessed Abode, so that when we walk into a church we get the feeling we are in the infinite bliss that name designates for a believing human being. For a believing human being, Heaven denotes Christ the Lord, that word having Him alone in view.

I think of all this as I find myself praying before the Blessed Sacrament. I think of all this, and as I do so, I am filled

[2] Again, this is Rich's own translation of the Hebrew.—ED.

with compassion for the Jewish people who have no Christ on their altar to turn to for comfort in their innumerable earthly needs, for the kind of consolation to be had in Christ alone in His Eucharistic Presence.

Why don't men die of grief at the realization that they lack the faith to believe in the only true Church! How can the Jewish people endure being Jews and not Christians? How are they able to endure the lack of grace Christianity alone can supply them? It is Christ the Jewish people have to have for them to go through the sorrows of their earthly lot. "Hear, O heavens, and give ear, O earth; for the LORD has spoken: 'Sons have I reared and brought up, but they have rebelled against me. The ox knows its owner, and the ass its master's crib; but Israel does not know, my people does not understand'" (Is 1:2–3). It is of the Jewish people these words have been written, God foreseeing their sorrowful state for not knowing Him in the Person of His Son. I get a depressing feeling every time I pass a synagogue, knowing Christ has now transferred His presence from that place to where He exists in His Sacramental state. I think of all this, and a dreary feeling comes over me, and I pray for those who know not Christ in His Sacramental state. Not knowing Christ in that state, they do not have the grace to love the Love Itself Jesus is. "Come to me, all you who are weary and find life burdensome, and I will refresh you" [3] (Mt 11:28) our Lord says to the Jewish people.

How we should thank God for the fact that we are Catholics, so that we may in that way have Christ with us in the church near where we live. As Catholics, we don't have to

---

[3] This is Rich's paraphrase; the verse reads, "Come to me, all who labor and are heavy laden, and I will give you rest" (New American Bible [NAB], 1970)—ED.

go far away to find Christ, seeing that in His Sacramental
Presence He resides at our very doorsteps in the nearest
church we happen to find ourselves, so that to have Heaven,
all we have to do is to step inside, and make an act of faith
in the Real Presence, seeing that in that way we can all rise
to the heights of the most sublime kind of prayer it is in
the province of a human being to be able to experience.

And although in the Old Testament God performed wondrous deeds, they're surpassed to an infinite degree in His
making Himself available to us in the Holy Eucharist. What
are the marvels performed by Moses compared to those performed by the priest during the act of consecration?

I know I am digressing. But is not our whole life a kind
of digression, digression from our home in Heaven to this
sad earthly exile where we cannot experience what they do
who have had the grace to depart from this life? We cannot
be happy in the present life but only in the one to come,
and it is in the realization of this truth that our sanctity
consists. Our sanctity consists in the realization that it is
only when we will be completely with Christ in the state
of glory that we, who are made in the image of God, will
attain full fruition, and not until that blessed day. Until that
blessed day we are going to remain the "foreigners" [4] on
this earth of which the psalmist speaks (Ps 39:12).

With the saints, it is either Jesus twenty-four hours of
the day, or not to have Him in their inner being. The saint
does nothing by halves, so his love for Christ falls into this
category. Once we get the grace to love Christ, it is hard
to have any love in our hearts for anything else God has
made, be this good and beautiful as it may. The psalmist
speaks of Christ being "fairer in beauty . . . than the sons of

---

[4] Rich's translation from the Hebrew; the RSV has "sojourner".—ED.

men" [5] (Ps 45:2), and it is this beauty of Christ's Being I fell in love with since the first day of my conversion. I feel sorry for my fellow Jews who fail to love the Love Itself Jesus is, and I shall never never fail to feel sorry for them on this account. A great Jewish convert, the Ven. Francis Libermann, once wrote these words about someone in his family who was not a Catholic. So and so, he said, "is not a Catholic." So and so, he said, "is still a Jew, and therefore nothing." People may consider these harsh words, but to me, they have always spoken the deepest truths that can be uttered, seeing that if we fail to be in Christ, we are in the eyes of God nothing at all, seeing that Christ constitutes the sole Reality this universe contains; without Christ rooted in our deep inner being, we are nothing at all. In fact without faith in Christ nothing has any meaning; at least without faith in Him nothing this world contains has any relevance for eternity, and not having any relevance for the life to come, what is there on this earth worth taking seriously. . . ?

I know that these are not the kind of thoughts which would be popular among a certain class of people. But these are the kind of thoughts which have been popular with every single man and woman who was blessed with the gift of faith in our Divine Lord. We have not been put on this earth in order to get along with our fellow human beings. We have been put on it for the sole purpose of seeking the truth and to follow that truth no matter where it will lead us. In my case, the quest for God's truth led me to the feet of St. Peter in the city of Rome, so it is for this reason I have the grace to find myself a member of the Mystical Body of Christ. We are not born to become this or that;

[5] Rich's translation; the RSV has "fairest of the sons of men".—ED.

we are born to be the truth-seekers God wishes us to be, the Truth our Lord Himself said He was in the words, "I am the Way, the Life and the Truth." Once he has received the grace to become a Catholic, the life of a convert becomes a song he will sing for the rest of his earthly days, and this is especially true of converts from Judaism, seeing all such go from darkness to the light to be had in Christ alone.

"Sing to him [to the Lord] a new song" (Ps 33:3), we are told by the divine psalmist, this song we sing when we get the grace to become Catholics. All others are in the category of those who said they cannot "sing a song of the Lord in a foreign land"[6] (Ps 137:4), the "foreign land" they were in prior to the gift of faith in the only true Church. And so, finding ourselves in the Church of Rome, we sing to the Lord the new song He asks we should sing to Him, a song having in itself the joy of heart which has been given him as a result of his new-found faith. And so, as a former member of Judaism, I sing this song with all those who are the recipients of a similar grace. With St. Paul we all say, "For I through the law died to the law, that I might live to God. I have been crucified with Christ; it is no longer I who live, but Christ who lives in me; and the life I now live in the flesh I live by faith in the Son of God, who loved me and gave himself for me. I do not nullify the grace of God; for if justification were through the law, then Christ died to no purpose" (Gal 2:19–21).

I have passed my eighty-seventh year, so where do we go from here? My "bags are packed," they have been packed since the first day I became a Catholic. Since the first day I became a Catholic I had only one thought: What am I doing in a world like this, so far away from the homeland

---

[6] Again, Rich's own translation.—ED.

of my soul Heaven is? The gates of Heaven having been opened up for me by my baptism, why stand outside like a prodigal son? I listen to the music from Heaven ringing in my inner hearing, so I long to be where this music comes from, in the angelic world where all the blessed souls now are. I think of all this, and as I do so I find myself drawing near the goal of my heart's desire Jesus in the state of glory is, so I wonder why am I being detained on this earth? But I realize God has His own reason for this kind of detention, so I say *fiat*, and with this word comes a peace of soul I would not exchange for all the wealth of the world. Still, in spite of the patience I have the grace to have from my having to be so far away from the home of the soul Heaven is, I look forward to the "Day of the Lord" when I shall get the grace to enter into the Kingdom of Heaven for which we pray when we say, "Thy kingdom come." I think of all this, and as I do so I call to mind the words in which the psalmist says, "Lead me out of my prison, that I may give thanks to your name"[7] (Ps 142:8). I too long to be set free from the prison of mortality so that with St. Paul I can be "freed from this life and be with Christ"[8] (Phil 1:23).

Charlie Rich was finally admitted to the union he so longed for in 1998, at the age of ninety-nine. He left behind an autobiography and a number of spiritual writings. Information on these, and on the books about him written by Ronda Chervin, can be found on the website www.friendsofcharlesrich.com.

---

[7] NAB, 1970 translation—ED.

[8] Rich's paraphrase; the RSV has "depart and be with Christ".—ED.

Jewish Knight of Columbus

Father Arthur B. Klyber, C.SS.R.

Arthur Klyber was born in 1900 in New York City, of Orthodox Jewish parents who had emigrated a few years earlier from Russia. He was orphaned as a young child and was raised with little Jewish education. At seventeen, on the eve of the U.S. entry into World War I, he enlisted in the navy; it was there that he came to know Catholics and the Catholic Faith, and he was baptized in 1920. On leaving the navy the following year, he joined the Redemptorists and was ordained a priest eleven years later.

From his seminary days on, he felt a special apostolate to his fellow Jews. Over his long life he wrote and distributed numerous books and pamphlets of apologetics emphasizing the Jewishness of the Catholic Faith and lectured extensively, all in addition to fulfilling his regular duties as a Redemptorist priest and missionary. In 1976 he founded, with Mark and Elasah Drogin, the Remnant of Israel to propagate his writings. After sixty-seven years of service as a Redemptorist priest Father Klyber died in 1999 at the age of ninety-nine. Remnant of Israel continues to carry on his

This account of Father Klyber's conversion was generously provided by Remnant of Israel. It originally appeared in a slightly different form in Ronda Chervin, ed., *The Ingrafting* (New Hope, Ky: Remnant of Israel, 1987). Used with permission.

work; more information on Father Klyber and his books can be found at its website, www.remnantofisrael.net.

The Klybers and the Laschinskys emigrated from Berdichev, Russia, to the ghetto of New York City about the year 1896. My Father, Samuel, married Julia Laschinsky who gave him four children, a girl and three boys, before she died at the age of 33. The girl died of tuberculosis, like my mother; and the three boys grew up in the big city.

Our family was strictly Jewish Orthodox on both sides. By 1910 both parents had died: I was then ten years old, and living in a Jewish orphanage with my two brothers. After two years I was placed with Jewish foster-parents until I graduated from grade school; and then went to live with my Uncle Morris and his wife Ethel, my mother's sister.

Despite three pleasant years and plenty of love in their truly religious home, I came away with only religious practices, but no religious convictions. Perhaps I would have acquired convictions if I had not left to join the Navy. My older brother has remained more or less a practicing Jew, but my younger brother became a Baptist and married into a Baptist family.

On April 5th, 1917, the eve of our war with Germany, young men of New York were enlisting like crazy, and I was one of them. At that moment if anyone had told me that within three years I would be a Catholic and that in the fourth I would begin studies for the priesthood I think I would have sneered at him.

Although I had had my Bar Mitzvah,[1] the thought of God had almost never occupied my mind. I may suppose

---

[1] The *Bar Mitzvah* is the ceremony marking a Jewish young man's coming of age, marked by a synagogue service in which he reads from the Torah (the first five books of the Hebrew Scriptures) for the first time. It is usually

that my devoted aunt and uncle hoped to confirm my Jewishness by their own good example as faithful Jews. Those two beloved relatives had never talked to me about Judaism, and my Bar Mitzvah ceremony was only a matter of five minutes, all done in Hebrew which I could read but did not understand.

At that time the only difference I knew between Jews and Christians was that Jews were not Christians, and that for some strange reason Christian boys used to beat up Jewish boys. I was without virtue so-called, although I had picked up a lasting sense of honesty (e.g., don't steal) through reading Horatio Alger's books for boys. These are based on the old proverb that "honesty is the best policy." The accent was on "policy", in the total silence about any *God*-given right of others to hold their money and property secure. Alger did prophesy rewards for such honesty, such as wealth and success in business. In spite of his rather pagan views, I don't regret his influence on me: it was the only moral instruction I acquired in my boyhood and young manhood.

After training at Newport, Rhode Island, I was detailed to the *USS Fulton*, a mother-ship of the Sixth Submarine Flotilla, then based in New London, Connecticut; and I remained with the Flotilla for the four years and four months of the service. Aboard the *Fulton* a shipmate named Bob Anderson and I struck up a warm and lasting friendship: we used to make shore liberties together. During the unforgettable flu-epidemic of 1918 Bob and I were transferred to the mother-ship *USS Alert*, a relic of the Spanish-American War, which still used sail as auxiliary power! Half of its crew was down with influenza. That very night of

---

accompanied by a festive celebration, somewhat analogous to a Catholic's confirmation.

the transfer, we sailed for the Mediterranean Sea escorting three submarines via Bermuda and the Azores Islands.

Eleven days later, while at anchor in Ponta Delgada in the Azores, came a Sunday on which Bob invited me to go ashore with him to Mass. I went along dumbly and without any notion of what the Mass or Christianity meant. The experience at the Mass in that small crowded church left me bored and unmoved, especially since I had to stand up through it all. I came away from it just as much (or maybe as little) a Jew as ever: but then maybe God did something which I didn't perceive.

Back aboard ship, we heard the electrifying news of the Armistice, along with the further cheery words that our ship had been ordered back to the States, this time not to Charleston, South Carolina, from which we left, but to San Pedro, California.

Some weeks after we had dropped anchor in the harbor (February 15, 1919) Bob invited me to his home in Los Angeles, about twenty-three miles inland. When I declined the invitation he baited me by mentioning their Jewish next-door neighbors who had three lovely daughters. The bait did not hook me, but I hooked myself out of curiosity to meet Bob's family, so I went along. The visit with Mrs. Anderson and all four of her sons was pleasant: the youngest was sixteen. After supper we went next door where the dear Jewish mother introduced her daughters to me and sat them down on a divan opposite me—for inspection, shall I say. Maybe you know that Jewish mammas are often utterly candid about offering their daughters for marriage.

Needless to say, I enjoyed the company of these fine girls, but decided not to cultivate their acquaintance. With the Andersons it was different. I became a weekend nuisance at their home, and gradually the boys introduced me to their exclusive gang of Catholic young men and women. It turned out that this companionship was "just what the doctor would have ordered." Of the twenty or so in the group I was the only non-Catholic. We all loved dancing and we did a lot of it. Picnics, swims on the Pacific beaches, mountain trips, and parties at their homes were regular weekend treats. This happy association lasted nearly two years. Though none of them ever asked me to become a Catholic, the example of their sincerely virtuous and religious lives must have had a deep though invisible influence on me.

I recall that my spiritual condition (if I can even call it that) shortly before my conversion was shabby: and I was heading for shipwreck on the rocks of loneliness. Still, as well as I can remember, I did not have any real conscience about sin, and I guess that was because I didn't have any practical belief in God. On one occasion, as I was ambling along a deserted street in San Pedro, I began suddenly to think it useless to be a "good boy".... What difference did it make anyway? I thought. I'll just go up to Los Angeles and have a good time the way many of my shipmates do. Lack of religion and purpose in life, as I saw it later, were partly responsible for that attitude. It is of interest that I did not carry out those dark plans which, as I learned after conversion, were contrary to God's will. It was at this crisis and in the nick of time that the Holy Spirit chose to come actively into my confused young life.

As I was waving to the Andersons one Sunday while they piled into their car for Mass, one of them shouted: "Like to come along?" Without further thought I hurried out to the car. In the church I was placed next to Bob. Now Bob was a silent customer, as the saying goes. Neither in the Azores at Mass, nor now at Mass did he offer even one word of explanation of what was happening. So, I bobbed up and down with Bob, or I stood up or I knelt, or sat down, but all those calisthenics didn't strengthen whatever weak spiritual muscles I might have had. As at the Azores, so now, I left Mass as unconverted and uninformed as ever. Yet I don't deny that the Holy Spirit may have tried to talk to me even then.

Perhaps a couple of Sundays later I was out riding with Mrs. Anderson and her son Paul. Our conversation was about things in general till suddenly out of the blue the dear lady asked me: "Arthur, why don't you become a Knight of Columbus?" Can you imagine any tactic so delicate as that Irish approach? And so comical? After a moment of speechless wonder I found my voice and replied: "Ah, who ever heard of a Jewish Knight of Columbus?" We both laughed, but she pursued the onslaught by saying: "Well, Arthur, you know it's not impossible."

So there. The message got to me but didn't *convert* me—at least not at the moment. The dear lady was brazenly asking me why I didn't become a Catholic. I merely chuckled, and then the conversation changed to other topics as suddenly as it had begun.

As I look back at that startling dialogue, I can't help regarding it as near preparation for what happened to me that same evening aboard a Pacific Electric train to San Pedro. I sat down for a comfortable relaxing ride, but it pleased the Lord of Heaven not to allow me to relax. On that twenty-three-mile ride the moment of Truth and the beginning of grace to accept it came to me without warning. In a clear sentence which I could not forget or reject, and without sound of human voice, I heard a question, "Why don't you become a Catholic?" The Holy Spirit, it seems, was at that moment more blunt and indelicate than was Mrs. Anderson. I suppose the Spirit was explaining that I *could* become a Jewish Knight of Columbus, if first I would become a Catholic. Curiously, I did receive all four degrees of knighthood within six months after my baptism.

Though the question on the train was alluring, it frightened me and started up a mental battle against conversion, which was to last for more than a week. My resistance didn't come from any Jewish doctrines or from any unwelcome teaching of the Church, since I didn't know any Jewish or Christian *doctrine*. My struggle came out of a real and immediate fear of losing all my relatives and friends back East if I should convert. Somehow I did know that such a loss of family could come about, though I don't know how I learned it. I knew only Jews who lived as Jews, and I had not heard of any who had been ostracized by their families for becoming Christians.

At the sub base that night I climbed into my bunk with a very troubled mind, and awoke next morning the same way. Inside of me a Jew and a Catholic were having a wrestling match: and this match continued for about eight days. I then put my foot down hard and decided, "I just can't do it and I will not do it: I can't bear the thought of losing my whole family and all my Jewish friends." With that decision I seemed to capture some mental peace, but the next day the wrestling began again. At a certain point the Jew in me began to yield, and I considered that maybe after all, my family would not throw me out. I also reflected that if they did, I still had a nucleus of friends here in the West. That was the consideration that brought me final peace of mind, and helped me to decide to "risk" conversion.

At once I wrote a short explanatory letter to Mrs. Anderson (I was too embarrassed to visit her) asking her to tell me what to do for a start. She expressed her joy at my decision and suggested I see my Navy Chaplain. She also

mentioned that she was mailing me two instruction books
exceedingly popular at that time: *The Faith of Our Fathers*
by Cardinal Gibbons; and *Conway's Question-Box*, both of
which, she said, her deceased husband had used in his conversion from Anglicanism. I later learned that Father Conway had a Jewish mother.

Next morning, when I stood before the Chaplain in his
office and announced that I wanted to be a Catholic, he
looked at me in astonishment and said with a good-natured
smile: "What! A Jew who wants to be a Catholic!?" After a
brief chat he handed me a small book to read and cau-
tioned me against being in a hurry to join the Church.
Believe it or not, the first half of that book was dedicated
to arguments *against* the Church. It could have ripped out
of me the precious, but uninstructed, Faith that I had. The
second half of the book compensated in some measure for
the dangerous developments in the first. I returned it with
the simple remark: "Chaplain, I still want to be a Catholic." He then arranged to give me a couple of instructions
himself; and said he would turn me over to a Catholic Chief
Petty Officer as my catechist. This fine shipmate gave me
excellent instruction every day for a month; and also incidentally instilled into me some of his own deep Faith: he
was at that time in the process of getting a simple discharge
from the Navy to begin his studies for the priesthood. One
of the books that Chief Yeoman Kenney (catechist) gave
me to read made me see with great clearness who Jesus
Christ was, and what He had done for the human race: its
title was: *Quo Vadis?* ("Where Are You Going?"). The author
was the famed Polish writer Sienkewicz whose books had
by that time been translated into every modern language.
My mind and heart at this happy time were like the mind
and heart of another completed Jew who much later said

to me: "Father, now that I believe that Jesus Christ is God just tell me what He wants me to do and I'll do it."

During the eight or nine days of my struggle about Faith I had my usual conversations and walks with Bob Anderson; but he didn't say a word about conversion. On one of those days he merely mentioned that the gang in Los Angeles were wondering why I hadn't come to see them for so long a time and were afraid they had offended me in some way. I remember mumbling something about just not feeling like visiting, and let it go at that. It was my own secret battle, and I felt I had to fight it out alone. I think it was the morning after my first talk with the Chaplain that I told Bob of my decision to become a Catholic. All he said was: "I felt all along that you were thinking about conversion." He had guessed it: he could read me well.

After that month of intensive instruction by Kenney, and my own greedy reading of any good Catholic book I could get, I was baptized in the Church of Mary Star of the Sea in San Pedro, with Bob as my godfather and Mrs. Anderson as my godmother. The unforgettable date was February 8, 1920, just thirty-three days before my twentieth birthday. The next day as I stepped aboard ship from the gangplank a friendly shipmate named Reynolds almost knocked me over when he reached out his hand and said cheerily: "Congratulations Art, I heard you were baptized." I thanked him, and wondered: "Can this guy be a Catholic and still have a girl in every port?!" When Reynolds saw my surprise he got serious and said: "Art, if my father ever found out all the things I have done he would kill me." I can't help feeling, however, that Reynolds turned out all right, and I feel the same about some other Catholic shipmates like him.

My baptism was followed by an intense interior joy which defies description. I am not afraid to say that joy of those

early days in the faith eclipsed even the joy of my ordination as a priest. In my long priestly experience I found that
most converts, and especially Jewish-converts, need such a
lift at baptism since most of them are punished severely by
their loved ones and their business associates. Those who
really love us air their bitterness in words something like
this: "You are a traitor against your own people: you have
betrayed the betrayed; you have gone over to the ranks of
the Christians, our enemies."

However, a Jew who has become a Christian does not
feel any degree a traitor to his people, but has actually come
to understand and love them more than ever. He wishes for
them with all his heart the saving Faith which he himself
has received. Completed Jews (converts) feel that they have
only become what all Jews expect to become when the
Messiah, for whose coming they still pray, finally arrives—at
His *Second* Coming. Come Lord: come to everyone.

O Adonai!

Sonia Katzmann (Sister Mary Samuele)

Sonia Katzmann was born in 1929 to Russian Jewish parents who had immigrated to the United States. Given a strictly orthodox Jewish upbringing, she found herself strongly drawn to the Catholic Church as a young woman. When her parents found out about her interest, it was the cause of great distress to them and of great suffering to Sonia. After their death she entered the Church, and then religious life, first as a Poor Clare and then as a Holy Spirit Adoration Sister. She died of cancer in 1978.

What follows is the "circular letter" written by her community. Many religious congregations circulate these when members die, to memorialize the deceased as well as to solicit prayers for the repose of their souls. The letter presents a luminous picture of a very beautiful, very Jewish soul, in love with Jesus and delighted to finish out her life consecrated to him as his bride.

This circular letter and permission to reprint it were graciously provided by the Holy Spirit Adoration Sisters convent in Bad Driburg, Germany.

The Holy Spirit Adoration Sisters have four convents in the United States: in Philadelphia; St. Louis, Mo.; Corpus Christi, Tex.; and, Lincoln, Neb. The addresses, as well as additional information on the order and its founder, can be found on their website: www.adorationsisters.org.

+ November 25, 1978

One sentence written about our deceased Sister Mary Samuele, Sonia Katzmann, who died a little over six months after her first profession, seems to summarize the sentiments of all the Sisters who wrote about her: "Good Sr. M. Samuele shared our life for a short time only, and during this time we learned to really love and treasure her."

Our Sister was the daughter of pious, strictly orthodox Russian Jewish parents. Her father once even let himself be fired from his job rather than work on the Sabbath. Sr. M. Samuele always retained vivid remembrances of the religious practices at home and in the synagogue. Some years after his marriage, Joseph Katzmann left Russia for the United States, intending to earn enough money to have his wife and their young daughter, Anna, follow him. The Russian Revolution intervened, and it was eleven years before the little family was again reunited in America. Thus Anna was nineteen years older than Sonia, born in Philadelphia on September 22, 1929. Their parents were simple but intelligent, capable people, who spoke six languages and set up their own business. In her early teens, despite her attendance at Hebrew School in addition to the regular school, Sonia lost interest in the Jewish services. She described how one evening as she took her place with her parents in the synagogue, she thought to herself, "I don't find God here." Thereafter she attended the services only for the sake of her parents.

After high school, Sonia worked as a clerk for seventeen years. At work a young woman began to speak to her of the Catholic Church, and Sonia's interest was sparked immediately. Intensely attracted to the Blessed Virgin, she obtained a rosary and hid it in her room. Her new-found religion opened up a new world for her but she said nothing to her parents. One day her mother discovered the rosary, knew what it meant and showed it to her husband. In anger he wanted to discard it, but his wife protested that it was a holy object to be treated with respect. After that, Sonia had to endure many difficult scenes with her father and sister. Her mother, though saddened, was more understanding. Sonia learned of the Poor Clares and became one of their benefactors, as also one of ours some years later. She began going to Mass but had to postpone becoming a Catholic until after the death of her parents. Years later, one Sunday she watched the people going to Communion, and struck with a longing to receive Jesus, she went to the pastor after Mass and made arrangements to take instructions in the Faith. She always recalled the day of her baptism as one of pure joy. When the thought of a religious vocation arose, she first turned to the Poor Clares. She was accepted by them, but for various reasons had to leave after a year. After spending long hours in prayer before the Blessed Sacrament, she again attempted to fulfill her desire for religious life by making the observer program at the Convent of Divine Love. Having received the acceptance to enter, she returned to her apartment only to gather her belongings and terminate her lease. She entered in July 1975, became a novice in May 1976 and was professed in May 1978.

Sr. M. Samuele relished the thought that she was part of both the Old and New Covenants, and one of her greatest delights was reading from the prophets and books of the Old Testament during the Divine Office or Mass. She had a strong, clear voice and was an excellent reader—she put her whole heart and soul into these readings, placing special expression into phrases she particularly liked. Once as a postulant, after practicing the "O Antiphons" before Christmas, Sister approached the choir directress with eyes full of wonder, saying how much it meant to her to sing "O

Adonai", the holy and awesome name of the Lord. One could often notice the same glow on her countenance on feast days such as the Presentation of the Lord and others so rich in Jewish tradition. Shortly before her death, Sister said that she thanked God every day that she had been born a Jew, because it paved her way to the fullness of Christianity.

The three years of Sr. M. Samuele's formation were not always easy, but she spoke of them as the happiest of her life. She was a very sensitive person and felt humiliated by the fact that she was older than her companions. Her feelings of inadequacy in the face of the talents of others sometimes caused her to withdraw at recreation, although she was a social person and loved to take part in the plays and skits for feast days. She had a flair for the dramatic and enjoyed making others laugh. Her special delight was playing the part of Father Arnold,[1] and she would put special effort into it so that he would be pleased with her impersonation from his place in Heaven. Sr. M. Samuele's inclination to be fearful and anxious caused her to react strongly at times to the words or actions of others and to be somewhat demanding on occasion. But she was also quick to recognize her faults, to accept correction, and to ask forgiveness. In fact, whenever she had been in a tense situation with another Sister, she would invariably be the first to apologize. But the quality which the Sisters recall most consistently is her outstanding spirit of gratitude. She took pains to express her thanks for the smallest things done for her, even for things that no one else usually thought of thanking for.

Sr. M. Samuele's novitiate companions were amazed at her wide knowledge and factual accuracy in a great variety

---

[1] St. Arnold Janssen, Founder of the Holy Spirit Adoration Sisters; see www.adorationsisters.org for more information on the Founder.—ED.

of subjects. The Sisters lovingly teased her as their "walking encyclopedia." Sister's love and profound respect for the beauty of creation revealed the true beauty hidden deep in her soul. Classical and operatic music could hold her interest for long periods, and she knew the names and composers of many symphonies, as well as interesting information on the composers' lives and work. She was very devoted to the welfare of her companions and rendered many helpful attentions. There was a childlike air about her as she let herself be shown and told what to do, and then she carried it out with conscientious fidelity. Sr. M. Samuele took organ lessons in the convent and applied herself with great zeal and interest to practicing. It was a notable sacrifice for her to think of never playing again after she became ill.

Sr. M. Samuele was professed only two months when it was discovered that cancer had affected many inner organs and even her brain. She was immediately hospitalized and given chemotherapy, which greatly relieved the pain. Sr. M. Victoria, her novice directress, writes:

The last four months of Sr. M. Samuele's life were nothing more than the breaking loose, in all its tenderness and fury, of God's love for her. She suffered intensely her first few days in the hospital. Once when we went to see her, she managed to say despite her pain, "He has broken me down completely. He can do whatever He wants with me." It seems that was what God was waiting for. After that he carried her "as a man carries his child, all along the way." Then began the flowering of her personality. She who could be rather negative in her outlook and had moods of melancholy, traits which we feared would be intensified by her illness, now was always in good spirits, interested in others and concerned about them. She never bewailed her fate or showed any bitterness or repining. She had always had a fine spirit of gratitude—now it flowed from her at the least provocation: gratitude to God, to her Sisters, to the doctors and nurses, her friends.

Sr. M. Samuele's love for the Congregation was very deep and almost daily she would speak about returning to the convent. But just when the doctors decided that they would allow her to do so, she took a turn for the worse. The cancer was beginning to attack the heart tissue, and she now required almost continuous care for the last week of her life. Of her last day, Sr. M. Gemma, her superior, writes:

> Together we prayed the vow formula, but when we came to the actual renewal of vows, Sr. M. Samuele gave a little sign that she wanted to pray this part alone. With gasping breath she prayed alone and inserted the words: "for life". After she had finished, she paused a moment, and then added, "This is forever." I stayed with Sister the last ten conscious hours of her life, and I treasure every moment. She remained her simple self until the end. She told me the priests she wanted invited to her funeral and the hymns she wanted sung. About 9:00 P.M. Sister lost consciousness and peacefully went home to the Lord at 3:30 the following morning.

Besides the priests she had wanted at her funeral, Bishop Lohmuller and four other priests concelebrated the Mass. The vicar for Religious, who knew Sister before her entrance, gave a stirring eulogy, and the chapel was filled to capacity. Cardinal Krol wrote our community a letter of personal condolence.

May she who loved our Congregation so much continue to pray for all of us.

I Have Called You by Name;
You Are Mine!

Ronda Chervin, Ph.D.

Ronda Chervin, Ph.D., has taught philosophy and theology on the faculties of Loyola Marymount University, St. John's Seminary of the Archdiocese of Los Angeles, and Franciscan University of Steubenville. She lectures widely and has authored over fifty books on Catholic thought, practice, and spirituality, as well as an autobiography, En Route to Eternity.[1] *More information about Ronda Chervin and her books may be found at www.rondachervin.com.*

Thinking back, I imagine that my twin sister and I were among the most alienated little children in New York City. I have never met anyone with our peculiar background. We were the children, born in 1937, of unmarried parents who met in the Communist party, but had left it shortly before our birth to become informers for the FBI. Apparently enraged Communists threatened to bomb our cradle.

Both father and mother, though militant atheists, had Jewish backgrounds, but neither had been brought up as a Jew— not even observing High Holy Days, either at home or at a synagogue.

[1] Ronda Chervin, *En Route to Eternity* (Ypsilanti, Mich.: Miriam Press, 1994).

As right-wing political atheists of Jewish ancestry, we didn't fit in with anyone around us: not with Catholics, not with the sprinkling of Protestants, certainly not with Orthodox religious Jews in full regalia, nor Reform Jews, nor Zionist atheist Jews, nor left-wing non-Zionist Jews. Later, as a Catholic, I realized that my desire to belong to an identifiable group forever and ever had a psychological as well as a theological reason.

My mother's parents were professional European Jews who had been invited by the Czar, at the end of the nineteenth century, to help modernize Russia. Once they arrived, they became fervent atheistic Communists. When news reached their city that the police were rounding up suspected revolutionaries in the squares to shoot them, my grandparents, their children, and some of the Polish servants, fled to the United States.

Although my grandfather, a doctor, practiced medicine among Jewish immigrants, mostly from Eastern Europe, the family never spoke Yiddish, a mixture of German and Hebrew. Instead, they exulted in being freethinking Socialist Americans whose brotherhood was with all mankind, certainly not with ghetto Jews.

My grandfather on my father's side was of Sephardic[2] Jewish ancestry—born in Curaçao, South America— a descendant of a Spanish family, De Sola, half of whom became Catholic during the Inquisition. He was from the Jewish half, and had migrated to the United States and become a Madison Avenue dentist. My grandfather De Sola never observed Jewish holidays. He was an atheist.

---

[2] Sephardic Jews are Jews from the Arab world or Spain. Jews from central or eastern Europe are known as Ashkenazi.

My paternal grandmother was a blond, fragile, Pennsylvania Dutch woman who met my handsome Hispanic grandfather in the dental chair. A deeply believing Christian, Grace Geist De Sola moved up the ladder economically and doctrinally from Quaker to Presbyterian to Episcopalian. She never missed a Sunday at church, prayed constantly for her atheistic husband, son, and grandchildren, and read the Bible night and day. She was forbidden on pain of never seeing us again to mention God or religion to us. After her death I inherited a copy of her Bible (printed back in 1876) and found inked messages throughout, such as, "Someday I pray that my granddaughters will read this passage."

From Heaven I hope she knows that both granddaughters became Christian leaders, albeit Roman Catholic. She insisted that her son, Ralph De Sola, be baptized and attend the Presbyterian church. Around confirmation time, my father, always brave, for good or evil, stood up in the congregation and announced that he was an atheist and walked out of the church.

Growing up, my parents had nothing but scorn and ridicule for my Christian grandmother. She was used as an example of how only weak and stupid people still believe in God, after Nietzsche and evolution had proved God dead, or nonexistent.

However, when we were eight years old, our parents separated for good. During this painful process, we were sent for a few weeks to our grandmother's summer cottage on Fire Island. I felt miserable being dumped for an indefinite period in the house of this grandmother who loved us tenderly but whom I thought of as an idiot and a weakling. Seeing her opportunity to introduce us to Jesus, Grace De Sola insisted, on pain of missing dessert, that we sing the famous children's song: "Jesus loves me, this I know! For the Bible tells me so.... Yes, Jesus loves me! The Bible tells me so." Even though, in loyalty to our parents, we acted as if we sang that hymn only under duress, I never forgot the words.

Was that the first time I heard You, Jesus, calling my name?

Fast forward: I was an eleven-year-old New York City girl sitting in public school at one of those old-fashioned wooden desks thoroughly defaced with graffiti carved by sixty years of bored pupils, the kind of desk that still had ink wells. Once a week we had show-and-tell. Preselected students had to get up and display, say, a toy plastic turtle from a Christmas trip to Florida with a two-sentence narrative. Amusing. No pressure except for the child who had to perform.

But this time something different happened. There was a pause. Probably set up by a Catholic teacher, a quiet boy none of us normally paid attention to came walking in wearing a long black robe with a white linen blouselike thing on top of it. He stood absolutely still, hands steepled in prayer, and started singing *Adeste Fidelis*. It was the first time I had ever heard sacred music. I listened in stunned, bewildered, but joyful, silence.

Was that You, my Jesus, calling my name?

At the time I didn't realize that this lad must have been an altar boy in the Catholic Church. My knowledge of Catholics was limited, negative, though in hindsight, somewhat humorous. We lived in the same neighborhood that is depicted in "West Side Story". Before the Puerto Ricans came it was part Jewish and part Irish Catholic. There were only about two Catholics at the public school because most Catholic children in those days went to the Catholic school. The only ones I recognized on the street were incipient or actual members of gangs. Why did I think they were Catholics? Because in those days all Catholic girls wore crucifixes around their necks, and the boys wore scapulars and sometimes also had rosaries dangling out of their pockets. Besides you could tell they were Catholics because they looked so mean. Also, since the girls also looked "sexy", I used to think that was a mark of a Catholic!

One day I was walking home with my sister and a group of preteen boys circled us.

"So, what are you? Are you Catholic?"

"No."

"Are you Protestant?"

"No."

"Are you Jewish?"

"No." (Our parents had never told us we had a Jewish ancestry.)

"So what are you?"

"We're atheists", we answered proudly. Having never heard of this category, they strolled off instead of beating us up as Christ-killing Jews.

Was that you, guardian angel, trying to protect us not only from physical harm but also from hatred of Catholics?

How did we find out we were Jewish? Well, the public school was ninety-nine percent Jewish. So on Jewish holidays everyone had a holiday. When we told our parents that we were the only ones at school besides two Catholics and one Protestant, they reluctantly admitted, "Well, you are Jews. You can stay home." Hurrah!

Summers in New York City were and are torrid. Before air conditioning, fathers would wait till there was no policeman in sight, bring down a big wrench, and open the fire hydrants so that the kids on the block could cool off. It was so much fun jumping up and down in the rushing water that Jewish kids forgot their fear of the Catholic kids and jumped in, too.

Affluent Jews sent their children off to summer camp in New England or Pennsylvania. Being poor after the separation of our parents, we went to the YMCA camp. Although the YMCA was only nominally Christian, there was a tradition of having a Christmas celebration right in the middle of the July session of the camp! A nativity was assembled, and the Christian counselors taught all of the campers how to sing carols. If the parents of Jewish children got wind of this, they were allowed to have their kids excused from the practice and the "idolatrous ceremony of kissing the little 'doll'". But my sister and I were atheists, so our mother didn't mind if we learned carols. Superstitious religious stuff was garbage as doctrine, but okay as just an old custom.

Hearing "Silent Night" and "Come Holy Night" sung not on the radio but live by beloved counselors, I was enchanted. Such beauty. Somehow different from the beauty of secular classical music or popular songs.

Was that you, Mother Mary, calling me by name?

Fast forward: junior high school English class. The assignment was to write a page about what you want to be when you grow up. It had to be done on the spot. "How can I know what I want to be, if I don't know the meaning of life?" I wrote spontaneously. I don't think I would have remembered this precocious philosophical question, a prophecy of my later choice to become a philosophy professor, had the teacher not given me an A+.

Was that You, Holy Spirit, calling me by name?

I transferred from City College of New York to the University of Rochester, mainly because I wanted to have the out-of-town living experience I had read about in books. Looking for pictures for my wall, I gravitated toward a cheap print of Salvador Dali's *Crucifixion*, just because of its aesthetic value, I think. As a result, in my dorm wing of almost entirely New York City Jews, all the other young women assumed I must be Catholic. When they found out otherwise, even though they were not very religious they suggested I take it down, since I was Jewish by culture if not by faith. I refused, without knowing why.

Was that You, my Jesus, calling me by name?

Like many, though not all, atheists, I was brought up to think the sexual morality of religious people was ridiculous. Out of fear of pregnancy, I had avoided going as far as sexual intercourse. But once I was on my own, my great wish was to shed my virginity as soon as I could find some attractive young man willing to initiate me. By God's providence I didn't get pregnant, since I would surely have had an illegal abortion if I had.

Was that You, Father of life, protecting me from lifelong guilt?

One of my friends happened to love the music of Bach. One afternoon he sat me down in the lounge and made me listen to Bach's "Wachet Auf". I didn't like choral music at all, but I sat riveted to the chair listening with profound attention to the sacred song.

Was that You, Jesus, calling me by name?

The third young man with whom I was intimate was a foreign student in the philosophy graduate program. He was a German who had been in the Hitler Youth as a teen, but who had been saved by a Catholic priest from remaining in that terrible movement. Many of his friends became

Catholic because of the ministry of that priest. He did not, yet he believed that Catholicism was the only salvation! He hoped to become a Catholic someday after sowing his wild oats. This man started feeding me books of apologetics, from G. K. Chesterton to Karl Adam. Not having ever read the New Testament, I hardly understood a word of these treatises. But something stuck because I started wanting to meet Catholics even after my relationship with the German broke up.

Was that you, Saint Mary Magdalene, calling me by name?

During a trip, a friend wanted to visit the National Museum of Art in Washington, D.C. Hanging on a wall was Dali's *Last Supper*. I didn't like the picture at all from an aesthetic point of view, but I felt glued to the spot. I stared and stared at the table and the Christ, feeling mystically drawn into it. Fifteen minutes later my Jewish friend had to drag me away.

Was that You, Jesus of the Eucharist, calling me by name?

Majoring in philosophy had been my way of searching for truth. In the secular universities I attended, skepticism was so much in vogue that by a year into graduate school I felt hopeless. Where was truth? Where was love? Why even live? In this frame of mind, during Thanksgiving vacation in New York City, 1958, my mother, who never watched TV during the day and never surfed channels, turned on a program called "The Catholic Hour". The guests were Dietrich von Hildebrand and Alice Jourdain (soon to become Alice von Hildebrand). They were talking about truth and love. Spontaneously I wrote a letter to them care of the station telling them of my unsuccessful search for truth.

It turned out they both lived on the West Side of New York City; Alice two blocks from me, Dietrich ten blocks. Alice invited me for a visit. Her roommate, Madeleine (later to become the wife of Lyman Stebbins, founder of Catholics United for the Faith), met me at the door and ushered me into a small room. There was this very European-looking woman (she was from Belgium) who looked at me with such intense interest that I was immediately drawn into her heart. She suggested I sit in on classes of Dietrich von Hildebrand and Balduin Schwarz, his disciple, at Fordham University. Balduin's son, Stephen, a philosophy graduate student, now a philosophy professor and pro-life apologist, could bring me up to the Bronx and show me around.

I sat in on a few classes. What impressed me most was the personal vitality and joy of these Catholic philosophers, rather than their ideas, which I didn't understand very well. The skepticism, relativism, and historicism that characterized most secular universities at that time left many of the professors sad and desiccated. Drawn to this joy, as well as the loving friendliness that everyone in this circle of Catholics extended to greet a newcomer, I quickly switched from Johns Hopkins to Fordham to continue my studies. That the wife of Balduin Schwarz was a Jewish woman converted from an atheistic background certainly also made my entry into this new phase of my life easier.

After a few months at Fordham, I could not help but wonder how the brilliant lay Catholics and the brilliant Jesuits in the philosophy department could believe those ideas such as the existence of God, the divinity of Christ, the reality of objective truth, moral absolutes, and the need for churchgoing. Obviously it was not only stupid and weak people who thought this way. What is more, in just a few sentences they could prove that there were universal ethical truths, and the mind could know them.

Was that You, Holy Spirit, removing roadblocks to my eventual conversion to the Absolute Truth that is a Trinity of Persons? Were You calling me by name?

I was sad to think that I would not be able to study with these wonderful people during the summer, since they spent every summer in Europe. By now I found it hard to enjoy my sinful relationships with cynical, if interesting, men. Unexpectedly, Professor Schwarz suggested I go on a Catholic art tour with them. My money problems could be solved by a scholarship. Later I realized this money was probably donated by one of the circle, in the hope that deeper acquaintance with my professors would facilitate conversion.

To understand the miraculous character of the events that follow, one must know I hated all but modern art. This was due to forced trips to museums as a child. I liked colorful impressionist pictures but nothing earlier than the nineteenth century, and certainly not old-fashioned Catholic art. And, even though by now I thought there was truth, I had no knowledge of God, Christ, or the Church and no interest in learning more. So, my only reason for going on the tour was to cling to my dear new friends.

The first miracle came when I saw Chartres Cathedral in France. I looked at the amazing shape of that church with the beautiful stained glass windows, and I started to cry. The line from Keats: "Beauty is truth, truth is beauty", came to mind, and I asked myself, "How could this be so beautiful if there is no truth to it, just medieval ignorance?"

Wasn't that You, God of Beauty, calling me by name?

The pilgrims on the Catholic art tour all went to daily Mass. I started going also out of curiosity. Seeing my noble, wise philosophy professor on his knees astounded and disgusted me. I wanted to yank him up and say no man should kneel. "You are the captain of your soul; you are the master of your fate."

Finding out that I had never read the New Testament, and seizing the moment of grace, Professor Schwarz, my godfather-to-be, searched through bookstores in southern France until he found a Bible in English for me.

Second miracle: on the tour bus, reading the Gospels without understanding much, I fell asleep. I had a dream. There was a large room with tables. Jesus and Mary were sitting with their backs to the wall. Mary beckoned me and said in Hebrew, "Come sit with us." (I don't know Hebrew, but in the dream I did.)

Wasn't that you, Blessed Lady of Zion, calling me by name?

Third miracle: acting on an impulse, I knelt on the floor of the hotel and said a skeptic's prayer I thought my professor had told me as a joke: "God, if there is a God, save my soul, if I have a soul." The next day we got to Lourdes. My godparents-to-be, the Schwarzes, were praying that I would not be put off by the rows of trinket vendors. I said, "I'm used to 42nd Street; nothing bothers me."

Fourth miracle: I was touched to the core by the "Immaculate Mary" hymn sung in many languages by the pilgrims in candlelight procession.

Wasn't that you, dear Immaculate Mother, calling me by name?

Fifth miracle: again, the art I thought I hated was used by God to reach me. In a museum in Florence I saw Da Vinci's unfinished *Nativity*. I looked at the Virgin Mary, so simple, pure, and sweet, and I wept. She had something I would never have: purity! For the first time I thought of myself as a sinner. I felt impelled to tell my mentors, sure they would banish me. Of course, they didn't. Jesus came to save sinners.

Wasn't that you, our Lady, calling me by name?

Sixth miracle: the face of Christ in a tapestry of Raphael came alive, not for the others, but just for me!

Wasn't that You, my Jesus, calling me by name?

Seventh miracle: the tour included seeing Pope Pius XII at Saint Peter's. I had dreaded being bored at museums, but having to be in a crowd watching the Pope, whom I vaguely thought of as dressed up in the gold that belonged to the poor, was more than I could stand. I would go shopping instead. My mild professor insisted I go. So I went. At the end of the ceremony the Pope was blessing the disabled and sick. It was hard to see him because of the crowd. My rather old, not very strong godfather-to-be lifted me up so I could see the charity on the face of the Holy Father. Pope Pius XII had exactly the same expression in his eyes as the living face of Jesus from the tapestry.

Wasn't that You, dear Holy Spirit, prompting my god-father? Wasn't that You, calling me by name?

Stunned by this profusion of supernatural happenings, but too much a thinker to proceed on that basis only, I studied books like C. S. Lewis' *Mere Christianity*. The chapter in which Lewis shows that it is no good fence-sitting by decid-ing Jesus was just a wonderful man or a prophet was an intellectual turning point. When a man claims to be divine, he is either really God, insane, or a liar. Since no one thinks Jesus was insane or a liar, He must have been divine. Read-ing books of Chesterton and Cardinal Newman made becoming a Catholic seem inevitable.

Wasn't that You, dear Holy Trinity, Mother Mary, guard-ian angel, all you saints, especially Saint Edith Stein, calling me by name?

On January 4, 1959, at the age of twenty-one, I was baptized. There has never been a moment in my life when I have regretted being a Catholic. Later my twin sister, mother, and husband became Catholics, making us into a Hebrew-Catholic family. (The way God saved them and me during the rest of my long life can be found in my autobiography, *En Route to Eternity*, as well as in other of my books.)

I recently came upon a prayer-poem of mine on the theme of being called my name. I imagine it fits all of our stories:

TUNNEL OF LOVE

Digging through
the tunnel of time,
sometimes I hear
Your song loudly,
sometimes faint,
sometimes my own
is weak,
sometimes a
full-throated cry.
When we meet,
no more signals,
deep silence,
as You carry me
into eternity.

Called to Fulfillment

David Moss

"Do not think that I have come to abolish the
law and the prophets; I have come not to abolish them
but to fulfil them."

(Mt 5:17)

*David Moss was born of Russian Jewish immigrant parents in
New York City in 1941. After working at IBM as an engineer for
twenty-two years, an extraordinary experience, recounted below, led
him to the Catholic Faith. He now serves full time as the President of the Association of Hebrew Catholics, which is working to
preserve the identity and heritage of Catholics of Jewish origin
within the Church. More information on the organization and its
aims and activities can be found at www.hebrewcatholic.org.*

As I have reflected on my own life, and as I have reflected on
the story of the People Israel, it has seemed to me that both
present a story of healing that which was *wounded* and of finding that which was *yearned* for. These were not stories of
renouncing what was, but rather of fulfilling, of completing,
of perfecting the promise and hope of who we are, of who
God made us to be. And finally that fulfilling, completing,
perfecting was made possible through "*the mystery hidden for
ages and generations but now made manifest to his saints*" (Col 1:26).

We who have responded to this mystery and have begun to experience the transformation that is taking place in our souls can only express awe and gratitude. How can we understand the mysteries of grace that have so affected us and have apparently had so little impact on others? How can we understand why we have faith, why we have been enabled to recognize our Lord in a moment of grace, and have further been enabled to say "yes, I will follow" in another moment? How can we understand all the elements that have brought us to the incomprehensible privilege of entering into an unanticipated union with God through the Holy One of Israel, our Creator and Savior, our Lord in the Holy Eucharist?

After reading *Salvation is From the Jews*,[1] which has helped us all understand a little more of that "mystery hidden for ages", I offer my own story, a mystery of grace enabling this soul, through the undeserved mercy of our Lord, to find the healing and meaning he searched for.

In 1941, in Brooklyn, New York, I was born David Moskowitz to my Jewish parents, Elsie and Lester Moskowitz. Like many others seeking work, my father changed our last name to one less noticeably Jewish, *Moss*. Thus, two years after I arrived, my sister Rosalind was born with *Moss* as her last name, and two and a half years later came my sister Susan.

We grew up in a Conservative[2] Jewish home. My memories of those early years are good, with especially warm feelings from visits to the synagogue and the celebration of the various holy days of the Jewish year. Memories after age nine, when our parents split apart, took on a mixed

---

[1] Roy Schoeman, *Salvation is from the Jews* (San Fransisco: Ignatius Press, 2003).

[2] See footnote 3, p. ix, above.—ED.

cast, many of which were very painful. Life became somewhat more complex as our mother returned to work to support her three children. The celebration of the holidays now often took place in the homes of relatives. My Bar Mitzvah was made possible through the generous help of a great aunt and uncle, both survivors of the Holocaust.

Although the Bar Mitzvah is a very important moment in the life of a young Jewish male, when at age thirteen he assumes the adult responsibility of keeping the commandments, it was for me the catalyst into much consideration of my Jewish traditions and heritage and, in fact, all religious traditions.

Like many others at that age, innocent in the ways of the world, I had already begun to notice the disparity between what was preached by my elders and what was practiced. The negative views that were casually spoken and received about non-Jewish people, especially in contrast to the high ethical norms that we were taught, began to have their effect on my views.

The neighborhoods where we grew up in Brooklyn were largely Catholic. Though I understood nothing about Christianity, I had grown to love the Christmas carols, especially those about the Mother and her Son. It was not too long before I discovered the most beautiful music that I had ever heard, that of the "Ave Maria" by Schubert. (I also love the version by Bach-Gounod.) I am today convinced that this music was the instrument that our Blessed Mother used to penetrate and soften my heart, hook me, and slowly reel me in through the succeeding decades.

As with my own heritage, experiences with some of the Catholics I encountered provided good memories. Yet other experiences added to my developing view of the irrelevance of religious beliefs and traditions. For instance, nine boys, all members of one family, took their turns beating me up because I was a "Christ-killer". In another example, in my naïveté I went into a Catholic jewelry store to purchase a Star of David on a chain for my mother to wear around her neck. Instead of the clerk informing me that they didn't sell Jewish items, she said: "We don't sell to Jews."

As I thought about my own heritage, I wondered what all the study, all the prayers, all the traditions amounted to if, as a people, we remained closed in on ourselves, if we regarded all other peoples in negative terms, if we succumbed to a type of pride, for which I could see no justification, that we were somehow better or more privileged. It didn't seem to me that we were better than anyone else. And what kind of privilege, I thought, was the Holocaust?

My thoughts about the Catholicism that I had come to know followed a similar pattern. All of this talk about "love" and a Savior resulted in my getting beat up and being treated disrespectfully in a store. In one Catholic home, I watched the late teen and early adult sons treat their mother like a slave as they got dressed to go out on a date.

There was one man that I met who, it seemed to me, truly reflected what it meant to be a good Jew or Catholic. He was a black man who served as the janitor of an apartment building near where we lived. He actually lived in the basement of this building. His "apartment" consisted of a single room, open on two sides to the basement, one wall being the foundation wall of the building, the other being a simple fence separating his room from a public walkway. One of his duties was to burn garbage, tossed down a chute opening on each of the floors of the building, in the basement incinerator. The odors from this garbage, mixed with the smells of cat urine and spray, permeated the air. Added to the odors was the dust from the coal bin that faced the open side of his room. Another of his duties was to run a large coal furnace in the basement to heat the water that eventually ended up in the apartment radiators.

This man, whose dwelling place was so humble, whose life was largely solitary and subjected to the bigoted attitudes of some, who served those who lived in the apartment building for a small stipend and a place to live—was a man I had the great honor to spend some time with and grow to love. We played checkers, and I listened to his stories. Sometimes he would advise me on how to deal with the anti-Semitism I encountered. Although I heard many harsh words about blacks, and pejorative terms from Catholics and Jews when blacks were referred to, from this man I only heard good words. He never complained, always saw the good in people, always made excuses for their poor behavior, and never spoke about religion. Yet, he seemed to exemplify many of the virtues that I have since learned about. It was only later in my life that I would come truly to appreciate this man. I am truly sorry that I can't remember his name, but I hope this mention will serve to honor him. And I also hope to greet him when I pass over.

Within a year or two after my Bar Mitzvah, I came to believe that the beliefs and traditions of my heritage—as well as those of the dominant majority, the Christians—were constructed by men to serve the needs of men. Whatever truth there was to the notion of "God", these truths were not very obvious. In fact, as I continued to read, I came more and more to think that the whole idea of "God" was invented by men, enshrined in beliefs and traditions that developed over time to provide answers to our most fundamental questions, and some comfort in the face of tragedy and death.

So, I turned away from the beliefs and traditions of my heritage, and from any other as well. Yet, to turn away from one's beliefs and traditions was also to turn away from the whole matrix of values those beliefs and traditions supported. Of course, some of the values of that heritage had already become part of my formation. Having turned away, I was not ready to go out and lie and steal and kill. Yet, I knew that beyond my preference, I no longer had a rationale for why lying and stealing and killing were objectively wrong. More importantly, I no longer knew what life in general and my life in particular meant. I no longer knew if anything had any real objective value. Thus was I launched upon the path to discover the meaning of life, if there was any. This was not for me simply an academic exercise, but a necessity that enabled me to survive intellectually and physically.

My first two years of high school were spent at Brooklyn Tech, where the curriculum provided an introduction to aeronautical engineering. My mother remarried, and we all moved to Toronto, Canada. There, we established and ran a dry cleaning and laundry business. My sisters went to local public schools, and I completed high school at Central Tech, where I achieved a diploma in aircraft mechanics.

Family problems arose, and soon after graduation, I left home and returned to New York City. While engaged in a variety of jobs to pay my bills, I entered Brooklyn College, desiring to engage the learning of those who went before me in my pursuit of meaning and truth. But my education was not to be confined to academia alone. Though I was never an active member, I tentatively subscribed to the thinking of many of the leading liberal, progressive, and Socialist groups in the nation. These included the American Humanist Association, the American Ethical Union, the Students for a Democratic Society, and others.

These groups had given up what they believed were archaic notions of God, religion, and the restrictive morality that often seemed to focus on sexual behavior. Yet they seemed committed to ideas of social justice, economic welfare, universal equality, and the like.

Eventually, I distanced myself from these groups as I came to believe that the premises upon which they built their organizations were at least as illusory as the premises I had turned away from.

In 1964 I got married in a civil ceremony to Janet, a woman of Protestant background who had also lost her childhood faith. We moved to Poughkeepsie, New York, where I got a job with IBM. Over the next fourteen years, we had three children and adopted a fourth. I resumed my college studies, first at Marist College and finally at Vassar College.

My studies began with mathematics where I was for a short time convinced that we could find formulas to explain everything. I moved on to explore the liberal arts, including psychology, sociology, anthropology, economics, and politics. In each field, I took the introductory course plus one or two more. In each field, I came to believe that the real value of these disciplines was in their record of observed behavior. More often than not, it seemed to me, the theories of human behavior or of reality the practitioners in these fields constructed were built on shifting sand. However one would evaluate the fruit of these disciplines, they did not seem to contribute any objective input to my questions regarding the meaning of life.

I eventually turned to the study of philosophy. This field was immensely more satisfying than the others, if for no other reason than that some of the questions philosophy dealt with were similar to the questions I had. I moved through the history of philosophy as I had moved through my studies in the liberal arts: superficially and quickly. My intention was not to immerse myself in any particular philosophical area or school of thought. Rather, I was looking for a doorway that would lead me to an understanding of what meaning, what value my life had.

As I studied each philosopher or school of philosophy, I would experience the elation of new ideas and answers to questions that the previous philosopher or school had not been able to answer. As I tried to live in the clothes of these new ideas, I would soon discover that they also led to an impasse, or that they could not be lived as they were described, or that they were as illusory as what had preceded them. And from elation, I would experience a tremendous letdown.

Throughout this period, the meaning and love I experienced with my family was at times overwhelmed by the sense that, ultimately, none of it mattered. Nothing mattered: all the love and hate, all the sacrifices and self-centered behaviors, all the education and ignorance, all that was moral or good or beautiful didn't matter. It would all become dust, indistinguishable from all the other dust of the universe. And this bag of absurdity and meaninglessness that I carried on my back was getting heavier.

What sustained me through these times was the thought that men did in fact find answers to difficult and enduring questions, such as the cure for disease or the objective knowledge that enabled men to go and return from the moon. And it was these thoughts that formed a kind of faith that undergirded my search, the faith that there was an objective reality and that it was knowable.

From my studies at college and my discussions at work, I went through two major changes of perspective. Both occurred in the mid-1970s. The first was a conversion from a pro-abortion to a pro-life position. Previously, without any real investigation on my part, I had trustingly accepted the liberal arguments that had been put forth to free women from their sexual bondage. Now, having undertaken a study of the biology of life and reproduction, prompted by some colleagues at IBM, I quickly saw abortion as the unjustifiable killing of human beings in the earliest stages of their life. As a Jew whose people had just recently experienced the Holocaust, I was even more at a loss to understand how anyone could condone abortion—especially those who were Jewish. I got involved in the pro-life movement because I *knew* that here was one of the most important battles in the history of mankind, that is, if life had any ultimate meaning.

My other conversion moved me from a liberal to a conservative perspective in social matters. At some point in my studies in the liberal arts, I started to follow through the references listed in the notes and bibliographies of the required reading. And I actually began to review some of the referenced material and follow through on their references. I discovered that some of the required reading for the courses I was enrolled in were providing interpretations of the subject matter in accord with a secular humanistic ideology. Of course, the readings were not advertised as such, and I was not alarmed since what I read accorded somewhat with my own biases of that time. But through the literature that the references led me to, I discovered another whole world of understanding, another way of interpreting the same subject matter studied in these courses. And this world made more sense to me.

I found that my sensitivities, including compassion for the poor, the suffering, and the oppressed, continued to feel most comfortably at home among liberals. Meanwhile, my appreciation for human nature and social order moved me into conservative circles. Here I began to come to terms with the deformation of human personality and character. I would eventually learn to recognize these deformations as the consequence of original sin. And the reconciliation between my liberal and conservative sides would eventually take place in Catholic social teaching.

In the same period, when our oldest son was about five, our family started attending a Southern Baptist church. Janet and I decided that we wanted the support that a church could provide in helping to inculcate moral values in our children. Regarding faith in God and the specifically Christian beliefs of the Baptists, we felt the children would be free to choose what to believe, as we had and as most other children did, when they reached their teen years.

As this was my first experience with a Christian community, I was very impressed by the love we experienced among the members of this church. Naturally, they were only too ready to help us explore their beliefs, in the hope that we too would become Christian. A couple of years later, Janet was able to return briefly to her childhood faith, professing belief in Jesus and getting involved in church activities. I continued in my studies, now with the added spice of occasional discussions with Baptist men.

I knew that the Baptists in this church and the Catholics in the local pro-life movement were all praying for my conversion. But my interactions with both groups, while pleasant and nonconfrontational, made little impact on what I believed. I now acknowledge a much greater efficacy to their prayers.

In fact, the Baptists and the Catholics helped bring me to a new crisis. The exuberant joyful sounds of the Baptists made me aware of how little I was able to make any joyful sounds. The serene peaceful faith of some Catholics, especially in the midst of suffering, made me even more aware

of how unable I was to connect with any rationale for serenity and peace, especially in the midst of suffering. Like salt
in a wound, my acquaintance with these Christians only
served to emphasize the meaninglessness of my life.

As I noted early in my story, I now believe Mary was
with me on my journey and, through her maternal inter-
cessions, helped me move forward toward the gift of faith.
From the time we began attending the Baptist church, many
"coincidences" began to occur. I will relate just one.

An IBM and Catholic pro-life colleague, Herb Flanagan,
with whom I had many philosophical discussions, also began
to help me understand the difference between Catholics and
Baptists. At one point, he suggested that I walk through
the woods behind IBM and kneel in prayer before the Blessed
Sacrament for a few moments during my lunch hour. To
honor this friend, I would leave work at 11:45 A.M., walk
through the woods and arrive at Saint Martin de Porres
Catholic Church at 11:55. I would then proceed to recite a
doubter's prayer suggested by Herb for five to ten minutes.
Having completed this exercise, I would hurriedly make
my exit before Mass began at 12:15 P.M.

One day, I left work late and ran through the woods,
wanting to be faithful to my promise to Herb. As I ran, the
words "Saul, Saul, why do you persecute me?" repeated
themselves over and over in my head. I suppose I had heard
them in a sermon at the Baptist church, but if so, it was
not recently. Why were these words repeating themselves,
like a tune that one can't silence?

I arrived at the church about 12:10. I was going to simply
kneel, say one prayer, and get out. But it was too late. The
people were all arriving, and I did not want to call attention
to myself. The Mass began, and the people rose, and they knelt,
and they sat, and they crossed themselves, and ... Oy!

The Scripture readings, which I had paid no attention to, were over, and the priest began his homily. The first words out of his mouth were, "Saul, Saul, why do you persecute me?" This was the feast day of the conversion of another Jew, Saul, now known as Saint Paul. Needless to say, I was very moved, my spine continuing to tingle as I returned through the woods to IBM. But I was convinced that the answers to my questions were not going to emerge from mere coincidences.

My studies had provided reasonable answers to a lot of questions, but not to those I was obsessed with. There were three questions I had written on my blackboard at IBM to which I had not been able to find adequate answers. Somehow I came to think that I would find the meaning of life bound up in the answers to these questions. The questions were:

1. How does one explain the fact of *existence*? Not only that something exists, but that there is a reality that is *existence*?

2. How does one explain sacrificial love? I was thinking of the soldier, who against every instinct for survival, throws himself on a grenade to save his buddies. I also thought of the mothers I knew growing up in Brooklyn who took care of their children and husbands and homes all day and then went out on a second or third shift to clean offices on their knees. The money they earned was put in the cookie jar for their children's education. How did one explain such self-donation?

3. How does one explain the sense of *ought*? This was not a virtue that one could learn. Nor did it have to do with the keeping or breaking of a

commandment. It was rather like a little internal nudge directing one to a good deed, a good deed that might very well go unrecognized. I thought of a man who missed an important business appointment by taking the time to pick up a wallet and return it to the old man who had dropped it. Where did this sense that he *ought* to return the wallet come from?

As I sat back in my chair and stared at these questions, having exhausted every avenue I could think of to study and find answers, a feeling of dread and the ultimate blackness of a meaningless life settled upon me. As I found myself slipping into a despair that I feared I would not recover from, I remembered my youth and I cried out, "God, if You really exist, I need to know now."

I cannot adequately describe what took place next. I can only say what it seemed like and what I can remember. My office at IBM vanished, and I appeared to be in the sky, in clouds. They parted, the sun shone on me, and they came back together. I was back in my office at IBM.

And I was no longer the same. The feelings of despair and blackness disappeared, and all the baggage of meaninglessness and absurdity I had carried all those years was gone. I now knew there was a God. And I now knew that my life had meaning and purpose. I knew the answers to those questions on my blackboard. And I knew the answer to a question I had never asked: I knew that Jesus was the Messiah and the Divine Son of God.

I sat stunned in my chair, trying to take in what had just occurred. I knew that I wanted to capture this moment somehow, so that I would not later explain it away as a daydream or an illusion prompted by an undigested morsel of food. So I took off through the woods and went to the priest who served as pastor of the church I had been praying in. I told him that I needed to tell my experience to someone who would understand and whom I could approach some time later for confirmation that it had actually taken place. After listening to me, he asked me if I wanted to become a Catholic. "Heavens no, Father", I responded.

But what was I to do now? There was so much to think about, so much to learn, so much time to make up. I began to talk with both the Baptists and the Catholics. Oy! Two thousand years of history can certainly muddle a message, I thought. And why didn't my Jewish people believe in Jesus?

Since I was going to the Baptist church, and since I recognized myself as a man who had committed many sins in my life, it was not hard for me to follow the suggestion of my Baptist friends. In July or August 1978, I walked down the aisle of this Baptist church, publicly acknowledging my status as a sinner and asking Jesus to come into my life. I didn't understand all the theology, but they showed me the appropriate verses of Scripture, and I responded. The next step was baptism. For the Baptists, baptism is a public ritual symbolizing the rebirth that supposedly took place in my soul when I accepted Jesus into my life. My Catholic friends explained baptism as the sacrament that not only symbolized rebirth but effected it as well. Whatever graces were imparted when I walked down the aisle in the Baptist church were intended by God, they assured me, to bring me to the sacrament of baptism.

How would I decide, in a reasonably short period of time, what baptism meant? After all, there were many sincere adults in both camps, men and women who loved Jesus and attempted to live their lives in accord with His will. In both camps, there were pastors and scholars and missionaries who had committed their lives to Jesus in accord with the understanding of their church. How was I, who knew virtually nothing, going to decide who was right?

Someone then asked if I believed that Jesus wanted me to be baptized? "Yes", I said. "Well then, why not get baptized and let Jesus teach you what it means?" That seemed to me a good suggestion. I didn't want to join any church yet because I had too many questions regarding the Christian faith. To be baptized in a Catholic church meant that I would become a Catholic. The Baptists found a verse in Scripture that let me be baptized without joining their church. So once again, I remained with my Baptist friends, and in September I was baptized by full immersion in their baptismal pool. Although I had no revelations or insights at the time of my baptism, the pace of my spiritual journey quickened.

Approximately two weeks later, I woke up from a night's sleep with a clear answer to the question of what baptism meant. Not only did I now understand that baptism was a sacrament and the means of our regeneration, but much that I had studied for more than twenty years came together like a jigsaw puzzle. I was overcome with amazement and joy as I realized that the Catholic Church was the Church that Jesus established. Study and understanding would come later, but now I would look for a priest to begin the process of entering the one, holy, apostolic, and catholic church.

With the decision to enter the Catholic Church, I entered a terrible period in which a multitude of voices filled my head, uttering pure filth and blasphemous arguments against Jesus, against the Church, and against me, my personality, my manhood, and so forth. I struggled with feelings that I was joining the persecutors of my people and betraying them and the God of our fathers. I slept very little, and after about a week and a half, my friend Herb brought me to a priest at a Knights of Columbus hall.

After some discussion, this priest advised me not to make any decision until the torment within my head ceased, and I was at peace again. Then, he said, if I wanted to rescind my decision to enter the Church, at least the decision would not emerge from an emotionally turbulent state. He assured me that the turbulence would end soon. And it did, a little more than a week later. When it ended, I knew a peace that I had never experienced before in my life. There were no doubts within me about my continued journey into the Church. Now to find a priest for instruction.

The first priest I approached handed me a book entitled *Christ amongst Us*. Within a couple of days I returned the book with the first one hundred pages marked up. If what the author of this book professed was the Catholic Faith, then I would have no part in it. The author, a priest, has since been laicized and married. The book has also lost its imprimatur.

The next priest was associate pastor in a local church. When I was taken to a garden in the back of the church to speak with him, he was sitting in lotus fashion on a bench, praying, I supposed, with his eyes rolled back in his head. I wondered if he was one of these mystical types I had heard about. We began to walk through the garden and talk. He was easy to talk to, and I thought that perhaps I had found the one who would provide my instruction—until he began to talk about Mary.

I had a number of questions concerning prayers to Mary and to the saints. But this priest's concerns about Mary seemed to me altogether bizarre. He found a relationship with Mary a problem because "Mary", he said, "makes my mother look bad."

The next priest was recommended to me because of the inspiring homilies he gave at Sunday Mass. He was a religious order priest, and he helped out at the local parish. One evening, I went to the monastery where he lived. He greeted me in civilian clothes, which was a little disappointing, but understandable since he was at his home. After a short conversation, he felt the need to disabuse me of some superstitions that I appeared to be on the verge of adopting. Superstitions? He meant notions like the Virgin Birth, the actual Resurrection of Jesus, the transformation of a cracker into the Body and Blood of Christ, and so on. When I asked him how he could celebrate Mass, how could he say what he did with the beliefs he held, he responded that he had no trouble with the words—he just meant something different. He assured me that he was a biblical scholar. If I would study Scripture with him, I would see that his understanding was correct. I responded that I might have been interested in his approach if I were interested in doing my own thing. However, I was not interested in starting another non-Catholic Christian group but in learning from the Church that Jesus established. And I left.

I turned to Herb with the lament that I had struck out. A few days later, he called and promised me that the following recommendation would be the last I would need. Father Andrew Apostoli was giving a presentation on Padre Pio at a church in Poughkeepsie. I went to the presentation and was completely overwhelmed and inspired by the life and holiness of the Padre. I met Father Apostoli, and he invited me to visit him at Saint Lawrence Monastery in Beacon, New York. At the time, Father Apostoli was the superior at this Capuchin monastery and was not able to spend the time with me. Instead, he assigned Father Peter Napoli to my case.

Father Peter was a wonderful priest who grew up in Brooklyn. He knew as much as I did, if not more, about Judaism and had many Jewish friends. He was God's gift to me and helped me over all the obstacles that remained, most especially concerning prayers to Mary and the saints.

In February 1979, at Saint Lawrence Monastery, I was received into the Church in two days of liturgy, prayer, and celebration that included a conditional baptism, confirmation, first confession, and First Communion. The music played at Mass included a hymn, "Amazing Grace", to help smooth the transition from my Baptist experience. It was a wonderful transition.

Over 150 people, most from the local pro-life movement, showed up to witness my entrance into the Church. When I inquired why so many that I didn't know showed up, I learned that the Body of Christ was always joyous when the Shepherd rescued another of His lost sheep. Additionally, I learned that my entrance into the Church served to encourage others who, through the 1960s and 1970s, had become more aware of the many who were leaving the Church than of those who were entering here. The fact that I was a Jew, someone told me, made the event even rarer and more inspiring.

In those two days of my entrance, it seemed like my feet never touched the floor. I was overwhelmed by the liturgy and by the graces that were flooding my soul. I remember two distinct impressions. The first was that I had come home. "Home"—what a wonderful word. After more than twenty-three years wandering through a spiritual desert, like the prodigal son, I had returned to the house of the Father of Abraham, Isaac, Jacob, and Jesus. And in returning home, I discovered the meaning that I had left so long ago. Although adapted to each individual soul, the meaning of every person's life was simply based on the reality of love and truth. And love and truth were based upon the reality of God.

The second distinct impression I experienced that day was that I was once again *Jewish*. Though it seemed consistent with the sense of "coming home", I didn't understand then the significance of this impression. Eventually, I came to see that in coming home, I had reclaimed my Jewish heritage, but it was now fulfilled in Jesus and His Church. A Hebrew Catholic woman in Israel, from an Orthodox Jewish background, conveyed a similar sense to me when she described Catholicism as the Judaism of the Redemption.

However, from the time of my entrance into the Church, my identity as a Jew within the Church kept pestering me, producing a type of restlessness and yearning for something I couldn't identify. A few years later, I met Monsignor Eugene Kevane who introduced me to Elias Friedman, O.C.D. It was Father Friedman's analysis of Jewish identity that helped me come to grips with the restlessness and yearnings that dwelt within me.

My restlessness was, I believe, connected to my being a member of a people with a vocation: the *irrevocable calling* of their election, as Saint Paul describes it (Rom 11:29). But without the collective presence of the People Israel within the Church, the calling was not being exercised. My yearning was for my people to come to know their Messiah, *the Way, the Truth, and the Life*, the fulfillment of the promises God had made to their fathers.

In his Letter to the Romans, Saint Paul describes a similar restlessness and yearning:

I am speaking the truth in Christ, I am not lying; my conscience bears me witness in the Holy Spirit, that I have

great sorrow and unceasing anguish in my heart. For I could
wish that I myself were accursed and cut off from Christ
for the sake of my brethren, my kinsmen by race. They are
Israelites, and to them belong the sonship, the glory, the
covenants, the giving of the law, the worship, and the promises; to them belong the patriarchs, and of their race, according to the flesh, is the Christ who is God over all, blessed
for ever. Amen. (Rom 9:1–5)

Further on, he adds: ". . . as regards election they are beloved
for the sake of their forefathers. For the gifts and the call of
God are irrevocable" (Rom 11:28–29).

In 1979, the year that I entered the Church, Father Friedman launched the Association of Hebrew Catholics (AHC)
with the help of Andrew Sholl, a Holocaust survivor. Simply stated, the mission of the AHC is to gather Jews who
have entered the Church and help them live out their God-
given irrevocable calling through their collective witness of
Jesus and His Church.

Since the day of my baptism, my life has changed dramatically. Eventually, Janet divorced me. Later on, the Church
would provide me with a decree of matrimonial nullity. At
the invitation of Monsignor Kevane, I joined the AHC with
Ronda Chervin, Ph.D., and a number of other Hebrew Catholics. And at Monsignor Kevane's urging, I founded the
Miriam Press and in 1987 published Father Friedman's *Jewish Identity*. A few years later, I assumed responsibility for
publishing the AHC publication, *The Hebrew Catholic*. And
in 1994, upon my retirement from IBM, Father Friedman
appointed me President.

Meanwhile, across the continent, the woman who was
my *b'shert* (Hebrew for "destined other"), Kathleen, was
undergoing her own transformation in Christ. Having also
entered the Church in 1979, she was seeking the Lord and

the calling of her life. We eventually met and worked together for two years.

On May 1, 2001, the Feast of Saint Joseph, Kathleen and I were married. Now, our unique paths were joined for our good and that of our mutual calling in the work of the AHC. In September 2001, we relocated to Ypsilanti, Michigan, hoping to further the development of the AHC in association with Ave Maria College. While that hope has not been realized in the ways we had expected, the AHC has gained the approbation and blessing of our Bishop Carl Mengeling.

As I began the story of my spiritual journey, so I end it, in utter awe and gratitude. God has given our life its ultimate meaning: the fulfillment of life, now and eternally, in Jesus and His Church with the entire communion of saints. And within that life, He has given us a special mission concerning our people, the People Israel.

I will be eternally grateful for all the people who have helped me on my journey. There are so many who have prayed, have answered questions, and whose lives have served to give me a glimpse of our Lord and the meaning of His life, death, and Resurrection. There are so many that I look forward to meeting and thanking when I pass over. For now, I would like to acknowledge publicly and thank our Blessed Mother Miriam; my godfather Herb Flanagan; Father Andrew Apostoli; Saint Pio; Father Peter Napoli; Monsignor Eugene Kevane; Father Elias Friedman, O.C.D.; Faye Sisson, and Father Eugene Keane.

In the Gospel of Luke, we sing the Magnificat with Mary, Ark of the Covenant: "My soul magnifies the Lord, and my spirit rejoices in God my Savior, ... for he who is mighty has done great things for me, and holy is his name" (Lk 1:46, 49). And a bit further on we sing the Benedictus, with Zechariah:

> Blessed be the Lord God of Israel, for he has visited and redeemed his people, and has raised up a horn of salvation for us in the house of his servant David, as he spoke by the mouth of his holy prophets from of old, that we should be saved from our enemies, and from the hand of all who hate us; to perform the mercy promised to our fathers, and to remember his holy covenant, the oath which he swore to our father Abraham, to grant us that we, being delivered from the hand of our enemies, might serve him without fear, in holiness and righteousness before him all the days of our life. (Lk 1:68–75)

In the Gospel of Matthew, our Lord tells His people: "O Jerusalem, Jerusalem, ... I tell you, you will not see me again, until you say, 'Blessed is he who comes in the name of the Lord'" (Mt 23:37, 39). And in the *Catechism of the Catholic Church* we read that: "The glorious Messiah's coming is suspended at every moment of history until His recognition by '*all Israel*'..." (CCC, no. 674). May our lives and our efforts hasten the day when "*all Israel*" shall proclaim, "Blessed is He who comes in the Name of the Lord!"

All This and Heaven, Too

Rosalind Moss

Rosalind Moss is full-time apologist and evangelist on the staff of Catholic Answers, a nonprofit apostolate dedicated to promoting the Catholic faith, and travels the world speaking and teaching at parishes and conferences. She appears frequently on Catholic radio and television and is the editor of a book of Jewish convert stories entitled Home at Last: Eleven Who Found Their Way to the Catholic Church *(El Cajon, Calif.: Catholic Answers, 2000). She may be reached at www.catholic.com.*

It was the 1960s. I was young, single, Jewish, and on my own in New York. The headline shot through me like an arrow aimed straight at my heart: "Nuns have received permission to shorten their habits to knee length." I've tried in vain now, some forty years later, to track down the exact headline, paper, and date. But the news item wasn't limited to newspapers alone. It aired over local radio. And it went through me as if it were *my* news, and my loss.

What had nuns' habits to do with me? Nothing. I was Jewish. I had been taught from childhood that there were basically two kinds of people in this world: Jewish and non-Jewish. So what had these ladies in long black habits to do with me? They were foreign to my world. Yet I

knew that, *whoever* they were, they were in the world to affect the world for God. But, alas, I thought, the world has affected them.

What a deep sadness came over me. It was right at the start of the miniskirt era, and I supposed the shortened hemlines were a religious accommodation to the fashion, or, at least, to the increasingly *self*-focused leanings of the day. Somehow I felt robbed of what was never mine to begin with.

I was born in 1943 to Jewish parents of Russian and Hungarian descent. My brother, David, was born "David Moskowitz" two years earlier. Within those two years, my father shortened our name to "Moss". It was easier for him to get work with a name that was not so obviously Jewish. In the same manner, my mother's maiden name, Brodsky, became Brody as her brother, my uncle, strove also to feed his family. I was the first *born* "Moss". My sister, Susan, who arrived almost three years later, was the second.

We grew up in a multiethnic neighborhood in Brooklyn in what today would be considered a fairly conservative Jewish home. We kept quite separate from the world around us in our younger years and loved living the life and traditions of our family and of our people. It was more than religion that we lived; it was who we were as a people, as God's people, united in our very existence to the Jewish people not only throughout the world but throughout the centuries.

L'Shana Tovah![1] What joy those greetings brought. It was Rosh Hashanah, the Jewish New Year, and David would

---

[1] "For a good year!" in Hebrew, shortened from "May you be inscribed in the Book of Life for a good year!" It is the traditional greeting for Rosh Hashanah.

be out in the street in front of our apartment building in Brooklyn blowing the *shofar* in union with millions of *shofars* across the globe calling the Jewish people to repentance and to the beginning of the Ten Days of Awe that would conclude with Yom Kippur, the Day of Atonement.

At sundown, *Erev Yom Kippur*[2] (literally: the Eve of the Day of Covering), we would walk to *shul* (synagogue). That began our fast, which would end the following sundown. Early the next morning we would return to the synagogue to pray with the entire community and to make atonement for our sins in the hope that our names would be written in the Book of Life.

We loved it. *I* loved it. We weren't Orthodox, but one family in our apartment building was. And David and I would spend several Saturdays with them as children of six and eight years, just for the privilege of sitting in the dark on *Shabbos*[3] and to enter more fully into who we were as a people.

Every tradition, every High Holy Day, every feast, told us who we were—and who God was—and His purpose for us as a people, which was, above all, to *continue* as a people in faithful loving obedience and service to the God who formed us for Himself. And every observance united us with the generations that had gone before, whose perseverance paved the way for us, as we would also do for future generations.

---

[2] Hebrew for "Eve of Yom Kippur". Jewish holidays begin at sundown the preceding evening, hence *Erev Yom Kippur* is the start of Yom Kippur.

[3] Yiddish for "Sabbath", referring to the Saturday Sabbath observed in Judaism. Since the Sabbath laws prohibit the lighting of fires, Orthodox Jews interpret this also to prohibit the turning on of electric lights.

Sukkot,[4] *Simchat Torah,*[5] *Hanukkah,*[6] *Purim,*[7] *Shavuot.*[8]
We loved them all. There was not one that any of us dreaded
or that we "had" to participate in. We loved who we were.
We loved the family we were. We loved being part of the
Jewish people throughout the world. And we loved belong-
ing to the God of Abraham, Isaac, and Jacob.

But the celebration of celebrations, the feast that topped
all others in people, preparation, and participation was *Pesach*
(Passover). After all, it was the celebration of our deliverance from slavery in Egypt. Surely it was a *remembrance* of
that first Passover under Moses 3,500 years or so prior. But
in delivering Israel from Pharaoh's hand, God delivered *us.*
We went through the sea. *We* sang "Dayenu": "Had G-d[9]
brought us out of Egypt and not split the sea for us—Dayenu!
[it would have been enough].... Had He sustained us in
the wilderness for forty years, and not fed us with manna—
Dayenu!" The past was made present, and we not only sang

[4] The "Feast of Booths" celebrates God's bounty in the fall harvest.

[5] Literally "Rejoicing in the Torah", the celebration of the word of God,
which takes place in the fall at the close of the annual cycle of Torah readings.

[6] Literally "Consecration", the eight-day festival that celebrates the recon-
secration of the Temple in 164 B.C. (recounted in 1 and 2 Maccabees). It
usually falls around Christmas.

[7] Literally "Lots", referring to the day, chosen by lots, in 356 B.C. when all
the Jews in Persia were to be massacred. The Jews were saved by the intervention of the Jewess Queen Esther, and the day became a joyous holiday.

[8] Literally meaning both "sevens" and "weeks", it falls exactly seven weeks
(forty-nine days) after Passover, and commemorates the giving of the Torah
to Moses on Mount Sinai. In this it closely mirrors the Christian Feast of
Pentecost, which falls seven weeks (fifty days) after Easter and commemorates the giving of the "new law" (cf. Rom 7:6), "written not with ink but
with the Spirit of the living God, not on tablets of stone but on tablets of
human hearts" (2 Cor 3:3).

[9] Out of respect for the sacredness of the name of God the Jewish custom
is not to spell it out but to replace the vowel with a hyphen.

but *knew* of God's outstretched arm to *us*, the beneficiaries of all that had gone before.

And all the while we sang, all the while we prayed, all the while we partook of the food of the Passover Seder, the door was kept ajar for Elijah, who was to announce the arrival of the *Maschiah* (Messiah). I'm sure we spoke of *Maschiah*[10] at other times of the year, but at Passover we waited. One of these years He will come. One of these years *Mashiach* will take us—all of us! from the four corners of the earth—and bring us to Jerusalem, where we belong. And He will set up His Kingdom and reign—a Kingdom of peace and beauty and goodness. And there will be sadness and war no more. Life will be as God intended it to be.

I was eleven, the year of David's Bar Mitzvah, when it was my turn to go to the door that had been left open for Elijah, to see if *this* was the year he would be waiting outside. It never for a moment occurred to me that he could not be at *our* door if he had come for the Jews of the entire world. I remember my little legs trembling as I approached the door and peeked into the hallway to look for the long-expected Guest.

Empty. Nothing stirring. No one was there. With slight disappointment and maybe a bit of relief—after all, what *would* it be like when Messiah came?—I announced to the family that Elijah wasn't there; Messiah wasn't upon us.

So what's a family to do? What else? Go on with the feast and don't forget to sing as we leave, *L'shana ha'ba-ah b'Yerushalayim*. ("Next year in Jerusalem.") Why? Because that's where we'll be when Messiah comes. And he *will* come.

---

[10] Jews frequently use "Messiah" as a proper name, much as Christian's use "Christ". Both, of course, mean "the anointed one", the former from Hebrew, the latter from Greek.

So! He didn't come *this* year, so he'll come *next* year—*next year in Jerusalem!*

At times I wondered if it were really true. Is there really a Messiah? But, I believed there was. I certainly *wanted* there to be a Messiah. It was the only hope the world had. It was the only hope *I* was beginning to have. Our home life had changed dramatically just three years earlier. My parents had gone through a difficult separation and subsequent divorce. Five years later, a second marriage would eventually result in even greater calamity for us all.

I recall wondering, about that time, perhaps from about ten years of age on, why we (mankind) were on the earth. Why do we exist? For what purpose? And to what end? Once we die, will our lives on earth have mattered?

I don't remember thinking or even knowing about Heaven or Hell. We knew God was good and perfect in His ways. He would do what was right with His own when we died. That did not mean an automatic ticket to be with God, just the understanding that if we had not turned from God during this life, we would be okay. We need not fear.

But neither did I *think* of eternity, other than at a funeral service. I had enough to do trying to figure out the meaning of life on *earth*. In fact, I recall walking to public school, about 5th grade, with girls who were Catholic. Every so often they would speak of Heaven and eternity. Their conversation and focus frightened me. It seemed to me that they were more focused on the "afterlife" than on things here on earth. What *good* were they *here and now*? I would think. What danger might they present in the midst of earthly realities if this present life was not their focus?

David seemed off in his own world thinking about the meaning of life. Somewhere in his teens he declared himself an atheist! David! An atheist? How can you *know* there's no God? How can you be a *Jew* and abandon belief in God?

But David was not denying Judaism or our heritage. It was that both Judaism and the God of the Jewish people, as we understood Him, left too many unanswered questions. The need of the human heart—at least the need and questions of David's heart—were not met through the knowledge and experience of our upbringing.

I too struggled. And though, as time passed, David's conclusions appeared somewhat plausible to me, I never reached them. "I am because of what is", I reasoned. "*If* there's a God, therefore I am. If there's *no* God, *therefore* I am. My knowledge or lack of it doesn't *determine* what is, so why know?" How would *knowing* change your life? Into my twenties, I labeled myself an "agnostic", but I never truly abandoned belief in the existence of God.

In the ten years that followed, I had about the most active social life a single gal could have in the "Big Apple". I held top positions with three New York corporations, rode horseback, danced 'til the wee hours of the morning, and had everything the world could give. Only one thing was lacking: a reason to exist. No amount of love, money, or success could fill the interior emptiness I lived with. I was so sure the right relationship, one that would lead to marriage, would be the answer. But that day had come and gone a few years earlier. I had been twenty, single, free, and in love. There was nothing in the way. Nothing except my longing heart that, it began to seem, no amount of human love could fill. How can this not be it? How can the height of human love on earth not fill the deepest longings of my heart? And if love and marriage are not the answer, what is?

There had been no answer. But I had known I could not allow myself to enter into the permanent bond of marriage with someone, even a wonderful someone, with the deepest need of my heart for meaning and purpose still unmet. I broke off our engagement and continued to live life as I had before, striving to get out of bed in the morning without a reason to do so, holding "impressive" positions in the business world that only magnified for me the emptiness I faced.

By now, David had married a "fellow atheist", a lovely gal who had been raised in a nominal Protestant home. That was hard on my parents, who were not at their wedding. David and Janet decided they would raise their children without religion, knowing each could choose a religion for himself when older. But the oldest, approaching seven years, began coming home from school and play with questions about what "we" believe, what "we" were. And so David and Janet decided to find a religion they could take on for the family, just, as I understood it, to give the children a sense of identification. They could still make their own choices when they were older.

Janet, in time, and unknown to me, had come to believe in Christ through a small Baptist church within walking distance from their upstate New York home. David continued reading, and every once in a while adopted some "ism" that seemed to hold the answers to life. None of them passed the test of time.

It was the summer of 1975 when I received a call from David telling me that he and Janet had been on this search:

". . . and Janet has joined the Baptist church. It's just through the woods behind our house."

(Not that I was thrilled, but Janet wasn't Jewish; no real problem there.) "And *you*, David?"

"I don't know. I'm still searching."

"And the children?"

"Well, we decided they would follow Janet for now, since she has a direction. When I come to my truth, I'll deal with that then."

We hung up the phone, and I stood in disbelief. *David* was going to allow his children to worship a *man*? Prophet, teacher, whoever Christ was, *we're Jews!* And *if* there's a God, we don't need to go through anyone!

I visited their home in Poughkeepsie, New York, that summer. Sunday morning came: "Ros, we're going to church. You're welcome to join us." Janet's words were warm, inviting, and genuine. How could I blame *her*? She had a right to her belief. But the *children*.

I wanted to go. I wanted to see what David was allowing his children to be exposed to. David joined us. I tried not to show the anger that welled up inside me as we entered that church. How foreign it was to all I had known and to who we were. I sat in a pew next to David and Janet—the children were off to Sunday School—and braced myself for whatever came next.

It could not have been too far into the service when the choir sang a song I had never heard before—how *could* I have? I was hardly paying attention to the words, yet all of a sudden they went straight through me, as if they had a life of their own:

> Grace, grace, God's grace,
> Grace that will pardon and cleanse within;
> Grace, grace, God's grace,
> Grace that is greater than all our sin.

It felt as if a ten-pound brick had been placed on my heart. It was the weight of love. Not the love of the people around me, but a love that was utterly foreign to my life.

Again the chorus pierced my being: *Grace that is greater than all our sin.*

"Grace that is greater than *my* sin?" *What* sin? I wasn't sure God existed. Who would I sin against? Man? He's my equal.

I was hit with a love that was not mine, and a sin that was. Despite every effort to keep what was happening inside me to myself, I broke down sobbing at the end of that service. Janet and the folks around me were smiling from ear to ear and eagerly began telling me about Christ. *Oh no you don't*, I thought to myself. "Get away from me with those words!" I would not give them the chance. "I know what I'm feeling. Don't you tell me Christ is the reason for it!"

David was more than curious about my response. After all, *he* was the one searching, not I. As I left their house to catch a 6:00 A.M. train Monday morning, David slipped me a small, two-by-four-inch black book. In a whisper he said, "Read this, Ros. Let me know what you think."

I opened it on the train. It was a New Testament. Oy! No one on the train even knew me, yet I wouldn't dare read that thing in public! I tried briefly to read it in the privacy of my apartment back in Manhattan, but to no avail.

It was on a Sunday afternoon the following month, while walking through Central Park, that I was overwhelmed with the presence of "something", something—dare I say it?—supernatural. In an instant, I was engulfed somehow in a pocket of space, surrounded only by trees and the sky above. I was still in the middle of Central Park, but the sound of bicyclers, skaters, the nearby ballgame, music, etc., became very faint. I couldn't see a soul, only the trees and sky. And I stood still in my tree cocoon looking up. It lasted less than a minute. But when it was over, I knew, I think for the first time, that there was a supernatural presence in the world. And it flooded me with a sense of peace unlike any I had known.

Four months later, now Christmas 1975, I visited David and Janet one last time to bid them farewell prior to my move to California the following month. Never could I have anticipated the cataclysmic change that would take place in our lives following that visit. In his continuing search for truth, David had come across an article that said there was such a thing as Jewish people—alive, today, on the face of the earth—who believe that *Jesus Christ*—a name I had never pronounced in my life—was the *Jewish Messiah* the rest of the world is waiting for. I sat in shock. I was thirty-two years old and had never heard such a thing in my life.

"*Jewish* people believe this?" It didn't matter to me who believed what in the world. But *Jewish* people? They believe that the *Messiah*, the only hope the world has, was here—on *earth—already!*

"And no one knows that He came? He didn't make an *impact* when He came? He didn't establish His Kingdom? We're not back in Jerusalem? There's no peace? And He *left?*"

There would be nothing left—no hope—nothing! "*It's insane!*" I shouted.

"I didn't say it was true", David calmly responded. "That's what this article says, and it also says the Jews who believe this are mostly out in California. They go by several names: *Hebrew Christians, Messianic Jews, Jews for Jesus.*

"You know what?" I concluded in short order, "there are all kinds of troubled people in this world. Jews are just as entitled to be troubled as everyone else. You *cannot* be Jewish and believe in Jesus. But you *can* be Jewish and be troubled. So if there are troubled Jews who believe this, it has nothing to do with truth and certainly nothing to do with me!"

That was that. I moved to Santa Monica, California, the following month as planned. Within three months, while walking through an arts and crafts festival near UCLA on a Sunday afternoon, I saw off in the distance a hippie-ish looking fellow in his twenties with a beard and a T-shirt that read "Jews for Jesus".

Don't tell me they really exist out here! I went over to speak with the young man to find out how troubled these folks truly were. His name was Mitch. He was Jewish. And he believed that Jesus Christ was the Jewish Messiah. But his belief about Christ did not stop there. He believed Christ was God. GOD?

How can you take that in? How can *anyone* take that in? How can he—a Jew—believe a *man* is *God*? How can anyone *look* on God and *live*?

I had assumed back in New York that these were troubled people. This confirmed it. You don't need to spend time figuring out how a man can be God. He can't. End of story.

But Mitch handed me a tract. It read, "If being born hasn't given you much satisfaction, try being born again. ☺" (The happy face was included.)

"Born again"? How can a person be born *again*? You can't come out of your mother's womb a second time, so what does it mean? What *could* it mean? I wouldn't show it—not to that young man (at least I *tried* not to)—but that little tract shot a knife through my heart. No one knew the purposelessness that filled my busy days. No one knew the longing for love and meaning and a reason to exist I lived with. Unlike David, I never searched, figuring there was little chance that, even if true meaning *did* exist, I would ever find it.

But *oh*, to start life again. Would that help, if I could start again from the beginning? No matter, it's an impossibility.

Born again? What could that mean? *Is* there hope? Mitch explained that God created us for a relationship with Him, that we could not only know that God *exists*, but also *know Him*, personally.

Twilight Zone, it seemed to me. But what had I to lose in checking out this neurosis of theirs? For five months I listened. For five months they took me through Old Testament prophecies that pointed, they believed, to the Messiah. I tried to remain solid in my unbelief, frightened at the thought of falling prey to their thinking. But my defenses were a poor shield against a few verses from Isaiah which pierced me through.

> For to us a child is born,
>   to us a son is given;
> and the government will be upon his shoulder,
>   and his name will be called
> Wonderful Counselor, Mighty God,
>
> Everlasting Father, Prince of Peace.
>
> (Is 9:6)

> Therefore the Lord himself will give you a sign. Behold, a virgin shall conceive and bear a son, and shall call his name Immanuel" [i.e., "God with us"].
>
> (Is 7:14)

And then this:

> Who has believed what we have heard?
> And to whom has the arm of the LORD been revealed?
> For he grew up before him like a young plant,
>   and like a root out of dry ground;
> he had no form or comeliness that we should look
>   at him,
>   and no beauty that we should desire him.

He was despised and rejected by men;
  a man of sorrows, and acquainted with grief;
and as one from whom men hide their faces
  he was despised, and we esteemed him not.

Surely he has borne our griefs
  and carried our sorrows;
yet we esteemed him stricken,
  struck down by God, and afflicted.
But he was wounded for our transgressions,
  he was bruised for our iniquities;
upon him was the chastisement that made us whole,
  and with his stripes we are healed.

(Is 53:1–5)

Why hadn't I heard those Scriptures before? I don't know. After all, we weren't that knowledgeable about our faith. In any case, they don't prove that Christ is the Messiah. And they certainly don't prove He is God!

For five months these "Jewish believers" told me that Christ died for *my* sins and for the sins of the entire world. The words they spoke were in English, but they might as well have spoken a foreign language. There was no way for me to make sense out of what they were saying.

It was at a Hawaiian restaurant in August of 1976 that my life would change—utterly, radically, and forever. There I sat with twelve "Jews for Jesus". Twelve of them and me. Twelve *Evangelical Protestant* "Jews for Jesus" and me. I didn't know what an Evangelical Protestant was! And there they started in on me again: "Christ died for your sins, Ros, and the sins of the whole world."

"Okay, hold it right there", I stopped them short. "I have no clue what that language is about. I have no way to understand what you're saying. For the sake of this discussion, let's say things happened as you say: Christ died for *my* sins, your sins, and the sins of the world. Let's say He did it. My question is, '*What for? Why* did He do it? What was in *His mind* when He did that?'"

They took me through the sacrificial system of the Old Testament, which I never knew through all my years in synagogue. They explained that we come into the world separated from God. Separated. From *God*? (Would *that* explain my constant pain and emptiness? I thought silently.) They explained "original sin", the sin of our first parents that plunged the entire world into sin. They told me that the Scriptures state that the wages of sin is death. The *wages*—our "salary", what we've earned, what is *due* us!—is death.

And they explained that "death" means "separation". "For example," they said, "if you stick a pin in a corpse, there's no response, because death is an inability to respond to life. So, Ros, stick a *spiritual* pin in you, there's also no response. Because the things of God are foolishness to the *natural* man—i.e., the one yet in a state of separation from God. (They were quoting from the New Testament,[11] but of course I did not know that. In fact, they quoted from Scripture most of the evening without my knowing they were doing so. They knew I did not think the New Testament was a kosher book, so they told me they were quoting Scripture only when it was from the Old.)

They explained that God is a holy God who must punish sin. I understood that, but I had never reached the conclusion they brought me to that night, that if God gave us what we truly deserve, we would be dead and separated from Him forever.

[11] See 1 Cor 2:14.

But God, they quickly added, is also is a *loving God* who created us for a relationship with Him. And then they unfolded the most incredible story the world would ever hear, which, at the age of thirty-two, I was hearing for the first time. They told me in the hours that followed how God, in His love, without compromising His holiness, provided the way for us—fallen children of Adam and Eve—to be restored to a relationship with Him.

They walked me through the story of the Exodus, which I knew well, and the deliverance of the children of Israel from over four hundred years of slavery in Egypt to the foot of Mount Sinai, where Moses and Aaron would build an altar of sacrifice to God. The Israelites, according to the Law given Moses on the Mountain, would bring lambs to the altar as a sin offering for their own sins and for the sins of the nation. Why a sin offering? Because God said that without the shedding of blood there can be no remission or forgiveness of sin. While still at the foot of Mount Sinai, God would write through his servant, Moses: "For the life of the flesh is in the blood; and I have given it for you upon the altar to make atonement for your souls; for it is the blood that makes atonement, by reason of the life" (Lev 17:11). And so the Israelites would bring lambs or goats or bulls to the altar, whatever the specific sin offering required. And if it was a lamb, such as the Passover lamb had been prior to their leaving Egypt, it would be a one-year-old male from the flock, without blemish or spot. As an act of identification with the lamb, the individual bringing the lamb to the altar would put his hand on the lamb's head. It was a symbolic act that would paint a picture of the sins of that individual passing from him onto the lamb. And the lamb—who was innocent—but who, symbolically, had taken upon himself the sins of the individual—was then sacrificed. And the blood of the slain lamb was shed upon the altar as an offering to God, in payment for the individual's sins.

Why? I questioned. Why would God put an innocent animal to death for *my* sins? He should put *me* to death instead. It made no sense. But it began to get through to me that *sin* was no light matter to God, if He would do that.

They told me that the blood of thousands—no, millions—of lambs slain over 1,500 years of that Mosaic sacrificial system could never take away sin. They were a *kippur*, a covering, for sin. Nor had those sacrifices any power to perfect the worshipper or change his heart. The Israelites would return home and continue to sin over and over again and to offer sacrifices over and over again.

Not one sacrifice or all of them together could take away sin, *but every sacrifice and all of them together were a sign*, they told me, a sign that would point to the One who would come and take upon Himself, not the sin of one person for a time, but the sin of all men, of everyone who had ever lived and who ever would be born, for all time.

And with that, they took me, for the first time, to a scene in the *New* Testament. It was the appearance of Jesus as he came to be baptized by John the Baptist in the Jordan River. Recognizing immediately who it was that was walking toward him, John proclaimed to the Jewish crowd who had come to be baptized by him: "Behold, the Lamb of God, who takes away the sin of the world!" (Jn 1:29). The *Lamb? The* Lamb? The Lamb to which every Old Testament sacrifice pointed?

I was shattered. I could hardly believe what I had just heard. I thought silently to myself (though my body was visibly trembling), "If one little four-legged lamb, under the Old Testament sacrificial system, could take upon itself the sin of a single individual, temporarily, for a time, what then could the blood of *God's Son* do on that Cross, the Altar of altars? If *He* is the Lamb of God, His would be the only perfect and acceptable sacrifice, not just for Israel's sins but for the sins of the *entire world*.

I was speechless. And in shock. I knew it was true. My hang-up all this time was that a *man* cannot be God. I realized that night that, indeed, a man *cannot* be God. But if God *is*, if He exists, *God* can become a man! He can do anything He wants to do and I'm not about to tell Him how to be God!

I knew it was true. But it would take another two months for me to work through fear and pride and whatever other baggage I carried and give myself to that incomparable Lamb. It was on the evening (7:00 P.M.) of October 17, 1976, that I asked the "Lord Jesus Christ" to come to live within me and to take my life. I felt like I was jumping off a cliff. It was all or nothing at all. Either He was God and would show me what it meant to come into relationship with Him, or He was not. I would be patient and wait.

But my "wait" lasted one night's sleep. I awoke the following morning feeling like a *Martian* on planet earth. Oh, how the words of Scripture—mere words on a page before—now flooded my heart: "if anyone is in Christ, he is a new creation; old things have passed away; behold, all things have become new" (2 Cor 5:17)[12]. Indeed I was new. The *world* was new to me. The emptiness of my heart was gone. And, at last, at last, I had a reason to live for every second I breathed.

"Oh," I thought, "if the world only knew the One who said, 'I have come that they may have life, and that they

---

[12] New King James Version translation.

may have it more abundantly' "![13] (Jn 10:10). There weren't enough ways to thank Him. I couldn't learn the hymns fast enough to praise Him!

O for a *thousand* tongues to sing my great Redeemer's praise!

Amazing love, how can it be! That *Thou my God* shouldst die for me!

Loved with everlasting love, led by grace that love to know; Spirit, breathing from above, Thou hast taught me it is so! Oh, this full and perfect peace! Oh, this transport all divine! In a love which cannot cease, I am His, and He is mine.

Oh the *happiness* that was mine—and hope, and love, and purpose, and meaning, and *life* beyond all I had ever known.

"Is that so?" inquired my Jewish friends? "So what's your purpose?"

"To know God!"

"To know God? What kind of purpose is that?"

"It's *everything*", I would answer. "To know God is to know the One who made us. It's to know the One who loved us and gave Himself for us. It's to know our very reason for existence."

"But how can you, a Jew, believe in Jesus Christ?"

"Isn't it a very Jewish thing to believe in the Jewish Messiah? His name is not 'Jesus Christ'. His name is 'Jesus', a Greek translation of the Hebrew *Yeshua* (in English, Joshua). It means 'God saves.' His *title* is 'Christ', which, too, is the Greek translation of the Hebrew word *Mashiach* (in English, Messiah). It means 'Anointed One'. He is *Yeshua haMashiach*, or, translated, *Jesus the Christ*."

---

[13] Ibid.

I called David in New York to tell him I had come to believe in the Messiah—*God* come to earth! He quickly identified me as an Evangelical Protestant, and perhaps somewhere in the Fundamentalist camp. I hadn't yet understood. All I knew was that I was a Christian, a follower of the Christ, the Jewish Messiah, the Hope of Israel.

One year later, David called to tell me that he, too, had come to believe in Christ. Oh, what joy! What we did not know at the time was that Susan, living in Michigan, would have a profound experience of the presence of Christ about that same time. Hers was a very different journey. It would be some years hence before Susan would come to understand more fully who Christ is and the gift of His atonement for sin. But how utterly amazing that three siblings, three *Jewish* siblings, living in different parts of the country, and with little to no contact for the most part, would come to believe in the Messiah, and within the same period of time. Oh, the deep, *deep* love of God!

As David and I rejoiced over the phone, he introduced a somewhat serious note. "Something's wrong, though, Ros. How can it be that so many godly men (Protestant pastors) who love God and who study the Word of God with sincerity, humility, and all the tools of interpretation, come out with so many different interpretations of Scripture—and in crucial matters? Our Lord prayed that we would be *one* as He and the Father are one. How could Christ have established His Church, given us the Scriptures and not left us a way to know what He meant by what He said?"

My feeble responses—that we simply do the best we can, that we see now through a glass dimly, that one day we'll know as we are known—did not satisfy David. "What parent", he would ask, "would give birth to a child and let that child fend for himself to find out where to get food and who should teach him what? God", he reasoned, "is a more perfect Father than any human father. Would He adopt us into His family, make us His children, and then leave us orphans to fend for ourselves, to find out where to get true food, and, in this case, the Bread of Life?"

It made no sense to David that such a description fit the God he had come to believe in. And so he set out to find out if our Lord established *a* Church (versus thousands of denominations, with new ones springing up daily), if it was possible to find out what it was, and if it still existed after two thousand years. That's a journey which my beloved brother has related himself in this very book. But here's the portion of his journey that sent an unbelievable shock through my system.

One year had passed since David had come to believe in Christ. In studying the origins of the divisions within Christianity, David, particularly through a faithful core of prolife advocates, had begun to look into the Catholic Church, and, more, he had begun to study with a Catholic monk! *Double Oy!* I flew to New York to rescue David from the monk! How could his search for the "true Church on earth" have led him to the *Catholic* Church? Didn't he know that the Catholic Church was a part of *Satan's* system? Didn't he know it was the "whore of Babylon"?

I knew that! My first Bible study as a new Christian was taught by an *ex*-Catholic, who had been taught by an *ex*-priest, who taught me that the Catholic Church was a false religious system leading millions astray. And my brother is looking into *that*? As far as I was concerned, the monk was an agent of the devil himself sent to lead my brother into error! The three of us met and wrestled over matters of faith for over two hours.

It was Christmas Eve 1978. David had invited me to join him for Midnight Mass. He wasn't Catholic (yet), but was increasingly drawn. I wanted to go; I wanted to see what David's problem was. I had never been in a Catholic church before.

We sat through the Mass, which I knew absolutely nothing about, other than what I was told by those who assured me it was "Satan's system" and, therefore, Satan's territory. But as the Mass began, some things began to seem awfully familiar. They weren't Christian things, as I knew them. *They were Jewish.* How could this be? And why? The dignity and reverence of the formal procession with the Scripture held high resembled the procession with the Torah during the synagogue service. The posture of the people and priests as they prayed seemed Jewish. And the *prayers* of the priest behind the altar: "Blessed are you, Lord, God of all creation. Through your goodness we have this bread to offer, which earth has given and human hands have made. It will become the bread of life."

"Could it be?" I thought back to *Shabbos*, to the Sabbath prayers of our Jewish home: "*Baruch ata Adonai Elohenu Melech haOlam hamotzi lechem min ha'aretz.*" ("Blessed art Thou, O Lord, our God, King of the Universe, who brings forth bread from the earth.") The entire manner of worship, of prayer, even the music in some way resembled the synagogue service.

I watched in stunned silence. We left at the end, neither of us, of course, having received Communion. As we descended the steps of the church, David asked, "What did you think?" It took the entire half-hour ride home for me to be able to speak. I sat in shock. "David," I said at long last, "*that* is a synagogue, but with Christ!"

"That's right!" He was elated.

"No, that's wrong!"

I was sick. What was David's problem? Did he have a hang-up from our Jewish background—the aesthetics, the liturgy? Didn't he understand that Christ (not liturgy, not the priesthood, etc.) was the end to which all things pointed?

One year later David was Catholic.

"Is your brother a Christian?" my Evangelical friends would ask.

"I *thought* he was," I would answer, "but he's *Catholic* now, so I don't know!"

Blessed be God that he indeed *was* a Christian, a Christian who had discovered the fullness of Judaism and of Christianity beyond all I understood at the time. Though I had come to believe in Christ a year before David, it was his search that led me to the Messiah. And it was David who first gave me a copy of *This Rock*, the Catholic apologetics magazine published by Catholic Answers (my full-time employer now for the past six years). And it was through *This Rock* that I learned of Scott Hahn, that beloved former Presbyterian Minister and Seminary Professor whose tape series set me on an unstoppable journey all the way to the "synagogue with Christ", the Catholic Church.

It was through Scott's tapes that I first heard a most helpful and revealing statement made about fifty years earlier by a Catholic Bishop by the name of Fulton Sheen: "There are not one hundred people in America who hate the Catholic Church," Bishop Sheen would say, "but there are millions who hate what they mistakenly think the Catholic Church teaches."

Those words resounded through my journey over and over again as I discovered the multitude of misconceptions I had been taught about the Catholic Church. I don't blame those who taught me; they simply passed on to me what they had been given. I will be grateful for all eternity for those Protestant pastors and lay men and women who taught me to love God and to love His word. Their lives lived fully for Christ caused me all the more to hunger for truth. And it led me home to the full measure of the Church on earth.

There is no subject I did not uncover of all that separates Evangelicals from Catholics. But I discovered that it is not doctrinal matters only that separate the brethren. It is a *way of seeing*, a way I would come to discover, in time, that was utterly, beautifully, wonderfully, and intensely Catholic. The journey lasted almost five years, five agonizing years. In my heart, I think I knew Catholicism was true. But I couldn't get there. How could *I* be *Catholic!*

One day, a cousin from Brooklyn visited. He knew I was a Christian but knew nothing of my search into the Catholic Church. Along the way, he related a story of a gal he had met on the beach who, he said, "was like *you*, Rosalind: a 'Jew for Jesus'. Only *she* went *all the way* and became Catholic!"

How did he *know*, I thought? How did *he* know that to go "all the way" was to become Catholic?

It was at the Easter Vigil of 1995 at the Church of Saint Joseph in Millbrook, New York, that I entered at last the *one, holy, catholic, and apostolic* Church. Since I had been baptized as an Evangelical, I received the sacrament of confirmation, and I received the Eucharist, the Jewish Messiah, the God of Abraham, Isaac, and Jacob, on my tongue. I know, I know—it's impossible! How could God become Bread? The same way He can become a man. He is God. Is anything impossible for Him?

I sobbed uncontrollably through the rest of the Mass. Monsignor James T. O'Connor, the pastor of Saint Joseph's, dismissing the people at the end of that glorious evening, said, "We've done the greatest thing tonight that anyone can do—receive people into the Church." His happiness at our finding our way home to the Church the Messiah founded (though Monsignor O'Connor played no small part in that journey) filled me with deep love and unceasing gratitude.

Has the road since that glorious day always been easy? Oh no. *Will* it be? No. There are many who do not and who *cannot* understand, many who call me a traitor to our people, even one set of cousins who, to this day, will not allow me in their house. Their anger and unbelief is understandable to me. It is not a mystery. *My belief* is the mystery. I would say, with Saul, who became the Apostle Paul, "I count everything as loss because of the surpassing worth of knowing Christ Jesus my Lord" (Phil 3:8).

In the fullness of Judaism, which is the Catholic Church, I have now the *whole* Christ—*all* that God has given in giving us His Church: the sacraments, the communion of saints, a Mother—a *Jewish* Mother, the Mother of the Jewish Messiah!—and, above all, the unbelievable *condescension* of a God who not only gave Himself *for* us on Calvary, but who even gives Himself *to* us as our daily Food.

Christianity is not a Gentile religion. It is a Jewish religion that was given to encompass the entire world and every soul in it. It is looked upon as a Gentile faith in today's world because most of the world is Gentile, and Christianity has spread throughout the earth, as well it should. But it was begun by a Jewish carpenter, who was "God with us" and who "came to his own" (Jn 1:11), i.e., the Jewish people. His followers all were Jewish. Christianity was looked upon as a *Jewish* sect in the first century. The question then was, "Do you have to first be *Jewish* to believe in Jesus?"

The answer to that question was no. But the first Christians were solely Jews who were doing a very Jewish thing: following the Jewish Messiah. The Church was founded on Israel, on twelve Jewish disciples. But the disbelief and misunderstandings of that day on the part of many were not unlike those of our own day. There was great joy in following *Yeshua*[14], but the cost was high. So the author of the Letter to the Hebrews, in the first century, wrote *to the Hebrews*—i.e., to Jewish believers in Messiah, who, as a result of their faith, were often ostracized from the synagogue and their entire families and communities, from all they had known and loved.

Yes, the cost of following Messiah was high, but the cost of reverting back to the Law, i.e., to pre-messianic Judaism— the Judaism that existed under Moses, before Messiah came— was higher. The Torah could never save. It could only point us to the One who could—to the Lamb, who did not come to abolish the Law, He said, but to fulfill it.[15] "The Law", wrote Paul, "was our schoolmaster to bring us to Christ" (Gal 3:24).[16]

The Letter to the Hebrews was written to first-century Jews who thought that this Jesus, this *Yeshua*, was the long-awaited Messiah of Israel, but who were afraid to put their faith on the line. They witnessed the pain of their fellow brethren who had been cut off from their families, and they feared the price of following Messiah was too high. So they sat on the fence. And the writer of Hebrews says to them in essence: "Don't sit on the fence, don't throw away your confidence; don't turn back. Come all the way to Christ.

[14] The name "Jesus" in Hebrew.
[15] See Mt 5:17.
[16] King James Version.

Come all the way to salvation. Christ is *better* than Moses! Moses was a *servant* in God's house; Christ is the *Son*. Christ is better than the *angels*! *They* worship *Him*! Christ is better than all that went before. His priesthood is *superior* to the priesthood of Aaron. He offers a *better* sacrifice, a *better* priesthood, a *better* covenant, a *better* country. There's more to gain in suffering for Christ than in going back to the Law that prefigured its fulfillment!"

Oh, if only certain spokesmen within our *Catholic* fold would understand the message of Hebrews—and of the entire New Covenant for that matter. I refer to those who propose—against all Church teaching—that the Jewish people today can be saved under the covenant God made with Moses. "God is faithful to His promises", they say. But of course God is faithful to His promises. That is precisely why He sent the promised Messiah.

How unthinkable it is to any Jew that the Messiah would come for everyone *but* Israel! Would He come *through* the Jews but not *for* the Jews? Can we love the Jewish people and withhold from them knowledge of the very Deliverer *they* gave to the world? If Christ is *not* the Messiah of the Jewish people, He is *no one's* Messiah. Yes, He will come a second time to gather to Himself all who have believed in Him and to establish a Kingdom of everlasting righteousness. But it is He also who came the first time, as a dying Lamb to take upon Himself the sin of the world.

That's why He was put to death *Erev Pesach*.[17] He was the final Passover Lamb. But unlike other sacrificial lambs, this Lamb rose from the dead to give life to all who will put their trust in Him. Just as the Israelites were instructed

---

[17] Hebrew for "Passover Eve".

to eat the lamb,[18] so too are we, the people of the "Israel of God"[19], the Church, to eat the Lamb—*the* Lamb who is Christ.

It was to the *Jews* that Jesus said, ". . . unless you eat the flesh of the Son of man and drink his blood, you have no life in you. . . . For my flesh is food indeed, and my blood is drink indeed" (Jn 6:53–55). Many walked away because they understood what He was saying and could not handle it.

In my Evangelical years, I was taught that the "bread" of which our Lord spoke was merely *symbolic* of His flesh, and the cup only *symbolic* of His blood. But, Jesus said to the Jewish nation, "It was not Moses who gave you the bread from heaven; my Father gives you the true bread from heaven. For the bread of God is that which comes down from heaven, and gives life to the world. . . . I am the bread of life" (Jn 6:32–35).

What an eye-opening day it was for me when I connected the *manna* of their wilderness wanderings to the *Bread of Life*. I had come to understand that every feast of the Mosaic Covenant, that every article of furniture in the tabernacle, indeed the tabernacle itself, was a sign, a type, that pointed to the reality that was Christ and that had its fulfillment in Him. If the "bread" of which Christ spoke and of which He partook at the Last Supper were merely a *symbol*, then the manna of the Old Covenant did *not* point to Christ; it pointed to a *symbol* (matzo), which then pointed to Christ.

But if the manna pointed directly to Christ—the *living* bread come down from heaven[20]—that would be consistent

---

[18] Ex 12:8.
[19] Gal 6:16.
[20] Jn 6:51.

with every other Old Testament type. The reality is always greater than the shadow. The manna was miraculous. Would a miraculous sign point to an inferior, i.e., natural piece of matzo? What sort of fulfillment would that be? But if the manna (bread from heaven) points to Him, the true Bread from Heaven, the reality indeed is greater than the sign!

If non-Catholic Christians only knew the full measure of God's love to us in giving us Himself, they would flock to the Catholic Church and to the Eucharist on bended knee. And if the sons and daughters of Abraham, Isaac, and Jacob knew that their Messiah *has* come, that He has established His *New* Covenant *with Israel*, as the prophet Jeremiah foretold,[21] and through Israel to the world, and that He has given us Himself, the Living Bread, the True Manna from Heaven, they would flock to Him as well—yes, on bended knee. And like the Jewish doubting Thomas, they would cry out with every Jewish and non-Jewish believer throughout the world, "My Lord and my God!"

Omein.[22] May it be.

I almost forgot to tell you. My parents' initial response to our faith was to shut us, including David's children, out of their lives. It was a difficult time of separation for us all. But, in time, both my parents (mother and stepfather) gave their lives to their Jewish Messiah through that little Baptist church in upstate New York where the love of God first flooded my heart. And they sat down to the Passover table the following year and drank a cup of Manischewitz wine to the Messiah who had come! My sister, Susan, also gave her life to Christ and serves Him now with her whole heart through the deaconess, hospital chaplaincy, and outreach min-

[21] Jer 31:31–34.
[22] "Amen" in Yiddish.

istries of the Lutheran Church Missouri Synod. *Baruch haShem!*[23]

One more thing! I began this story with my initial response as a Jewish girl to a news item in the 1960s about nuns' habits being shortened. Now I'll come full circle and tell you that forty years later (*forty* seems to be God's favorite figure in the preparation of His people!)—if Messiah grants the desires which He, I believe, has planted in *this* Hebrew-Catholic heart—I long to restore the years the locusts have eaten with an order of Sisters that will not only return their hemline to the floor, but the habit—as the glorious sign to God that it is—to the world!

Blessed Mother of the Hope of Israel, pray for us! *Baruch haba b'Shem Adonai!* (Blessed is He who comes in the name of the Lord!)

---

[23] Literally "Blessed be the Name", the standard Jewish blessing of God in Hebrew. The name of God is not used out of respect for the sanctity of God, and "the name" is substituted.

Where Time Becomes Space

Judith Cabaud

Since obtaining her degrees at New York University and at the Sorbonne in Paris forty years ago, Judith Cabaud has been living in France. Her passions have always been her nine children, and now her grandchildren, and her writing. She lives with her husband in a small provincial town in central France, where she teaches English and American civilization, and writes. Her books include her spiritual autobiography Where Time Becomes Space, *a historical biography, a novel, and several works on the life of Eugenio Zolli, including a biography that has been translated into four languages. She can be contacted at judithcabaud@wanadoo.fr.*

As far back as I can remember, as a little Jewish girl born and brought up in Brooklyn, New York, a deep-rooted sense of curiosity and a capacity for discovery were among the essential traits of my character. Paradoxically, I was able to observe things from afar and, at the same time, become very involved with everything I touched. My life from the beginning, without my knowing it, was always to unfold in this way, in the light of God's grace.

My parents were the hard-working, American-born off-spring of Jewish immigrants who had arrived in the United States from Russia and Poland with the great wave of the

nineteen hundreds. My mother and father got married the
year of the Wall Street Crash. They ignored the Great
Depression, so busy were they at trying to make ends meet
in their tiny hardware store. Two sons were born to them
within four years, and I came into the world a little later,
the year Pearl Harbor was attacked. Despite the war raging
in Europe and in the Pacific, it was a grand time for my
parents who had come into some prosperity; they had hopes
and ambitions to turn their precious children into typical
American boys and girls.

The rift was precisely there, however; our grandparents
were witnesses to the past, to our roots and our religion,
and they spoke only Yiddish. Family feasts brought together
near and distant relatives during Jewish holidays. My grandfather would perform the liturgy of the Seder with great
diligence. This could last for two hours, while the little
ones were dying to eat. But the image of his piety and my
father's extreme respect for his parents remained forever
ingrained in my memory.

When I was enrolled in Public School 233 around the corner from our house, there was very little change in the people I met daily: the majority of pupils and teachers were Jewish.
I could not even imagine who or what non-Jews were like—
with the exception of a few Italians whose children went on
Sunday mornings to some far-off church wearing lacy dresses
and dark suits. To be a "real American" was therefore a myth
that belonged to the more affluent people. The simple souls
in my family could not even fathom a choice: you were a Jew
and you were an American. There was no incompatibility—
dual identity signaled simply a dual way of life.

Since other religious beliefs remained far away, no one
needed to ask questions. On the holy day of Yom Kippur,
God opened His registers for Life and Death, and Jews were

catalogued according to their merits. But the atonement made for past sins was a kind of tribal ceremony that belonged to a codified tradition—and tradition *was* religion. As a matter of fact, it was defined as a "way of life" to which other tribe members could add: "whether you like it or not!" By that time, I wondered: the image of God as a super bookkeeper in the American society of progress and technology seemed not only anachronistic, but paradoxical: He who created Heaven and earth, stars and planets, fauna and flora, mountains and rivers, man and woman, could He, on the Day of Atonement, be like someone taking inventory in a grocery store?

At Hebrew school, we learned to write the alphabet and recite prayers. Bible stories were illustrated by the pupils, and our eyes would fall constantly on a large map entitled *Zion*. The stories remained just stories. No one pointed out that it was God who had inspired them, and that they were of another order than Grimm's fairy tales or Greek mythology.

On television, which was still a novelty at the time, I watched a film about the life and Passion of Jesus Christ. I remember I cried bitter tears to see Jesus, who was so kind, carry His Cross. When I saw the inscription, "Jesus of Nazareth, King of the Jews", I was startled and said, "How come we didn't learn about Jesus too?" A few embarrassed smiles went around the room until someone said, "But we don't believe in that."

At Christmas time, stores were decorated with colored lights. People bought presents and evergreen trees. Something melancholy hung over our feast of Hanukkah. It may have been the pennies I received instead of presents. In any case, the victory of the Maccabees in the sacred Temple did not suffice to replace the magic of Christ's coming for a curious little girl. But He was so far away. How could I know?

Then, the discovery of nature, of the germination of seeds, of a cherry tree in bloom, would overwhelm me with emotion. How could this happen? How did that God of strange tales and bookkeeping fit into the marveling I felt in front of the majesty of His creation? It was all at once frightening and grandiose. Would I learn it at school? There were so many things I wanted to study. I even contrived projects on writing books about world history. But there was always so much more to learn. I gave up at the thought that I would have nothing to say.

The decisive element in these young years came to me in the form of music. I still remember listening to tunes sometimes and standing immobile, as though paralyzed, so as to catch each phrase. I would listen to my brothers—Arnold who could improvise wonderfully on the piano, playing popular songs with beautiful chords, and Sheldon who could make his accordion breathe in frantic rhythm. At the age of seven, my parents let me have piano lessons with the man who taught Sheldon the accordion. I learned folk tunes and sundry arrangements of some composers with names I had never heard of. By the age of ten, an initiation to instrumental music at school was going to change my life; an introduction to beauty would provide me with living proof that I had a soul. A new teacher at PS 233, a musician who was young and idealistic, was allowed to experiment with my fourth grade class. He taught us notes and rhythm, and then we could choose one of the four string instruments of the symphonic orchestra: violin, viola, cello, or bass. Everyone learned to play one of them. I chose the cello. Our teacher took us to our first concert at Carnegie Hall, and we discovered the composers with sometimes unpronounceable names. I was very impressed, but it was another day on which it struck finally like a bomb. Two of us were sent to audition for the All-City High School Orchestra, whose members were usually picked from the best high-school musicians of New York City. By chance, that year, thanks to a shortage of cellists, they were recruiting to fill in the missing seats behind the music stands. To my great surprise, after playing an easy piece by Telemann, a very nice man with a comforting smile told me I could join them by coming to rehearsals every Saturday morning. My musical knowledge was minimal because I had had very little formal instruction, other than at school. So I was a little dazed to have been selected.

Everyone was still sleeping that Saturday morning as I left the house in a great hurry, with my cello in its brown canvas bag. It was a windy November morning, and the icy air beat on my face as I walked to the bus stop; there, I met my classmate Linda. We took the bus and subway before arriving in the auditorium of Brooklyn Technical High School where rehearsals were held. The orchestra was on stage, and a man in shirt-sleeves was about to conduct. As we were late, we walked up on the side of the stage with our instruments. A kind college girl showed me where to sit and put a cello part in front of me.

The conductor had stopped for a moment and was beginning again, and I suddenly had the impression of being in Heaven. Two flutes were playing in unison the fugue of the first part of Bach's *Second Suite* for orchestra, and all the strings were dancing and carrying them in their triumph. Kindly, the college girl was trying to show me where we were on my part, but after a few minutes, I could not follow anymore. I could not see the page, because my eyes were all blurred by tears. A new day had dawned for me.

That beautiful music of Bach was an intimation of Heaven. It came from somewhere, from Someone; so there *was* something else in the world.

I played in the All-City High School Orchestra for four years, and every Saturday morning was like entering the enchanted cavern of Ali Baba to find new caches of jewels: Liszt, Sibelius, Brahms, Bach, Wagner, Smetana.... The music of the masters was imbued with timelessness, while the world outside was full of people rushing toward a precipice. Arriving at the age of adolescence with this absolute nature, it was impossible not to see that the society in which I lived was solely based on appearances, not only physical, but moral as well. The Ten Commandments were rules that were often transgressed in very subtle ways. What counted was what could be seen. In this pleasure-seeking environment provided by adults, adolescents could go haywire, as long as the external picture remained intact. And so it was also for religion. Jewish observance ranged from strict Orthodoxy to "Reformed" trends in which we had the choice of the prescriptions of the Law that appealed more or less to us. We lit candles on Friday night; we could eat kosher at home (not outside). We respected Jewish holidays by sending cards for Rosh Hashanah; we lit a candle each night for Hanukkah. Passover was more like a Jewish Thanksgiving for us than anything else. All this was supposed to be somewhere in the Bible. Actually, we were never really sure of biblical origins because we never read the Bible.

The second decisive event of my girlhood was the loss of my father. Although he had always been preoccupied by his business, we had shared a common taste for adventure when he took us on trips all along the eastern seaboard. One day, when his head ached too much, he consented to see a doctor. He found out the truth by overhearing a phone conversation between my mother and the specialist who condemned him to live but another year. At the age of forty-six, he was face to face with death. He took medicine with depressive side effects and, like Macbeth, could sleep no more. Superficial people and jealous relatives told him he wouldn't die so young, that it was a psychosomatic problem, that he should see a psychiatrist, after all. Father tried to approach God and went to the synagogue on Saturdays, but the strength and intimacy he was yearning for were stifled and blocked by tradition.

Then, past the flat humid plains of the coastline, down beyond the happy golden fields of corn in Virginia, where light-brown tobacco leaves mellowed in tall smoke houses, and blacks bought doughnuts at the back door of a diner reserved for whites, there, in a red brick hospital building of North Carolina, surrounded by green trees and people with a southern drawl, my father was dying. He had been taken there as a last resort for a cure, but I remember his resigned expression when he left the house he knew he would never see again.

For my Christmas vacation, I was called to his bedside. The rooms of the hospital were decorated with streamers and balloons for the New Year, and one evening, in the penumbra of a sick and sweet-smelling corridor, I bade him good-bye unknowing, unrealizing, unthinking. Back at school in Brooklyn, less than two weeks passed before I was told on the backseat of a taxi cab: "It's all over"; and I needed a few seconds to understand that my aunt was talking about my father. The day of his funeral, something died within me too: I lost all worldly ambition for the wealth and fortune that had killed my father. What I was looking for could not be bought with money.

Solitude hung over our little house as the seasons began to pass again. My mother would escape its gnawing presence by spending her long days in the hardware store, and both my brothers by then were married. Only music and studies could keep me from the boredom that was lurking in the shadows of my life. I made bids for affection, but nothing would fulfil that unexplainable yearning I had for absolute love. Later, as a student at NYU, I fell into complete revolt against religion and society. When my grandparents died, the last vestiges of Jewish tradition disappeared for me. I was now on the last stepping-stone toward moral misery, incapable of finding that "great love" I was looking for. I fell in love with a handsome medical student who tore my heart to shreds. I indulged in psychoanalytical theories and scorned social conformity. I ignored the inevitable pitfalls of this dangerous materialistic attitude. My deception in love had given me a thin crust of cynicism, but I was waiting for my soul to become completely hardened, like clay baking in the sun. I thought true love belonged to romantic myth now, because it was inaccessible. The world was filled with selfishness and pleasure-seeking ambition. The only salvation I could perceive was illusive: temporary blue skies thanks to music and literature.

Then came the third and final event that transformed my life: my junior year in France. One of my teachers at Tilden High School had sent his daughter to Paris for one year. I don't know why her experience appealed so much to me. I knew nothing about France, but I had a burning desire to learn French and visit that country. Was it that tiny flame that Providence allows to blaze up at the mention of an experience that one day is to save us?

As soon as I set foot off the *SS Rotterdam*, which had sailed full steam across the Atlantic in that Fall of 1960, I was greeted by my French teacher's brother, Jean. The young man had come from Paris with a car to help me bring my luggage to his sister's flat. I was to board with her for the first three months of my coming school year. I was immediately certain that I had landed on another planet: driving down long avenues lined with green trees, gothic cathedrals, ancient monuments, stained-glass windows, and sundry castles along the way. Everything was lit up at night, to remind people that it was not a dream. How could I brood on my sorrows when I found myself amidst such gratuitous beauty, answering my yearning for disinterested love?

After three weeks of perpetual discovery, I enrolled at the Sorbonne where I would follow the curriculum called *civilisation française*. I took courses in French language and literature, history, philosophy, and art. I visited museums every week and attended theatre performances at the *Comédie-française*. In the required reading I sampled most of the French thinkers of the seventeenth and eighteenth centuries, but it was Blaise Pascal who finally caught me.

I had encountered Pascal back at NYU; he had intrigued me, but I didn't know why. Now I met him again as he emerged through the light and history of his time—and I could understand much more French. As a scientist, he was not merely a specialist in his own field, but a thinker in all fields. At last, here was someone asking questions not only about scientific phenomena, but about the very existence of the universe. Before, I had not paid much attention to the fact that the work of Pascal tends to persuade his reader toward Christianity, because I was not interested in religion. What moved me was his cosmic perspective. This was not the philosopher proving a series of abstractions. On the contrary, he was very concrete about his notion of infinity, while torment dominated his language: "The eternal silence of these infinite spaces frightens me."

I was frightened too. Wasn't I also "floating" between
the two infinities of greatness and smallness? I appreciated
his analysis of the "misery of man without God". How well
did I understand it: vanity, anxiety, self-love, imagination,
habit, pride. Did I need a better doctor to have a more
precise diagnosis? Wasn't my flight from home and society
a flight from myself?

After identifying for me the sickness my soul was dying
of, he told me what we are; our true state of being, our
human condition. Man is not the center of things but is in
the middle of things—that is, uncertain, "floating" in a universe whose limits escape us. And yet, man could be considered as great because of his consciousness of things. Here
my pseudoscientific ideas were shaken. It gave me a keen
awareness of my own shortsightedness. Then, my reflection
came to a standstill before what I considered as a wall: "Man
is only a subject full of error, natural and ineffaceable without grace."

In grace lay the entire mystery.

It was a cold December evening. Frost was forming on
the window as the long winter night was lowering in late
afternoon, and Jean came over to keep me company. He sat
reading in an armchair while I pored over the pages of Pascal's
Pensées. We had had another argument, as always, about
religion, and he seemed very discouraged by my indifferent
attitude.

I had come to a passage that explains our nature through
Christianity. Curiosity pushed me on: How can Pascal *prove*
the Christian religion to be true? No reading, however
noble, can coerce human liberty. I was quite sure of myself.
I could cope with anything in an objective way. But this
reasoning and logic brought me to the edge of the precipice. Pascal summed up the Jewish religion better than

any Rabbi I had ever known. The prophecies of the Old Testament were the stumbling blocks of modern Judaism. For the first time in my life, in spite of my Hebrew school education, I found out that we were awaiting the Messiah, a Savior to redeem our fallen humanity. This One would certainly have a big job of rooting out the evil and wickedness I could perceive. But who was this Messiah? Everything turns on the Person of Jesus Christ "that both Testaments regard, the Old Testament in its expectation, the New in its model, as their center." Now, at least, I understood why and for what we were a Chosen People.

Millions of stars were sparkling in that cold December night, and rays of ineffable light were pouring down through the darkness toward me. Unbearable emotion swelled my heart, and tears came to relieve the aching, throbbing truth. Something inside me was whispering and telling and showing me, in this gushing of sudden brightness all around me: *"Jesus Christ is God! Jesus Christ is God!"*

Five minutes before I was one person; now I was another. Mist and fog had lifted off the highest mountaintops for me, and their summits, which I would now have to climb, were perfectly bright and visible, in a pure sky of azure. Trembling and aware, I opened my lips to form the words "I believe."

Jean looked up at me. He was astonished. He had given me up, humanly speaking. This experience of grace cannot be defined. Only sudden images can evoke the mysterious free gift of God. Within me was the unending sound of amorous certainty, telling me that I had arrived, that here was the only essential truth for which we are born, and that eventually I would understand. And a chorus of angels, maybe those of our numerous children and grandchildren to come later, must have rejoiced in that winter night as one of the lost sheep of Israel found its Shepherd.

The next day I knew I hadn't dreamed or imagined it; that same sweet certainty was inhabiting me. It was enveloping me and was stronger than any human impulse. I went to the window of my room, and as though struck by a superior force from outside myself, I fell on my knees and wept. I didn't know how to pray, but words came automatically to my lips: "Holy Mary, Mother of God, pray for me."

I went outside and walked down the Rue Saint Jacques, still dazed. The only thought in my head was to find a church. I wandered past the butcher shop, where the nice man with a big grin used to sell me chops. Across from the small grocery store where I bought homemade yogurt was the Church of Saint Jacques.

Everything looked the same, yet everything was different. Nothing appeared changed, and yet everything was—because I knew that God existed and Jesus Christ was God. Everything was singing His presence to my ears. I thought, "If He exists, then everything exists because of Him; everything exists in Him and He in everything." This blaring light in my soul was showing me His realm. Before, I was groping in the dark. This light was His will, and His will had now taken me by the hand so that the Holy Spirit might lead me to where I had to go. I entered the dark vestibule of the church, went inside, and knelt at a prie-dieu. There was no one else—simply a small red lamp on the main altar. I didn't know what to do, so I just stayed there to let my confusion pass. Later that morning I would read more Pascal. To read of the miracles of Christ was almost superfluous, the greatest miracle having been to make me see, though I was blind, to make me hear, though I was deaf, to make me praise God, though I was dumb.

The image used in the Gospels for the state of the sick soul is that of a sick body. But, because a single body cannot be sick enough to express it properly, there had to be more than one. Thus we find the deaf man, the dumb man, the blind man, the paralytic, dead Lazarus, the man possessed of a devil. All these put together are in the sick soul. In later years I came to see that the miracles of God are permanent. However, it is only in certain moments that we can peer through the veil and see them "at work", in certain moments that we are disposed to that grace, to that divine energy that makes an explosion on the sun a mere spark.

As I came out of the church and walked slowly back to my room, I didn't know what to do. So I let myself be led by the hand of God, which grasped my own and indicated from time to time: "This is what you have to do."

Jean came to see me again and looked at me, wondering if he hadn't dreamed. I told him about going to the church that morning and that, though I didn't know what to do, I was nevertheless quite happy and at peace.

Of course, I thought of the inevitable reaction of my family. Because all religion was a matter of social conformity to them (and to most others I knew), it would be difficult to explain to them that my conversion had come from profound conviction, not convention. And even if I had all the best arguments in the world, I could not explain that light, that sweet certainty, that presence of One in whose hand I had now placed my own. I nevertheless worried about my mother, because I had caused her enough heartache. But when the sun shines, even though everyone says it is night, could I deny the day? Jean had brought a small package with two books, a missal and the synoptic Gospels. I was eager to know what happens at Mass for, having seen it, I was intrigued and wanted to know its meaning. I read through the missal completely and was amazed. The Mass had nothing of a sociological character; rather, it represented the reality of sacrifice, still occurring in the present as a continuation of its occurrence in the past.

Everything was logical now, because if Christ is God, there can never be too many signs of adoration, too many genuflections, and so the Mass was full of them. We went directly to the Church of Saint Jacques and found a low, evening Mass being said in the Chapel of the Blessed Sacrament. I sat in a corner and watched. "Send forth Thy light and Thy truth; they have conducted me and brought me unto Thy holy hill, and into Thy tabernacles. And I will go to the altar of God, to God who giveth joy to my youth . . ." (Ps 42:3–4, Vulgate).

Then, after saying a few more prayers, the priest raised a round, unleavened piece of bread to offer it, and a chalice with wine. And oh! how strange it was, to come here and find all these unknown people sitting with me, as though at my grandfather's table, at the Passover Seder, when we had watched the eldest member of the family bless and offer the matzo, the bread that was unleavened because the children of Israel did not have time to let it rise. And I felt the bitter herbs, in the taste of my sins still acrid in my mouth. And the ten plagues of Egypt were the symbols of my misery without God, the plagues of pride, of hatred, of sensuality, which had come to confound me and ruin my soul.

In the great silence of Egypt we had awaited the exterminating angel. There had been a glass of wine in the middle of the table, and I used to watch it, back in Brooklyn.

My brother would say that an angel of God[1] was going to
pass and would take a sip. He even opened the front door,
looking at me with a half-ironic smile, and I had thought,
as a child, that the amount of wine in the glass had diminished during the meal. It was folklore, no doubt, to most,
for few believed that the angel of God had really come by,
but as for me, I was sure!

What had saved us from the destruction that God had
sent the Egyptians? What had prevented us from having
our firstborn die on that terrible night, if not the blood of
the sacrificed lamb that had been smeared on the doors of
the Israelites? And it had been the decisive argument for
Pharaoh to let Israel go.

And who was that Lamb, promised throughout the Old
Testament, who freed us from the Egypt that kept us enslaved
within ourselves, enslaved to our sin and our hypocrisy?
That Lamb of God was Jesus Christ, who came to lead us
out of slavery and into the Promised Land, not the material
land of the flesh but the land of spiritual life, where we
would be reunited with our Lord God and be able to rest
in Him. Meanwhile, He had nourished Israel's children with
manna in the desert. Jesus had multiplied bread for the thousands, and now, at this very minute, in this holy Mass, we
were offering the Lamb whose Blood, smeared on our hearts,
would save us, redeem us, deliver us, and nourish us.

Jesus had been at the Seder table with His apostles, and
lo, having proved that He was the Son of God by accom-
plishing the prophecies of the Scriptures, and by performing many miracles, he preceded, at this last Seder, the sacrifice

---

[1] Properly speaking, it is the Prophet Elijah, who will return shortly before
the coming of the Messiah to announce his imminent arrival (Mal 4:5), who
is awaited at the Passover Seder.—ED.

of the Cross with the offering of His Body and Blood. "For
this is the chalice of my blood, of the new and eternal testament: the mystery of faith which shall be shed for you
and for many unto the forgiveness of sins." [2] Nothing surprised me in this. He who was that light and that sweetness, only He could have created the universe, for creation
is love. Only He could exist in three Persons, the Father,
the Son, and the Holy Spirit. Is it not as easy for Him to
exist in such a way as to have created millions of galaxies?
Could He not, therefore, change the bread and wine of the
Seder into His Body and Blood and give us the Eucharist?

Could He not have redeemed us on the Cross, once and
for all, though a single tear would have sufficed for God to
pay God? I understood this because His light was the overwhelming love I had always yearned for. Only as a baby in
the arms of my mother and father had I, perhaps, known
such an experience. I was loved and I loved—not an interested love for pleasure or for purpose, but a love through
grace, through the free gift of God. Love had led Him to
the Cross because evil is rife in the world. And love leads
Him ever now to sacrifice in the Mass.

This allowed me, at last, to begin to understand the Jewish religion. Through Jesus Christ, I could interpret the symbols of the Old Testament, which now became meaningful.
What I had previously learned of the Old Testament was
like seeing the first act of a play and not knowing what
comes next. The Jews, perplexed by the ancient prophecies
of Daniel, Isaiah, Hosea, and Ezekiel, had grown weary of
waiting and had taken refuge, as it were, in the Talmud—in
myriad prescriptions on the purity of their food and clothes

---

[2] Canon of the Mass, *St. Joseph's Daily Missal* (New York: Catholic Book
Publishing Co., 1950), p. 566.

and actions. This gave them a good conscience, but they did not seem to bother about the Author of it all. He had chosen them to take His message to the world—the promise of the Redeemer, the Messiah, who was to come for all the others too, for all the nations. How could they content themselves with fulfillment of laws while remaining indifferent to their mission?

At the time, I realized these things in an intuitive way, but there was much more to discover before I could comprehend what this new spiritual life entailed. In fact, many years were needed and many yet to come. For the moment, I had arrived only at the crossroads and had recognized the right direction in which I was to travel.

I had to think now about baptism, which was completely novel to me, the idea of being born anew. I had never even thought about conversion, especially because of my antipathy toward organized religion. Strange as it may seem, however, I no longer had any objections, as long as this compelling new light shone before the eyes of my soul. It was very strange, during the instructions I received in the following months, that I was never surprised by any doctrine of the Church, and I almost felt that I knew them already—as if God, by an infused light, gave all of His secret treasure to me at once.

Summer arrived in Paris, and people walked the streets on sultry nights. At Montmartre, in the shadow of the Basilica of the Sacred Heart, where one came to adore Christ exposed in the Eucharist at all hours,[3] the trees were full green, and artists were showing their paintings. On one such night, I fell asleep and dreamed I saw the

---

[3] Perpetual adoration of the Blessed Sacrament has continued uninterrupted in the Basilica of Sacre Coeur since 1885.

living room of my parents' house in Brooklyn. My mother was standing at the front door to admit suitors. I was sad and very pale. The doorbell rang, and it was Jean. I saw him in color, though the rest of my dream was in black and white. I said, "That's the one I want to marry." Mother looked puzzled and said to me, "But the others are very nice. What makes him any better?"

And I answered, "I love his soul."

A few months later, in the sacristy of the Church of Our Lady of Victories, a very old priest with shaky hands asked me if I would accept all the children the Lord would deign to send me and if I would educate them in the Church. I answered with great relief and joy that I was only waiting for the chance to do so.

The following year, on the twenty-first of April, the Vigil of the Resurrection, I donned a white robe with the other catechumens and into the dark church we carried the luminous flame from outdoors to share it with those who were waiting inside. *Lumen Christi*. They had slain a lamb whose blood had consecrated the doorposts of Israel's children, and they had made the first Seder in haste. . . . Now the Lamb of God was Jesus Christ, whose ignominious death on the Cross blotted out the sin of Adam. "This is, therefore, the night which purified the darkness of sinners by the light of a pillar. . . . This is the night in which, destroying the bonds of death, Christ arose victoriously from the grave." The Egyptians had decided to pursue them and trap them between the desert and a vast sea. Pharaoh was exulting in his new scheme. Israel's children felt the heat of the sand and the weight of their packs. Mothers were weary, and babies were crying. The old and the sick were heavy to carry, and the huge indomitable sea loomed before them. Pharaoh's troops were approaching in a cloud of dust. The heavenly Father

opened the Red Sea with a great wind in His might and
brought Israel's children to the other side with dry feet.

I went up to the main altar and knelt at the edge. Baptismal water flowed onto my forehead, and the waves of
the Jordan were pouring onto the Red Sea tide.

> Mary Magdalene came to the tomb early, while it was still
> dark, and saw that the stone had been taken away from the
> tomb.... Mary stood weeping outside the tomb, and as she
> wept she stooped to look into the tomb; and she saw two
> angels in white, sitting where the body of Jesus had lain,
> one at the head and one at the feet. They said to her,
> "Woman, why are you weeping?" She said to them, "Because
> they have taken away my Lord, and I do not know where
> they have laid him." Saying this, she turned round and saw
> Jesus standing, but she did not know that it was Jesus....
> Supposing him to be the gardener, she said to him, "Sir, if
> you have carried him away, tell me where you have laid
> him, and I will take him away." Jesus said to her, "Mary."
> She turned and said to him in Hebrew, "Rabboni!" (which
> means Teacher). (Jn 20:1, 11–16)

After two years of big city life, Jean and I had the opportunity to move to the country, to a large provincial manor
in the region of Auvergne. On the clearest days, across the
woods, you can see the blue outline of the Puy de Dome
mountain and the distant chain of France's ancient volca-
noes. We learned to farm the land—to plough, to plant,
and to harvest. Through the labor of each season, through
the presence of our children growing up by our side, in the
silence of a tree in bloom and a field where potatoes grew,
we felt closer to God. I had been brought up in the cult of
becoming "somebody". If you're so smart, why aren't you
rich? Now we became "nobodies" in the eyes of the world.
We didn't get rich by farming, and we had a large family.

After so many years of university studies and diplomas, I discovered the most interesting and fascinating vocation of womankind in motherhood. This was true "liberation" from the futile strivings of the world.

At the time of Christ, sincere believers expected the Messiah to be a liberator from Roman occupation, a sovereign, a king who with his army would reorganize the Promised Land. The Jews too were waiting for a "somebody". And who was this Jesus who didn't have a cradle to His name? All His life He was a professional "nobody". How could a Son of God be so poor? There they were, confusing the Messiah with a material goal. The prophets had warned them beforehand, but to no avail.

The time was ripe now to continue on my road. I always kept the bright light of grace in my memory, but another thought was obsessing me—what is "inner life"? The saints write of God in such intimate terms that they could as well be His lovers. Saint Teresa of Avila was one of my favorites.

I was driving along the country road and meditating on all these things. After dropping off the older children at school, I was going to have the blade of the circular saw sharpened. It was the season for cutting down trees and planting new ones. Although the Church was being besieged by post–Vatican Council II fever and every other priest was racing ahead to bring things "up-to-date", we felt temporarily protected in our rural environment.

My car bounced down the little road on my way back home. I stopped at the church, thinking that my errand had caused me to miss the First Friday Mass that morning, and that there would be time just to say a prayer. When I entered it was only the Offertory; so I could attend most of the Mass after all. I was full of distractions, still thinking of my errands, but I tried to collect my thoughts and pay attention to what was going on. I felt ashamed, thinking of the small advantage I took of the many graces God kept sending me, of my numerous defects, which harassed me still, and of that gnawing sense of unworthiness.... I took refuge in meditating on Mary Magdalene and wished I could have stayed at the Lord's feet the way she had, pouring perfume on them and drying them with her hair ... to be there, at his feet.... I thought of union in death, union with loved ones, and still more of a union that seemed unattainable, with God Himself, who had revealed Himself in the lives of saints—who were so remote from me.

A bell tinkled, and I prayed with the few people present for that First Friday, a Mass to the Sacred Heart of Jesus on a gray windy day. At Communion, I went up last and received the Host.

I was kneeling at my place when I felt at first a confusion, then an emotion, then more than an emotion, as my senses were numb—a sort of ecstasy. It was as if I heard the most beautiful music, and more.... As if I saw the most beautiful sight, and more.... For a few seconds, or minutes (there was no time), I was inhabited by the Real Presence of Christ in the Eucharist. He came to me; I came to Him. My eyes closed, I saw without seeing.... A white tunic of incomparable texture, enveloping me—huge, immense, like the sea, engulfing me. Above, there was a face in a shadow, a contour without features, overwhelming, all-inspiring. In a flash, I heard myself say: "You are so beautiful, so beautiful."

Though everything was the same on the outside by the end of the Mass, my heart was aflame and so swollen with emotion that I found myself bathed in tears, with a smile on my lips. New peace and new love ... I was in love. I was in love like a schoolgirl. I had found my greatest love.

I had seen His star (it was a Jewish star). I had followed His light, and now it stood over the crib in Bethlehem, so that I could adore Him. He was beauty, radiance, splendor. He came into the depth of my soul, and I saw Him there, and it was love at first sight. He was magnificence, sublimity.

It lasted for about three months that way, and I was still in love like a newlywed. He left me out in the desert after that, but it didn't matter anymore, because I knew from then on that He was there.

Now more than forty years have gone by. We have been blessed with nine children and presently twenty-five grandchildren. Our eldest son is a parish priest, and two granddaughters have taken the veil. When our youngest child went off to school, I became an English teacher at the local *lycée*. However, my favorite tasks are still writing and gardening. All the blessed things that have occurred in our family are gifts of the Sacred Heart of Jesus, and First Fridays have forever remained important days on the calendar.

Bethlehem was also a little town. Herod listened to his scribes and asked the three Wise Men to inform him if, on their journey, they found the Christ there. "They went their way; and behold, the star which they had seen in the East went before them, till it came to rest over the place where the child was. . . . And going inside, they saw the child with Mary his mother, and they fell down and worshiped him" (Mt 2:9–11).

They brought presents to the Christ Child—the gold of love, the incense of prayer, and the myrrh of penance. And observing the setting sun over the evergreen trees in the forest, we also go our way through the seasons, in the desert and in green meadows, through life and time, until the realization of our daily prayer to the heavenly Father is accomplished: Thy Kingdom come!

Sh'ma Yisrael to Hare Krishna
to Ave Maria

Marilyn Prever

Marilyn Prever is a retired homeschooler, mother of eight, grand-mother of many, and freelance writer. She has contributed articles to Homiletic and Pastoral Review, New Oxford Review, *and other publications. She lives in New Hampshire with her husband and their youngest children. She may be reached by email at phil.prever@verizon.net.*

How does a nice young Jewish mother from Brooklyn—that was me in 1971—end up sitting on the living room floor in a half-lotus position and telling her husband she is going to stay there chanting the Hare Krishna until he agrees to leave everything behind and take her and the children on the road, to a destination known only to God? Since the only one she knows of who has done anything like that is the Patriarch Abraham (only he didn't have a car), couldn't she at least chant the *Sh'ma Yisrael?* It's a long story....

When somebody suggested I write my story for a book about Jews coming into the Church, my first thought was that

Sh'ma Yisrael: the first two words, which also serve as the name, of the central prayer of Judaism from Deut 6:4. It begins, "Hear, O Israel: The LORD our God is one LORD; and you shall love the LORD your God with all your heart...."

I wasn't Jewish enough. I grew up in a culturally Jewish family, but the first time I saw the inside of a synagogue was on my wedding day, except for a Bar Mitzvah[1] or two when I was too young to remember. On my father's side I was three generations removed from any kind of Jewish observance—his immigrant parents took pride in being modern and American, which meant leaving all the ways of the *shtetl*[2] behind. My grandfather spoke with a thick Yiddish accent, and I remember him sitting on the porch wreathed in cigar smoke and reading the *Forverts*, a Yiddish newspaper, but he worked in the family hardware store seven days a week, right through the Sabbath. My mother's mother, on the other hand, was a devout and observant Jew, but somehow she was not able to pass on her religion to her children; as soon as they got out on their own, they ran to the Chinese restaurant to enjoy the guilty pleasures of shrimp and roast pork.

We kept up a few traditions for the sake of our Jewish identity. We lit the menorah[3] for Hanukkah, though I don't remember anyone saying any prayers, and on Passover we had a feast with all the traditional delicacies, which we called a Seder[4] even though there was no ceremony, just the food. ("Why is this night different from all other nights?" "Because we have matzo balls in the soup?")

My mother did make a few attempts to introduce a little religion into our lives. She lit the Sabbath candles for a while on Friday nights, and she always lit the *Yahrzeit*[5]

---

[1] See footnote 1 p. 98 above.

[2] Yiddish for a Jewish village.

[3] The eight-branched candlestick used in the celebration of Hanukkah.

[4] The ritual meal commemorating the Jews' Exodus from Egypt that inaugurates the Passover festival.

[5] The anniversary of the death of a relative which is traditionally observed with special prayers and the lighting of a "vigil" candle.

candles in remembrance of the dead. For a while also she
used to read a psalm to me and my sister every night, but
that ended when I annoyed her by giggling all through it.
The reason I was giggling was that it said, "Thou anointest
my head with oil. My cup runneth over", and I thought
"cup" was the Yiddish word *kop*, head, and I pictured my
head filled up with oil and running over.

I was given a children's Bible, and I found it both fascinating and terrifying. I loved the creation story and Jacob's
Ladder (Genesis is still my favorite book), but most of the
rest scared me—the story of Cain and Abel (God seemed
to be unfair); the Flood (there were gray corpses all around
Mount Ararat); and a picture of Esther dining with the king
and pointing her finger at Haman. A dog was coming out
from under the table, baring his teeth at Haman, and this
scared me, too. It never occurred to me to ask anybody to
explain these things. Looking back, I think now that fas-
cination and terror really are not a bad introduction to religion. At least it was separated in my mind from the dreary
secularism that surrounded me.

Judaism and Catholicism were the only two religions that
were at all real to me. We lived in Brooklyn, New York, where
moving a few blocks often meant moving into a whole different ethnic environment. First we lived on Fifty-seventh
Street, which was Italian and, of course, Catholic. The Catholics were very nice to us, and comfortable to be with because
Italian family life is very much like Jewish family life (everybody yells at each other, and they like to eat). Everyone bent
over backward to be respectful of our religion, even though
we didn't have any. We always stayed home from school on
the Jewish holy days, because the Catholics stayed home on
their holy days. Once my sister and I were staying with neighbors on Ash Wednesday, so they took us to church with them,

and we got ashes on our foreheads. My mother thought it was hilarious and told all the relatives. The only negative experience I had of Catholics was when an Italian friend hit me because I "killed Christ".

"It wasn't me; it was my grandfather!" I answered, out of some vague knowledge that there had been trouble between our ancestors. But these were grown-ups' problems; we were friends again the next day.

Then we moved to Fifty-fourth Street, which was a center of Hasidism, a form of Orthodox Judaism that emphasizes joy and mysticism. We lived in two different worlds. I watched them the way I would watch a movie about a foreign country, the men in their black coats, furred hats, beards, and *payis* (side locks), and the women in their wigs and ultramodest clothing, going off to *shul*[6] with their large families. The men used to dance in the streets together on the festival of *Simchat Torah* ("Rejoicing in the Law").

So I grew up in a normal, happy, although religion-free, family with parents who were loving and virtuous, but as soon as I hit adolescence I went unaccountably berserk and turned against almost everything my parents had taught me. The only causative factor I can think of was that I had been for some years turned loose in the public library without any guidance about what to read, and what I mostly read was modern philosophy, psychology, and popular science. I read Freud and Darwin, Nietzsche and Bertrand Russell, all the debunkers. I found it all fascinating and concluded that if these people were right (though I wasn't entirely sure of that) then it didn't make any sense to finish school, work, get married, have children, and do what everybody else was doing, because it all ended in death.

---

[6] Yiddish for "synagogue".

My best friend and I agreed that the lives our parents were living were meaningless, and there was no point in following them, and so, with the weird logic of fifteen-year-olds, we ran away and took a bus to upstate New York, where we planned to pass for eighteen (by wearing very high heels and lots of makeup) and get jobs and an apartment. We were a little fuzzy about how this would make life meaningful, but in any case the police immediately picked us up and sent us back home to our frantic parents. My friend turned out to be schizophrenic; I had no such excuse.

I met Phil, my future husband, at Brooklyn College, and we found right away that we had something in common besides our secular Jewish backgrounds: his best friend was in the same mental institution that mine was. Five months later we got married. It was 1962. We had our first two children, and for a while I found the meaning I was looking for. Parenthood did a lot to settle us down, as it often does, and indeed children are one of the great sources of meaning, and gifts of God. The only trouble is, they're not God, they're only children. So I became restless again, and so did my husband.

We decided our problem was that we needed to find our roots, and so we moved to Israel, intending to stay there for the rest of our lives, in the Promised Land among our own people. He got a job at Hebrew University, and the children and I stayed home, where I spent most of my time washing diapers in lukewarm water in a tub and reading *Time* magazine from cover to cover to assuage my homesickness for the land of my roots, America, where the streets were paved with gold, there were two-day weekends, and everybody spoke English. I couldn't learn Hebrew, being bad at languages and surrounded by other immigrants. The other women envied me because I had good American pots and pans, so I didn't even have the comfort of sympathy in my self-pity. We lived on codfish, spaghetti, eggplant, bread, cheese, oranges, and huge bars of chocolate, which were surprisingly cheap. I wrote brave letters full of lies to my family and friends in America.

The children thrived, but I developed a malaria-like illness that recurred every month or so and left me weak. Just when I thought I couldn't get any more miserable, the Egyptians started dropping bombs on us. This was 1967, and we were caught in the war with Egypt that would be known as the Six-Day War. We spent it huddled in the shelter listening to the airplanes overhead and hoping none of them was carrying a bomb with our name on it, except for the time Phil spent running through the streets finding his way to us and actually dodging bullets, just like in the movies, only not fun.

The soldiers came home with stories of angels fighting on the side of Israel, and Egyptian soldiers fleeing so fast that they left their boots behind in the desert. Even I felt patriotic. We had captured Jerusalem. The song "Yerushalayim Shel Zahav" (Jerusalem of Gold) had become popular just before the war broke out, and now everybody was singing it.

Much, much later I began to wonder about the significance of those six days in connection with the part of the Olivet Discourse where Jesus says, "Jerusalem will be trodden down by the Gentiles, until the times of the Gentiles are fulfilled" (Lk 21:24). But at the time, all we knew was that we had had enough. We were going home to our native land; we were not the stuff of which faithful Zionists are made.

I'll say one thing about our time in Israel, though: I did get religion there. I became a Buddhist.

You may wonder how it was that I didn't look into Judaism. So do I. Maybe it was the effect of my upbringing, or maybe the whole thing was just too foreign to me. I was very much a modern person, and the form of Buddhism I was taught seemed in many ways a very modern religion: empirical, agnostic, individualistic. I enrolled in a correspondence course from the Buddhist Society of London and tried to study the scriptures, do my meditation, and follow the Noble Eightfold Path, which is indeed noble and also extremely difficult, especially for a former Jewish-American Princess with very little self-discipline. The only time I ever mentioned it to anyone in Israel was to a young man who was kind enough not to laugh, and only suggested that I might be interested in looking into the Jewish mystical tradition. I wonder what would have happened if I had followed that lead.

I am convinced that the Year of Our Lord 1968 was some sort of watershed time when "principalities and powers, and the spiritual hosts of wickedness in the heavenly places" were slugging it out with the holy angels somewhere in the stratosphere. Israel had just recovered Jerusalem, possibly fulfilling a two-thousand-year-old prophecy; the Church was reeling from the aftermath of the Council; the war in Vietnam was tearing the U.S. apart; and the "hippie" counterculture was in full swing. We came back to find an America that seemed like a different country from the one we had left only a year ago.

We got swept up in the confusion and evils of the time. We got tear-gassed in Washington protesting the war in Vietnam, of which I understood nothing; I was only responding emotionally to the propaganda all around me. The protest was like a big party, the air thick with marijuana smoke, with Allen Ginsberg (another mixed-up Jew) trying to levitate the Pentagon by chanting mantras.

But we were more interested in religion than political activism, and religion meant the "Wisdom of the East", in the garbled and Americanized forms it took for young people in the sixties, led by such sages as the Beatles and a series of self-styled gurus and swamis who came over from India to make a quick buck from the innocent Yankees. The airports were full of young Americans in saffron robes and shaved heads, chanting Hare Krishna and begging. Oddly enough, it was young Jews and Catholics who filled the ranks of these religious sects out of all proportion to our numbers in the population as a whole.

Looking back now, I see my former self as a chip of wood being carried downstream by the current. How often did I sit back, take a deep breath, try to understand what was happening, and make a real choice?

I think what saved me (under the grace of God) was books. A classic introvert, I was not comfortable in social situations, much less mass movements. I had been a voracious reader since childhood, and my favorite reading was still philosophy, psychology, and science. (I soon dropped the psychology as too superficial and added religion.) Though I read many harmful books, I also read good ones, and the habit of reading serious books and thinking about what I was reading was something of an antidote to the tug of the current.

The Buddhist and Hindu scriptures, insofar as I understood them, which was not much, at least gave me an idea of what a serious, disciplined, and single-minded life should be like. They confirmed for me the basic morality of the natural law that is "written in our hearts". And they gave me a sense that the goal of life was something deep and mysterious and helped exorcise from my mind the dread of living in a meaningless universe.

The authors who finally led me home to the Church
were mainly three: C. S. Lewis, G. K. Chesterton, and Saint
Teresa of Avila. Lewis and Chesterton were the great Christian apologists who knew how to speak to the lost sheep of
the twentieth century, and Jews seem to have a special affinity for Saint Teresa, maybe because she was part Jewish
herself.

So I did slow down a little and think, but I ran into a
problem: there were two religious traditions competing for
my allegiance, the Hindu/Buddhist and the Christian. I
would have been happy to be a Buddhist except that it
was too difficult for me. In the form of Buddhism I was
taught, which was probably somewhat Westernized, there
was no conception of grace or of a Savior; everything
depended on your own will, and my will was weak. I
would wake up every morning determined to follow the
Eightfold Path with all my heart, and within an hour I
would have fallen into some besetting weakness or bad
habit. I never made any progress. I thought for a while
that the use of drugs like LSD could help me make spiritual progress (I was following Aldous Huxley at the time),
but I soon found that, whatever I thought I had discovered or experienced while under the influence of the drug,
it made no difference in my behavior the next day. It's all
very well to think you have come to *satori*[7] but not if you
find yourself losing your temper with the children two
hours later. I realized eventually that these drugs were spiritually dangerous and that they are forbidden with good
reason, but I had no idea at the time that the spiritual
world I had discovered included spirits that were evil and
much more powerful than I. Phil used to make the Sign

---

[7] A Zen Buddhist term for spiritual enlightenment.

of the Cross before a "trip", but I didn't have even that much protection.

Christianity, on the other hand, terrified me. My problem was the Cross. All the Christians I knew were Catholics, and they all had crucifixes on their walls and often around their necks—three-dimensional depictions of a man being tortured to death. Lord Buddha was beautiful and serene, rapt in contemplation, calling me to "the peace that passeth understanding"—only I couldn't get there. The Catholics offered a way, but it was by means of this awful, bloody Thing I couldn't face. At around the same time I read Chesterton's *The Everlasting Man*, and his argument for Christianity was so strong that I stayed up one entire night unsuccessfully trying to find a logical hole in it, finally putting the whole problem into the back of my mind where I kept unsolved mysteries that were better left alone.

At last the whole thing came to a head, for my husband as well as myself. We took one final LSD trip and together faced the fact that we were getting nowhere. I felt a sense of crisis—that if we didn't take some kind of definite step to turn around our lives right away, we would pass a point of no return. I began to believe in Hell.

Having read the Gospels (though with very little understanding), I latched on to the passage about leaving everything to follow Christ and decided that what we had to do was to put the children in the car, leave everything behind, and go on the road to seek God or salvation or enlightenment or whatever it was we needed, and we had to do it immediately or we never would. My husband was understandably not thrilled with this idea, so I sat down on the living-room floor in a half-lotus position and told him I was going to sit there and chant the Hare Krishna until he agreed to do what I wanted. (I don't know what I thought

I'd do when I got hungry or had to go to the bathroom; it was an Existential Moment and such things didn't bother me). I began to chant:

> Hare Krishna, Hare Krishna,
> Krishna, Krishna, Hare, Hare.
> Hare Rama . . .

(So now you see why I didn't choose the *Sh'ma*.) He decided the best thing to do was to consult the *I Ching*, a Chinese oracle. The answer he got was tailored to our situation: something about breaking away and going on a journey with another person.

We took our two daughters and went on the road, explaining to them as best we could what we were doing. They were four and six years old at this time and accepted it all with complete trust in us; they were used to adventures.

We were on the road for three days, and then we were converted. I know this sounds suspiciously symbolical, like Jonah in the whale or Jesus in the tomb, but I can't help it; that's how it happened. At first, needing some sort of direction, we had decided we would head for an *ashram* (a sort of monastery-and-retreat-center) in northern New England run by Baba Ram Dass, formerly Professor Richard Alpert of Harvard University. Together with the better-known Timothy Leary, he had "turned on, tuned in, and dropped out" and was now the head of a community which, we thought, would take us in or give us some guidance. But as it turned out, the whole group had moved to India. So we went back on the road, ending up in Brattleboro, Vermont. It was April, but it was snowing, and we didn't have warm clothes, so we spent the afternoon in the town library, reading to the children and wondering what would become of us. Then we got in the car and drove on. We passed a church, and I found the minister and told him we had "left everything to follow Christ" and needed a place to stay. (This sort of thing was not so unusual in those days. It was 1971, the time of the "Jesus freaks". We were freaks, all right, even if we weren't quite sure whose.)

He directed us to a Christian ministry founded to evangelize street people, and they took us in and evangelized us, quite successfully, since for us "the fullness of time" had come. They gave us a booklet called *The Four Spiritual Laws*, which was a good explanation of the *kerygma*, the proclamation of the Good News. They took us in overnight, and before we went to sleep I knelt down by the bed and prayed that God, if there was a personal God (I still was not sure), would let me know if Jesus was really the only way. I fell asleep feeling peaceful.

The next morning I got up early, had breakfast, and was worked on by a young woman who kept urging me to ask Jesus to be my personal Savior so I could be born again. I wanted to be born again, but I had a problem: How could I have faith in something when I didn't know if it was true? The whole thing seemed to me like a *koan*, a question given by a Zen master to his disciple that seems to have no logical answer and that the disciple struggles with till he breaks through to *satori*. She told me that she had felt the same way before her conversion, so she had hit on a compromise: she asked Jesus to be her Savior for the next twenty-four hours, and then, if He came through, she would commit her life to Him. This made sense to me. "O ye of little faith!" But God is gracious. We continued talking a while, standing in the kitchen, and suddenly it felt as if something broke inside me, and I got down on my knees there on the kitchen floor (surprising her very much, since Evangelical Protestants don't kneel) and asked Jesus to be my Savior for twenty-four hours.

When I stood up, everything was different. I forgot all about the twenty-four-hour deal. I believed. I had somehow crossed the divide and was safe on the other side. Soon afterward my husband came into the kitchen, and I told him what had happened. He sat down at the table and struggled within himself, except that for him it was less like a *koan* and more a matter of finding the will to do what he already believed was necessary. His own pilgrimage had been more direct than mine and had always included an attraction to the Catholic Church and some sort of belief in Christ. While he sat there, our older daughter came in and handed him a picture she had drawn. It was a picture of the empty tomb, with an angel beside it, and above it she had written the words, "HE IS NOT HERE, HE IS RISEN." (It was near Easter time, and we had taught the children Bible stories along with others.)

That did it. He surrendered. We were now both across the bridge, and the first thing we did was to tell the children about it, and let them know that we had discovered that Jesus was the One we should follow. We told them to ask Jesus to be their personal Savior, and they would be born again, too. They were happy to do it, because, as they told us later, "We always liked Jesus the best." All four of us were baptized soon afterward.

The first thing our newfound Lord and Savior told us to do was to go back to Brooklyn and tie up all the loose ends we had left: pay bills, return library books, and explain everything to the landlord, to my husband's employer, and above all to our long-suffering parents, who were not glad about it but hoped our new religion would at least help us become more normal. (My mother and father were baptized by our parish priest four years ago, two weeks before my father died.)

We moved to Vermont and began a new life, joining the church of the people who had converted us. We didn't ask ourselves whether this was "the true Church" or what its relationship was with other Christian churches; we had found our Savior here, and we simply stayed and learned. Later on there were difficulties, but our first year or so as Christians was in many ways an idyllic experience. Everything was new and fresh; we had found what we were looking for all our lives; and though we were poor (my husband was essentially unemployed for the next two years, and we lived on temporary jobs and charity), we knew we could trust our new-found Savior to feed and clothe us like the birds of the air and the lilies of the field. We had two more children (the grand total turned out to be eight). Our fellow Christians were extremely kind and welcoming, especially when they found out we were Jewish. Though we did run into some anti-semitism later on, most of the Christians we knew were rather philo-semites, having a special love for the Jewish people because Jesus was Jewish. We have also found this true among Catholics. The anti-semites, of course, get more publicity. For the first time in my life I began to understand what Judaism was all about and to feel that it was a privilege to be born Jewish. Even though I still had no knowledge of Judaism as it is lived, either now or in our Lord's day, I was beginning to catch on to what is called "salvation history".

We were just beginning to study the Bible and find our way in all this newness when we got into more trouble. This time it was a cult called the Children of God. A friend had gotten involved with them and invited us to come see a community that was really living like the early Church. We drove to visit the place. As we got near it, we reached a spot in the road where all of a sudden every one of us simultaneously felt the presence of some evil force. It was as if there was some sort of spiritual roadblock. We didn't know if it meant the devil was trying to keep us from joining this community, or if perhaps the place itself was evil. We prayed and started singing hymns, and the presence went away.

When we got to the place, it was a nightmare. Dozens of people were crowded into a small house in the country, and most of them were sick. They didn't believe in doctors—if you didn't get well, it was because you didn't have faith. They used all the cult techniques on us that became well-known later when these practices got into the news, but we knew nothing about them: they kept us from sleeping or eating enough, never let us be alone, and constantly drummed Bible verses and slogans into our ears until it had a hypnotic effect. The children were hungry, and it took me hours to get food for them—cold oatmeal and a glass of water. When we tried to object to their ideas out of our extremely limited store of Bible knowledge, they always had an answer. The burden of their doctrine was that they alone were following the true teaching of Jesus, as was plain from His own words, whereas the rest of the church had gotten worldly and was actually betraying Him. One thing we definitely had to do was to give up all our worldly possessions, like the rich young man, and of course it was to their organization we should give them, just as the early Christians sold everything and gave the money to the apostles to distribute to the poor.

To our naïve and ignorant ears, it was all near enough to the Gospel message to sound plausible (especially on an empty stomach and no sleep), and the radical nature of it appealed to my desire to do something heroic for my Lord. (Also I was pregnant with my third child and probably more suggestible than usual.) The one thing that made it impossible for me to join them was that they would take away my children to be "educated" in another city. That was something I just could not bear to allow, even if they fed them something better than cold oatmeal.

By this time my husband and our friends had had enough, and they decided we were leaving. We all literally ran out to the car, and some of our tormenters followed us, shouting, "What are you doing?" At this point I was saved by a grace that God had arranged for me beforehand: feeling unsure about what we were getting into, I had resolved before we started that, whatever happened, I would obey my husband. Whatever else the Bible said, I knew it said plainly, "Wives, obey your husbands." So when they asked what I was doing, I shouted, "Obeying my husband!" and ran into the car and slammed the door behind me, but not before I heard their parting shot, also from the Bible: "We must obey God rather than men!" I left my Bible and my pocketbook with all my papers behind. I was lucky I had my clothes on, or I might have run away naked like the young man who panicked when Jesus was arrested.

We had been there two days, but it felt like two weeks. Much later we heard that the law had caught up with this cult, and the leaders were in jail for the most appalling criminal conduct, both financial and sexual. But getting home was the easy part. I spent the next six months in a state of agony, believing I had betrayed the Lord, but unable to go back and do what I thought He wanted me to do.

Out of some kind of pride or misguided sense of honor, I battled this out alone. It was like being in a vise. Finally I sought the advice of a woman who was one of the few Christians I knew who took the implications of the Cross with full seriousness. I spoke in the most general terms, saying I believed Jesus had called me to do something that was a way for me to renounce everything for Him, but that I couldn't do it, and I couldn't live with my failure. She gave me a very wise answer; she said that if it had really been Jesus asking me to do this thing, He would have given me the grace to do it. These words gave me enough peace to get out of the vise. A while later, I was talking to this woman in the church basement, and I suddenly saw her whole face and head shining with light. The light was coming from inside her, and I remember thinking, "This must be what artists are trying to convey when they paint a halo." It scared me, not because it was something numinous, but because it was clearly the light of holiness I was seeing, and I wasn't fit to be in it. I mumbled some excuse and walked away as quickly as I could without actually running. There were two subsequent times in my life when I was in the presence of such felt holiness, though without the visible light: once I ran away, and the other time I stayed and talked with the man, to my eternal benefit. So my batting average at responding to holiness is not very good: one for three.

Though I was out of the vise, I still felt that something was missing in my Christian commitment, maybe as a result of that original twenty-four-hour deal. One week a visiting preacher came to our church and gave a series of talks, something like what Catholics used to call a "mission". I don't remember the details of what he said, but after the third talk, I experienced a moment of very quiet but authentic conversion, realizing that I had been trying to have Jesus as my Savior but not as my Lord. I shed a few tears and then immediately was calm again. The preacher held an altar call for those ready to commit themselves more fully to the Lord. We were to come up and sign a card that said,

"Lord Jesus: Anything, anytime, anywhere. I am ready." I was the first one in line.

By this time we were pretty well acclimatized and had gotten over the worst of what amounted to real culture shock. I had made some good friends, and I had learned the hard way that the Jewish humor I thought so hilarious didn't go over very well in a white Anglo-Saxon Protestant culture—it just gave them the idea that there was something wrong with me—and also that the loud and vociferous arguments that are the lifeblood of a Jewish conversation were nothing to them but bad manners, or maybe even a sign of incipient violence. I learned to conform. Sometimes I wondered if this was how black people used to feel who were "passing" as white. On the other hand, I was not very welcome among my own people when they found out I was a Christian and had gone over to the enemy. I didn't realize how much I missed my own kind till I had a funny experience one evening. We were out on the sidewalks giving out tracts, and I got into a conversation with a Jewish shopkeeper. When he found out I was Jewish, he started yelling at me in a loud voice, "What are you doing out on the street? Where is your family? What's this on your arm? [I had a skin rash.] Needle marks! You're shooting up drugs, aren't you? Go home, straighten up your life! . . ." And so on. I could have hugged him, he made me feel so nostalgic for Brooklyn. He was treating me like his own daughter, yelling at me with Jewish-style affection. Nobody had yelled at me in such a loving, fatherly way for a long time; it almost made me cry.

As time went on we became more and more dissatisfied with the narrowness of the teaching we were getting, and certain inconsistencies were becoming more and more troublesome. Once at a communion service, one of the elders, a lapsed Catholic, suggested that since we were Bible believers, maybe we ought to just believe Jesus' own words when He said, "This is My body; this is My blood." I had wondered about that myself, but the idea raised more questions than it settled: Did the bread and wine become His Body and Blood sometime during the service? When? Did it happen any time Christians got together to have a communion service? What about the crumbs? Did it remain His Body and Blood afterward? I had heard of people who gave the leftover bread to the chickens.

Earlier in our life as "Bible Christians" (we didn't consider ourselves Protestant) Phil had an experience that turned out to have long-term effects on our understanding. Enthusiastic about the way Jesus had fulfilled Old Testament prophecies, and not knowing enough to realize the complexity and difficulties involved, he decided one day while we were visiting our families in Brooklyn to go to the headquarters of the Hasidim and "present them with the claims of Christ". It was a brave thing for him to do, but they were more than ready for him: they turned him over to an expert, a man who had plenty of experience with young Jews converted into born-again Christians. The man knew the Hebrew Bible a lot better than we did and had an answer for everything.

He would have been surprised if he had known what the effect of his expertise was. Instead of leading us back to Judaism, it led us eventually to Catholicism, because it caused us to question our interpretation of the New Testament, especially the epistles of Saint Paul. We had been taught a doctrine of the relationship between law and grace that was supposedly Pauline, but it was full of contradictions. At the same time, a lapsed-Catholic friend had said something about a related matter that stuck in my mind: he said we interpreted the Gospels in the light of the Epistles and suggested that it should be the other way around.

By this time, as you can imagine, we were asking too many questions to be quite welcome in any Fundamentalist or Evangelical church. Phil was by now a college librarian in Claremont, New Hampshire, commuting from Brattleboro an hour each way, and we decided it was time to move. When we settled in to our new home, we both realized that we were not looking forward to joining one of the local Evangelical churches. One day I was sitting on a bench and began talking to another woman, and when she found out I was a Christian she invited me to join her church, saying it was "the friendliest church in town". Suddenly I knew that I couldn't stand to be part of a friendly Evangelical church ever again. I had had it with the social pressures, the anti-intellectualism, the doctrinal inconsistency, the compulsory smiley-face friendliness, the whole atmosphere. I wanted out. We took a long break from regular churchgoing, and it was like getting in out of the wind. We didn't realize how much pressure we had been under until it was gone. We started praying more, thinking more, and reading more widely. We even tried visiting various Christian churches just to see what they were like. We tried the Russian Orthodox (too foreign, but later I was to return) and a few others. We even went to a Catholic church— that is, Phil went to Mass there. I used to sneak in and pray sometimes, wondering what it was about Catholic churches that made it so much easier to pray there (knowing nothing about the reserved Eucharist), but I was afraid that if I went to Mass I would be spotted for an imposter for not knowing how to genuflect or make the Sign of the Cross and thrown out. Phil had been attracted to the Catholic Church for a long time and had gone to Mass occasionally when we lived in Brooklyn. In fact, he had headed for a Catholic church right after he was held up at knifepoint one day when he was a taxi driver. He wanted to thank God that he was still alive, and it seemed to him only natural to find a Catholic church to do it in.

As for me, it was back to my books, and this time I didn't have to wander around the library without guidance: God put the books of His choice directly into my hands. A small bookstore opened downtown, and when I went to explore it the proprietress, on hearing that I was interested in Christian books, insisted on giving me a large boxful of good, hardcover Catholic books donated to her by a monastery. She refused to let me pay for them, saying nobody would buy them anyway. I took these books home and devoured them all, falling in love with the Catholic Church. I met Frank Sheed, Thomas Merton, Ronald Knox, Karl Adam, Cardinal Newman, the Radio Replies priests, and many more. I had catechisms, apologetics, Church history, lives of saints, devotional books, conversion stories, even Catholic humor. The store went out of business two weeks later.

By the time I was halfway through these books, my mind was convinced and my whole soul was attracted to the Church. I was still a little afraid of the Blessed Virgin; the doctrine made sense, but Catholics talked about her as if she were a goddess. Phil, who took a longer time to accept all the doctrine, nevertheless helped me understand it. When I was struggling with the idea of Mary's perpetual virginity he pointed out that if even under the Old Covenant the vessels used for Temple worship would be defiled by any profane use, how much more unfitting would it be for the body of God's own Mother to bear an ordinary child. This not only solved my Marian problem but also made me realize that as a Protestant I had never fully appreciated the divinity of Christ.

I wrote to our pastor and his wife to let them know what direction I was taking. They were naturally alarmed and sent me a book by an ex-priest who had made a career out of anti-Catholicism. I read it in a state of fear, thinking that perhaps I was mistaken in my new beliefs and God had sent this book to set me straight. To my vast relief, there was nothing in the book that I couldn't answer easily from my study of apologetics. And, in an ironic twist, the author confirmed for me the belief that Mary was the Mother of God by the fact that when he tried to explain why she wasn't, he kept falling into heresy—I mean doctrines that even he would consider heresy. I earned fifty dollars writing up the incident for *Catholic Digest*.

But I started having doubts. I had absorbed a good dose of anti-Catholic prejudice from seven years of hearing about the Catholic Church as the "whore of Babylon" and the Pope as the Antichrist. What if it were true that the Catholic Church was Satan's great deception, designed to lead people like me away from "the simple gospel of Christ"? At this point I made another of my famous bad decisions: I consulted a Protestant prophet. I knew someone from my charismatic days who had the gift of prophecy. She didn't know I was interested in becoming a Catholic, and I reasoned that if I just asked her for a message from the Lord, maybe He would help me. So I told her I had certain questions about my spiritual life and asked her to see if she might have some words for me. She did, and my presumption cost me six more months in the vise. The words were deceptively innocent: "You will have the answers to your questions when you're willing to hear them."

To understand why these simple words put me into a state of such torment, you have to remember that I was the one who had been convinced that my loving Jesus wanted me and my children to spend the rest of our lives sick, miserable, and eating cold oatmeal. Somewhere deep in my mind was the conviction that if something gave me joy, it was probably not God's will for me, and if something was entirely hateful to me, it probably was. My real problem was that I was afraid to believe the good news that Jesus really did love me and that His plans for me were "peace and not disaster". After six months of making myself utterly miserable, I responded to an invitation to a Catholic charismatic prayer meeting, where everybody not only prayed but also fasted for me. The priest told them just to pray that I would find peace. The next day blessed peace settled into my soul in all quietness and simplicity. I was finally able to recognize that the joy I felt in discovering the Catholic Church was a sign of God's leading, not some trick of the devil.

We decided it was about time for us to talk to a priest. I had never in my whole life been within ten feet of a Catholic priest (except for getting those ashes on my forehead when I was little), and I still had that sense of fear and shyness that had kept me from going to Mass. I confided in a Catholic acquaintance, and she gave me the name of a young priest she said was easy to talk to.

He was—it was the things he said that were the trouble. When we mentioned that the stories of Enoch and Elijah helped us believe in the Assumption of our Lady, his attitude made it clear that anybody who took the Bible that literally must also believe in the tooth fairy. When we brought up the topic of birth control, intending to get instruction in natural family planning, he hastened to assure us that

"it's none of the Church's business what you do in the privacy of your bedroom." As I imagined all the mortal sins I
could commit with impunity, from first-degree murder to
blasphemy, simply by closing my bedroom door, I realized
that something serious must have happened to the Catholic
Church between the time all those books were written and
the present.

But God's timing is perfect. A reading of the major doc-
uments of Vatican II (in whose name all these aberrations
were taking place) reassured me that the Church had not
changed her teaching. Meetings with faithful priests and
lay people also gave us reassurance. Even the Modernist priest
we spoke to turned out to be a help, because he was so
impressed by the amount of reading we had done that he
excused us from taking instruction.

I was baptized conditionally along with three of our
four children; my husband and oldest child wanted more
time to think about it. This was a painful time for us.
There was one remaining stumbling block for Phil: the
history of anti-semitism in the Church. We knew that the
Protestants also had a lurid past when it came to the Jews,
but formally identifying himself with an institution that
had seemingly masterminded some of the worst atrocities
was a different story. One winter day he was sitting in the
town library reading books about Catholic anti-semitism,
and he happened to glance out the window, struck by the
pattern of the graveyard behind the library, black head-
stones stark against the snow. Suddenly some words came
into his mind: "Let the dead bury their dead, and come,
follow Me." He and our daughter were received into the
Church soon afterward.

That was more than a quarter of a century ago. I haven't
told anywhere near all the adventures we had while finding

our way into the Church, and there have been many more since then. Becoming a Catholic did not stop me from getting into trouble—now I just get into Catholic trouble. For example, there was my father's mysterious eleventh-hour baptism and the family explosion it caused ... or my strange career in the pro-life movement, which resulted in scenes like the one in the doctor's waiting room, where a social worker screamed at me that I was a murderer.... Or the time we got kicked out of the pro-life group we helped found, for saying the "H" word. (No, not "Hell" but "heresy".) One day I plan to tell the whole story.

What a Long, Strange Trip It's Been

Father Peter Sabbath

Father Peter Sabbath is currently serving as pastor of Holy Name of Jesus Church in Laval, Quebec, in the Archdiocese of Montreal. He may be reached by email at psabbath@sympatico.ca.

I was ordained a Catholic priest six years ago, at the age of fifty-two—a very late vocation. When I was young, becoming a priest was the last thing I ever dreamed of. I hardly knew any Catholics growing up; I was born Jewish and lived in a rather Jewish milieu in Montreal, and even though our family wasn't practicing very much—more or less the equivalent of Christmas and Easter Catholics—we did go to synagogue on the High Holy Days and celebrate Passover in the home. I had my Bar Mitzvah at the age of thirteen, but religion was not really a big part of our daily life. We never prayed at home. I had quite a bit of exposure to Protestants growing up—more so than to Catholics—because the educational laws of the time were such that if one didn't go to a Catholic parochial school or a Jewish religious school, one went to the Protestant school. That was the catch-all for everyone. So I attended a Protestant school from kindergarten through high school, where we began each day with the Our Father and learned Bible stories. I certainly had some exposure to Jesus in that way.

The preparation for my Bar Mitzvah consisted of going to an after-school program for a couple of hours twice a week for three years, which resulted in my learning more about the Jewish faith in a more organized way and also starting to pray for the first time in my life. This did touch me, and I think I felt drawn to have a life of prayer, to know God, but there was no context for it and no encouragement. Since I didn't really know anyone else who did that, it faded pretty quickly.

I had the usual high school experience, devoted to having a lot of fun, and then I went away to Boston University to study business, still more interested in having a good time—dating, traveling, etc.—than in anything else. Religion was just something "out there" that was not part of my world. After I left Boston, I came back to Montreal to study at Concordia University and switched my major from business to English literature with a minor in religion because a survey course as an elective had caught my interest. I think there was a hunger in me to know God, but it was very much in the background. I lived the typical life of the mid-sixties, eventually dropping out of university close to graduation, and traveling around with my dog and my girlfriend, going to Woodstock, all those kinds of things. Religion was far away. But there was a growing hunger to know God, although I would not have used the word "God" in those days; I thought of it in terms of needing to find meaning in my life. I looked around, and maybe like a lot of young people in the '60s, didn't see much that was drawing me. Get a job, earn money, raise a family—that was fine, but I had to know why I was here on earth. That began to consume me.

I moved out to Vancouver and lived a very solitary life for a while. It was then that I started to read a lot about

the spiritual life, primarily along the lines of Buddhism—
Alan Watts and people like that. I started a little Buddhist
meditation, Hindu yoga, and went to Berkeley, California,
and tried out a few spiritual practices that were popular
out there at the time. Still, ideas of God, of Christ, or of
prayer, were very foreign to me; I was even somewhat
hostile to those ideas. I would have said I was looking for
the "infinite" or the "eternal" rather than God. I actually
used to wince when I had to say "God" or "Jesus". A
turning point came when a Catholic friend suggested we
make a retreat one weekend at a monastery. "Sure, cool"
was my response—I had no idea what that was. So we
went to a Cistercian abbey not far from Montreal.

The experience touched me very deeply—just listening
to the Gregorian chant, being one with nature, the silence,
all these things were completely new to me and touched
something very deep inside. When I got back to Montreal
late that Sunday afternoon I tried to find a church—I just
wanted to be in a church. I tried a few places that were
locked up and gave up and forgot about it for a while. I
went back to my other way of life, but continued to pon-
der these things a little bit. I took some detours.

I was still adrift and finally decided to focus my search,
my life, a little more on finding God. I started meditating
more—I still wasn't comfortable talking about prayer. I heard
about a retreat house that was being set up, and I went and
spent some time there, and that's when things started to
open up in me. At the time I was living near a Benedictine
monastery outside Montreal, and I started spending a lot of
time there, too, just drinking in the silence and the solitude
of the Gregorian chant. I started to experience Christ and
God in my life. Gradually the barriers began to fall, and at
a certain point I received the gift of grace. I was desperate

to know God and felt that life wasn't worth living if I couldn't know Him, yet at the same time I had the awareness that I was receiving something from Him.

It was at Saint Joseph's Oratory in Montreal. I was there with a friend at Mass. The priest didn't seem too interested in what he was doing, and I almost got up and left, but decided to stay. At the moment of Consecration, when the priest raised the bread and said the prayer, I just knew that this was the Body of Christ at that moment. I felt something change within me. After Mass I got up and said, well, I'm Christian now. I believed at that moment, and it stayed with me. I had already pulled back from the '60s sort of lifestyle my friends were living and was living a fairly monastic sort of life, simply because that was the way I wanted to live—consecrated to God and immersed in the spiritual life. So I began living it in a Catholic environment, but still wasn't baptized for another couple of years. At a certain point I was making a retreat at the Benedictine monastery Saint Benoit du Lac, and I realized that I wanted to be able to receive the sacraments—it wasn't enough just to know Christ.

So I called one of the monks I knew there and said I wanted to be baptized.

He said, "That's great."

So I said, "Well, what are you waiting for?"

He said that it doesn't work like that, it takes a little preparation.

So I went through the RCIA program in a very simple way, and the same month he baptized me. It was during the octave of Easter, 1976, in the middle of the night, at the retreat house. Although most of my family and friends probably didn't ever fully understand my decision, they respected it. (Quite a few of them later came to my ordination in 1998, and having them there was very moving and meaningful to me.)

Initially I was discerning the call to the contemplative life. At the time of my baptism, after the celebrations were over and things calmed down, what came to my mind was that something had come to a conclusion that had begun in me as a child, when my parents took me to see a film called *The Robe*. The movie was based on the novel by Lloyd C. Douglas, which I found out later was responsible for many conversions to the Faith. I saw the film and never consciously thought about it again, but a seed was planted there that came to fruition at my baptism. I realized then that I was called to the Faith at a very young age.

Some years later my mother asked me why I had become a Catholic, and I told her a little bit, about the Eucharist and about my faith. When I told her that I had received the gift of Faith at Saint Joseph's Oratory, she turned a little pink, and I asked, "What's wrong?" She said, "Well, when you were young we used to live near there, and sometimes we'd walk up there just as a nice place to visit. One day it was raining, and we went inside; and, I don't know why, I never did it before or since, but I lit a candle for you in that place." And twenty years later, in that spot, I did receive the gift of Faith. These are mysteries we don't understand fully in this life.

I didn't think about the priesthood at that time. I was working at a retreat house. I worked there for many years, giving retreats, to clergy, to lay people, to religious, who came from many places, and at a certain point the house closed. I had began to feel a hunger to know about the reasons for my Faith and to explore that, so I went to Rome and began to study. The sabbatical in Rome turned into a longer period of study, and it was there that my vocation was formed a little more.

In Rome what struck me most of all was the intersection of the universal and the historical—the continuity from the beginnings of the Faith, from Peter. The people coming from all over the world for a common purpose was astounding, and to begin to study philosophy and theology, and then to see that the Faith is truly, in the words of Saint Thomas, the one divine science. Canon law, Scripture, Church history, all these disciplines are part of the same Faith and the same truth. It was a revelation for me to be learning about the continuity of the Faith and the history of the Church.

I was a permanent deacon attached to Saint Patrick's Basilica in Montreal at the time I went to Rome. When I came back from Rome and continued my service there, people started to approach me and suggest the priesthood as a possibility. Eventually the Bishop spoke to me a few times, and it went on from there. Now I am serving as a priest at a medium-size parish in a suburb of Montreal.

As a Catholic, I would say I feel more Jewish, and more in touch with my Jewish roots, than I ever did before.

God of Abraham, God of Mercy

Steven Block

Steven Block lives with his wife and family in New Mexico, where he currently serves the Faith as the Cantor and Director of Music at the Albuquerque parish of Our Lady of Perpetual Help Byzantine Rite.

My background is a mixture of Orthodox[1] and Conservative Jewry. My parents brought me up in a kosher home, but were relaxed about pleasurable pursuits, such as going to Broadway shows on the Sabbath or bringing nonkosher food into the home (as long as we ate on paper plates and used plastic silverware). At the same time, I was very close to my grandfather who was Orthodox (though not Hasidic) and a daily attendee at synagogue. I was brought up going to my grandfather's Orthodox *shul*[2] and, in my formative preteen and early teenage years, I very often attended without my parents, as I too was becoming more Orthodox.

My grandfather had a tremendous influence on the entire family, and, even though his children and grandchildren for the most part became cultural Jews, he was greatly revered as a true patriarch and mourned as a spiritual icon when he passed away in 1992. It is his image and his example that

---

[1] See footnote 3, p. ix above.—ED.
[2] Yiddish for "synagogue".

remains with me today, as I work through a daily prayer life that has its natural ups and downs, its dry spells and its ecstasies, its urgencies and its banalities. Come rain or shine, my grandfather was impelled to take the daily mile-long walk to *shul* before sunrise to lay *tefillin*.[3] Prayers were a regular and ordinary part of his day, and I owe him so much for showing me the way to constancy and discipline in the most important matter of our lives, the state of our souls. I hope, feel, and pray that this saintly man watches over me and my family, and that we will soon meet in Christ.

It was through my grandfather's quiet and unassertive influence that I was trained to be an Orthodox Jew and can pray in Hebrew fluently. As I entered my early teenage years I became more and more zealous in my faith, certainly exceeding the practice of my immediate family. However, by the time I left home to go to college at sixteen, I had somehow placed faith aside as irrelevant, while privately speaking in my mind to a personal God. As long as my peers didn't know about it, I could accept these silent and informal conversations that typically took place as I waited to fall asleep.

The six years that followed my leaving home were filled with a mixture of excitement and potential, but at the same time were an experience of immorality and depravity that I still regret. I can't emphasize enough how, while the sins of one's youth may ultimately be forgiven, the scars that have been generated only fade away with time, while still permanently marking a part of one's being. The results of such sinning must be fought against and wrestled with every day of one's life, and that is an ongoing sadness. One takes special

---

[3] "Phylacteries", small leather cases containing texts from the Hebrew Scriptures held to the forehead and the left arm by leather bands, worn by Jewish men during morning prayer.

and endless joy in the forgiveness given by God in the sacraments of baptism and reconciliation, but no sin is worth the effect it has on our ongoing nature and our relationship with Christ.

At the end of those six years, I went on to work on a doctorate in music with a soul that was spiritually and emotionally exhausted, and I was ready to be rescued again by my Lord and through the cultivation of a relationship with a woman whose faith, fidelity, genuineness, and depth of character remain far beyond what I've ever encountered in anyone else. In describing my wife, Stephanie, as a person with inner beauty, the cliché doesn't begin to do justice to her. She is outwardly beautiful and fair to the depths of her soul. My good fortune in having found her reflects a generosity beyond anything I can understand; as in the case of my grandfather, I continually question how poorly I've repaid her devotion to me.

Before meeting Stephanie, though, God first led me back to my Jewish roots, in the year I began my doctorate—1975—in California. In the following order, I began to pray daily from the *siddur*,[4] to attend *Shabbat*[5] services, work for the Jewish Center, and to lay *tefillin*. I then further explored my Orthodox background by studying with a Chabad[6] Rabbi and reading Rabbi Schneur Zalman's beautiful mystical classic, the *Tanya*.[7] During this year I essentially led the life of

[4] The Jewish prayer book.

[5] Hebrew for "Sabbath".

[6] "Chabad" is an outreach organization of the Hasidic community to more secular Jews.

[7] Rev. Shneur Zalman (1745–1812), the "Alter Rebbe", is the founder of the Chabad-Lubavitcher Hasidic movement. The basic principle of Zalman's thinking is that each person must individually develop wisdom, understanding, and "grasping" in order to form a bonding between Heaven and earth. The complete man serves God with heart, mind, and deed: the mind understanding, the heart feeling, and the "hand" performing.

a recluse, even while outwardly still social and participating fully in my studies. This was a year that was devoted to the reexamination of my life and my beliefs, and it was essential to my nature that I build on a spirituality that was innate, if not formally ordered.

Coincidentally, as I began a year in which my faith would bring me solace, I also struck up a writing relationship with Stephanie. We had been platonic friends in high school, and it was a natural part of my "recovery" that I should seek to reacquaint myself with those persons in my life I felt had solid character. It was thus that I learned of Stephanie's own conversion, and of the importance of the influence of her godparents, Dietrich and Alice von Hildebrand. During that year we engaged in the "ancient practice" of writing many pages to each other several times a week.[8] One of our invariable topics was that of faith, since I was in the midst of returning to a strong Jewish life and Stephanie was a few years past her own conversion. We argued back and forth about religion. My perspective was certainly colored by a background that was used to suspecting anti-semitism. Having grown up in a non-Jewish neighborhood, and having been taunted as I walked to *shul* wearing my yarmulke,[9] such anti-semitism literally was around every corner, and it was my natural first inclination to find criticism of Judaism in each word.

Stephanie's way was so gentle and loving that it was only through her kindness that I began to read faith-related literary classics and then, taking a major leap, reading the Gospels. My antipathy toward reading the New Testament

[8] We still have the large stacks of letters that it would be wise to put a match to before too long.

[9] The skullcap worn by Jewish men.

was so strong that I felt that reading it was sinful, tantamount to apostasy. It was no small matter that Stephanie was able to sooth my misgivings, three thousand miles away, and allow me to begin to understand a faith whose very foundation, Judaism, was the heart of my then rediscovery. I made two visits to Stephanie in that year and returned to live in New York City in June 1976.

When we married in January 1977, it was a mixed marriage. I continued to *daven*[10] on a daily basis, Stephanie attending the synagogue with me on Saturday and I, in turn, going to church with her on Sunday. We spent much time before our marriage working with a Rabbi, and arguing with friends and family, to arrive at this crazy crossroads whereby Stephanie and I were both going to be not only observant of our respective faiths, but also supportive of each other's sacramental and spiritual needs. Perhaps it is a testament to the strength of love that we were really able to fulfill this promise in the first year of our marriage. Love knows no bounds, and so it was only a matter of time for Christ's love to work His way into my heart from my first turning back to Him in the Jewish faith in September 1975 to my entrance into the Roman Catholic Church at Easter 1978.

There were many significant influences in my journey toward Catholicism, and it's impossible for me to identify a single circumstance as responsible for my decision to convert. I like to think that it was primarily simply living with Stephanie, watching her attend daily Mass, and experiencing her deep generosity to everyone. It was also seeing the constancy in other Catholic lay men, a constancy that reminded me of my grandfather, and getting to know thoughtful and reverent priests through Stephanie. This ordinary and

[10] Yiddish for "pray".

uncomplicated accumulation of Catholic practice was becoming a part of my own persona. It is also true that several works, especially Saint Augustine's *Confessions* and Thomas Merton's *Seven Storey Mountain*, had a special resonance for me that helped turn me toward Christ. Saint Augustine's repentance for his early life and Merton's accommodation of his intellectual and artistic life were models for the struggles I faced in contemplating Christ.

The birth of my son Isaac in October 1977 was a major turning point for me. He was born at home, and from the moment of Isaac's entrance into the world, in which I played a very personal role, I had a sudden new awareness of my responsibility for another's soul. I felt the awesomeness of that responsibility with an intensity that lasted for months. Soon after the birth I asked one of our priest friends if I could study with him in preparation for possible baptism. My decision to convert ultimately wasn't out of the fear that bringing up a child in two different faiths could be harmful—part of me still believes that good will could have carried us through. I simply felt overwhelmed by the great gift God had given us in a son—who did, incidentally, go through a ritual circumcision. The decision to name our son Isaac didn't come about through conscious and deliberate reflection over the implications of that name, and yet there certainly had to be at least a subconscious spiritual comprehension of its profundity. I've often meditated on the way my path to conversion culminated in naming my son after the first sacrificial lamb of our Jewish heritage, who stands in for the final sacrificial Lamb, Jesus, of our Catholic heritage. And the way I was the unconscious patriarch of . . . who knew what was to come?

One more circumstance that I think of as apocryphal, but which Stephanie asserts is at the heart of my conversion, is that during this same period of time I decided to compose a setting of the Mass as a present for Stephanie. In my profession as a composer, I'm called upon to work on commissions that don't necessarily reflect a personal involvement, and there have been many settings of the Mass in which the words provide simply a form, rather than spiritual substance, for the music to follow. I wasn't removed from the nature of the setting, since I did insert the *De profundis* psalm—the first movement I composed—at the heart of the Mass, and my rescue from "out of the depths" has always held a very real and personal central position in my relationship with God. As Stephanie tells it, though, it was when I was composing the Credo itself that my transformation from a hesitant student of Catholicism to a firm believer occurred; that is, it was in the setting of the very words of belief that I found conversion. For me, that assertion has too much theatricality at its heart for me to affirm it, but God has His own ways, and I'm sure that a plethora of everyday miracles regularly pass by us unnoticed.

It was very difficult for me to take the final steps toward baptism in that journey toward Easter. I had much trepidation, not the least of which was that I hadn't told my parents and other relatives that I was converting. My marriage to Stephanie had evoked such distress in my family (my brothers have often alluded to the incredible angst and family upheaval that became a regular part of their upbringing at that time) that it was obvious that the news of my baptism would have disastrous implications. Since my grandfather was still alive, I believe my parents would have needed to take the formal steps of disowning me and sitting *shiva*,[11] mourning me

---

[11] *Shiva* is the period of seven days of mourning that follows the death of a close relative.

as someone who had just died. I was grateful and eager to receive the advice from a priest that it would be prudent to wait for the right moment to share this with the family. All the same, it is ingrained in my nature that any kind of dishonesty is reprehensible, to the point where I can easily confuse proper tact and courtesy for duplicity. Therefore the decision to keep my baptism a secret took a serious toll on my psyche through the years.

On the night of my baptism, my hands were cold, I shivered, and I was visibly in such fear for my life that Stephanie kept on reminding me that I was not obliged to go through with the conversion.[12] I truly suffered "mortal fear". Those who believe my conversion was apostasy will view that fear and trembling as a prudent self-warning, but I recognize it as a last-ditch effort by Satan to divert my attention from Christ (would that I hadn't given the devil so many more opportunities since my baptism). That night however, when the first sprinklings of holy water seemed to burn my soul, was a night that I've never regretted, a night of peace and great relief in the certainty that my sinfulness was forgiven. Wretch that I am, I still cry at the thought of God's clemency in my life. To know God in the Eucharist has been also just as much an inconceivable mercy for this Jew, as has been His forgiveness.

As of this writing, I've lived the life of a Hebrew Catholic slightly longer than I lived life as only a Jew. So I can speak as a wizened veteran, and try to encourage anyone

[12] At no time did Stephanie ever pressure me into conversion or even bring up the subject. The announcement of my decision to her was a surprise in the sense that she hadn't been aware that I was studying privately with a priest (she silently, however, recognized my softening toward the Church). She would be mortified at the supposition that I converted for her sake, and yet her example was ever present.

on the brink to trust in Christ and take that leap of faith. I live the life of a fulfilled Jew and understand that I'm yet all the more accountable to God for having the rich background of intimately knowing the God of Abraham, Isaac, and Jacob through a more direct ascendancy and contact in worship, while also knowing the God of mercy who sent His Son to be an advocate on my behalf and to bring me to eternal life. While I wish I had a greater sense of how to avoid the mortal danger in which I continually place myself through my own sin—no, conversion does not guarantee holiness—I'm daily blessed by the sheer fact of my baptism into Christ. When I find myself wishing for foolish things—to be more handsome, to be wealthy—I can summon up the feelings inspired by my ancestors' false worship of the golden calf and couple them with the humility that Peter felt when he was justly chided by Christ in His tender mercy. When I find myself feeling battered by circumstances and tempted to resentment, I can not only look to Job for comfort and not only draw on the traditions of the Hasidim who found ways to deal with astonishing buffets in Eastern Europe, but I can also look at the One who was truly "battered" for my sake and know that my afflictions have already been redeemed. I only need to have the sense to continue to look upon Him. Perhaps it's the audacity of a Jew who has been reared to see himself as a member of the Chosen People that allows me to proclaim that Catholicism is yet another manifestation of how all that is good resides in the Jewish deposit of faith for which I "claim" Christ. It's for this reason that I believe in the inevitability that all Jews must eventually come to rest in the arms of our Savior—we may think we're headed to meet Elijah as the Messiah, but what a blessed and powerful surprise of holy joy it will be to meet a smiling and welcoming Christ in Elijah's place.[13]

With Stephanie and my children, we have built an observant home in which my daily prayer life as a Jew has been transformed into a daily prayer life in which we recite the Office, pray the Rosary, and attend Mass. We also recite the Sh'ma[14] daily, and our Catholic practice is informed by our Jewish background either explicitly, as when we celebrate the Passover Seder, or implicitly, as when we fast or go to confession and recall our roots in the Yom Kippur liturgy in which every Jew confesses a litany of sins as his own.

It's not in my nature to imbue everything I do with a Jewish hue, perhaps because I've never felt an affinity with those who are cultural Jews and who might, for example, sprinkle all conversation with Jewish aphorisms or, more likely, ethnic associations with Jewish foods such as *kishke*,[15] *kascha varnishkes*,[16] or *kugel*.[17] I can still taste and smell the noodle kugel that the *Rebbetzin* (Rabbi's wife) would have ready for the Orthodox congregation to eat at the end of the morning service on *Shabbat* (which lasted for about five to six hours), but the wonderful memory of that kugel has never been the heart of my identity as a Jew; my center has always been the absorption in Jewish worship and religious practice. In that sense I've lived an especially blessed life, to be able to experience a seamless spirituality in the

---

[13] Although the actual Jewish teaching is that Elijah will come back to announce the coming of the Messiah, some Jews confuse this with a belief that he will come back as the Messiah.

[14] The central prayer of the daily Jewish liturgy, drawn from Deut 6.

[15] Beef casing stuffed with a seasoned mixture, prepared by boiling and then roasting.

[16] A Russian-Jewish dish of buckwheat, pasta, and caramelized onions.

[17] A baked pudding of noodles or potatoes, eggs, and seasonings, traditionally eaten by Jews on the Sabbath.

very personal understanding of Jesus as the fulfillment of the promise in the Old Testament.

All the questions I asked as a child, some of these echoing Moses' own queries as he argues with God in the Torah, have truly been answered in Christ. Stepping into baptism turned out to be a very small step of continuity, rather than a running leap from one edge of a precipice over a chasm. It's a great privilege to be able personally to recognize Peter and Paul in their fullness as Jews, and Matthew as a quintessential Jewish writer. Those who are born Catholic cannot in the same way appreciate these apostles' common predilections, with which we Jews can identify as with our own.

I can trace my observant nature to my grandfather, who no doubt in turn could trace his religious passion to his ancestors, and I can only sit back in humility as I watch my own children (at this writing, the seventh and youngest is sixteen) all live observant lives of their own as they individually struggle with the extent to which their faith impacts their lives. I have a daughter who is a Dominican Sister who took on Edith Stein's name (Sister Teresa Benedicta), and her rootedness in a saint so dear to me as a Hebrew Catholic is a personal acknowledgment I don't deserve.[18] One of our sons is a very determined seminarian, and my oldest, Isaac, is completing his theological studies, after having completed a first degree in pure math. The others are also on interesting paths that are informed by a religiosity that I can see growing and becoming a more formal part of their lives at every turn. For each child, I see only their own determination in reaching to God and Christ's great generosity in responding to them. While I

---

[18] Edith Stein (St. Teresa Benedicta a Cruce) was a Jewish convert who perished at Auschwitz in World War II, who consciously sought her sacrifice as a martyr on behalf of the Jewish people.

see their blessed lives as an unfathomable counterpoint to my own sinful nature, I can hope that their virtues and perseverance will somehow pray me out of a Purgatory that I would be grateful to merit.

My children too are Jews. While they don't have the depth of memory informed by ethnic identity, they have inherited the better part in knowing their faith. Stephanie, who has no Jewish background, has, in her typical graciousness, played a major role in assuring their birthright. As a homeschooling mother she has taught them Hebrew, and she herself learned how to say various Jewish prayers, serving as a model Jewish mother. My children look up to my parents and cherish their grandparents' religious roots all the more, and even more so as my parents move in a natural progression toward greater observance in their later years.

When I first wrote about my conversion twelve years ago,[19] I was still at a point where I hadn't told my parents about my conversion. In that account one can see how haunted I was by that fact. We Jews face so many inherent obstacles in our moving toward Christ, and most of us experience the suffering of a Blessed Libermann[20] as we move toward conversion. I think this is a central anguish that we all face in individual ways, an agony that is unavoidable, but part of the price that is worth paying.

Over the years, I continue to think that my mother, in her own way, pleaded for a "don't ask, don't tell" policy, knowing in her heart that I had converted, but not wanting to have to make a public admission of the fact. When my parents at

[19] In *Bread from Heaven*, edited by Ronda Chervin and published by St. Bede's Press. More information on this, and other books of Dr. Chervin, can be found at www.rondachervin.com.

[20] Blessed Francis Libermann was born the son of an Orthodox Rabbi, to whom his conversion was a source of bitter grief.

one point considered retiring to live near us, I wrote the following to them in a letter addressing their possible move:

> Forgive me if I state the obvious, but I'm sure you realize that we are a Catholic family. While things are somewhat toned down for your visits out of respect for you and a desire to make you feel at ease, our prayer life as Catholics is a central fact of this household. There is no confusion for any of the children because they know that their Jewish heritage (and they are taught this heritage) is the backbone of their relationship to God in the Trinity, and there is no dissent from this.... From the start of my marriage, I have always kept my Jewish heritage and faith in God that you transmitted to me, though it is in a Catholic context here.

Does the above constitute an explicit admission? In my attempt to be charitable, I don't overtly state that I'm a baptized Catholic, but I believe my parents are intelligent enough to read between the lines. My parents simply responded that my letter was "beautiful" and "moving" and that they "understood" the feelings behind my conferring with them about their impending retirement—they instead moved to live near one of my brothers.

My conversion process hasn't been typical, but I know that my decision in how to approach my family was informed by and in tune with my parents' sensibilities, something it's very difficult for others to judge in objectivity. This is the most recent ending of a conversion story that continues, for none of us are ever finished with our ongoing conversion until death. For a Hebrew Catholic, there are several continuing conversions we make in our lives, always reconciling our Mosaic roots with our immersion in Christ, and all the while living richer and more bountiful lives as a result of our twice-blessed faith.

Oy Vey! He's Catholic!

Bob Fishman, B.S.C.D.

Bob Fishman currently resides with his wife, Karen, in Helena, Montana, where he is the Director of Religious Education for the Cathedral of Saint Helena. He hosts "The Catholic Hour" radio show, has hosted a number of television specials on EWTN and PBS, and speaks throughout the country promoting the truths of the Roman Catholic Church and her Jewish roots. He may be contacted through Saint Joseph Communications at 800-526-2151.

I'd like to tell my story of how Judaism led me to Christianity, Christianity led me back to Judaism, and finally my trip back to Judaism brought me home to the Catholic Church, which is truly the fulfillment of my original Jewish faith.

My parents were Jewish; my parents' parents were Jewish; there were no breaks in the line: no intermarriages; nobody had ever converted to Christianity or married a Christian. They were Jewish all the way back, but my parents were not religious Jews; they were Jews pretty much in name only. They did belong to a temple, but they only went maybe twice a year, on Rosh Hashanah and Yom Kippur, and that was about it. There wasn't a lot of Judaism in our household growing up; we celebrated Hanukkah and had a Passover meal here and there, but that was it.

When I was thirteen years old, I celebrated my Bar Mitzvah. To prepare for it I studied with a Rabbi for about six months and went to Hebrew school. The rite of passage that the Jews call Bar Mitzvah is one of the roots of the Catholic sacrament of confirmation. It's the point in a boy's life when he becomes an adult in the community and is recognized as a mature member of the congregation. This meant that I had the privilege of reading from the Torah—the first five books of the Old Testament: Genesis, Exodus, Leviticus, Numbers, and Deuteronomy—written on a beautiful scroll that is kept rolled up in the tabernacle.

After my Bar Mitzvah, my Judaism was basically over. I didn't go to temple regularly; as a matter of fact, I hardly went at all. It's a lot like some Catholic kids who after confirmation say, "it's over—I don't need to go to church." Nonetheless, despite the fact that I didn't attend temple, I had a hunger deep in my soul. I thirsted for knowledge of God. I didn't understand the reason, but I wanted something deeper; and so I started studying other faiths. I started studying Buddhism, meditation, transcendental meditation, and Zen, and my parents didn't have a problem with any of those belief systems. The only one they had a problem with was Christianity. I used to ask my Mom, "Why don't Jews believe in Jesus?" And she would always say the same thing (imagine a Jewish mother speaking), "I don't have to tell you why. This is my house; we don't believe in Jesus; that's all you need to know! We're Jewish!" All right, fine, so I started studying these other faiths that they didn't have problems with, but even then I never was fulfilled.

When I was seventeen, a friend of mine came and said, "Bob, I've got something for you."

"What is it?" I replied.

"It's a New Testament." He handed it to me. It was one of those little green New Testaments that say *New Testament, Psalms and Proverbs* on the cover. It fit really well in the back pocket of my jeans. My friend said, "Now just take it home and read the words in red. The words in red are what Jesus said."

"Words in red are what Jesus said—I can remember that." So I went home and sneaked up to my bedroom. This was a big deal for me; I was smuggling in contraband. I was really careful; I made sure no one was around, and everything was safe and secure before I brought out the forbidden book. I started to read the words in red, and I expected to find blatant anti-Jewish things that would explain why Jews don't believe in Jesus. But as I read the words in red, I discovered instead a Jewish Rabbi who talked about kingdoms, talked about love, talked about prayer, talked about God as our Father. This really blew me away. I was confused.

About that same time I graduated from high school and joined the navy. I didn't realize that when a Jew joins the service, he's asked if he keeps kosher. Now my parents never kept kosher; I didn't even know what keeping kosher really meant except that one doesn't eat bacon. But as I was sitting with the recruiter I remembered all the horror stories about the food in the military, and I thought eating better might be a good idea. So I said, "Yes, I keep kosher." The recruiter replied, "Great! We'll feed you kosher food, but you have to go to temple on Saturdays." That didn't sound so bad, so I agreed I'd go to temple.

Well, I made it to boot camp and was there for a couple of weeks when I ran into my first "born-again" Christian. I'd never met one of these guys before, and he was on fire! He found out I was Jewish, and he was convinced that I needed to be saved. I asked, "What do I need to be saved from?" and he gave me some tracts to read. He left tracts on my bed, on my footlocker, in my shoes, all over the place. I read the tracts, and I really didn't see anything bad in them, but on the back of the tracts there were two cartoons. It read, "Are you saved?" with boxes to check, yes or no. Next to the "yes" box was a cartoon of a guy kneeling at the throne of God, and next to the "no" box a cartoon of a guy with flames shooting out of him. Now, eternal damnation does not appeal to me, so I checked the "yes" box and handed it back to him. I told him, "There, I'm saved! Done!" He was disgusted and said, "No, that's not what it means."

I grew tired of this born-again guy because he just kept coming around and pestering me about being saved. I decided I wanted to answer this guy from a Jewish point of view. I went to my Rabbi one day, he was a young guy, and told him about this Christian. I told him I wanted to have a Jewish response to this pest, and I asked him to help me study about the Old Testament prophecies about the Messiah. We studied over three hundred prophecies about the Messiah. We debated over words and phrases. We consulted the great rabbinic teachings of the time to see if the prophecies were about Israel or the messianic kingdom. We looked at the Hebrew word *alma* to see if it meant virgin or young girl. Finally after looking at all of these prophecies, I came to the conclusion that the Messiah had to be Jesus.

It couldn't be anyone else. From the tribe of Judah. From the lineage of David. Born in Bethlehem. Would be wounded for our transgressions, bruised for our iniquities. Pierced, beaten, spat upon, and sold for thirty pieces of silver. Even the very donkey on which He rode into Jerusalem was prophesied hundreds of years before it ever happened. No other religious leader had that. No one ever

predicted where Buddha would be born. No one ever said
how Lao Tzu would die or what Plato's or Aristotle's ministry would be. There are no prophecies of any of the other
religious leaders. Christianity was different. There were over
three hundred prophecies of Jesus in the Old Testament alone.
This separates it from all other world religions. It had to be
Jesus, and I had no choice but to believe. His birth, life,
death, and Resurrection were predicted hundreds of years
before it ever happened. These prophecies, and the fact of
their fulfillment, literally changed my soul.

During this period of realization, I was transferred to Pen-
sacola, Florida, in the heart of the so-called "Bible Belt".
Actually, I think it is the "buckle" of the belt itself. I had
been there about two weeks when I was given a new roommate. He was a six-foot-five African American named "Tall
Paul". He came into my room, and we became fast friends.
He was from south Philadelphia and looked as if he had
seen some tough times in his life. Together we looked like
Mutt and Jeff.[1] He was this tall muscular black guy from
the streets, and I was this short little Jewish guy from the
suburbs. We got along splendidly. One night, over some
Dr. Pepper and Doritos, the subject of religion came up. I
was anxious to share what I had learned, and I just let it all
spill out. When I was finished I said, "Tall Paul, do you
know of a good church I could go too?"

"Brother Bob," he said, "have I got a church for you!"

"What kind of church is it?"

"It's a Pentecostal church", he responded with an obvious
excitement in his voice. "You come with me one time to
church, and if you don't like it you never have to come again."

---

[1] Characters from a comic-strip of the same name that ran from 1907 to
1982.

This was very intriguing to me, and Tall Paul was obviously thrilled at the prospect of my going with him. I had never been to an actual church service before, and I thought all of them were basically the same. I had wanted to be an observer and thought this would be the perfect opportunity. So I agreed to attend Sunday service with him.

As Sunday morning arrived I was in nervous anticipation of what was about to happen. As we drove to the church and parked outside, my heart was racing. After all, this was a completely foreign experience for me. While walking through the parking lot, Tall Paul turned to me and said, "I have a favor to ask you."

"What's that?" I answered.

"I want you to sit in the front row with me. Is that okay with you?"

I pondered his question for a moment, but having never been to a service before it did not matter to me where we sat. Front or back, I was just there for the experience. "Sure, we can sit in the front row." He seemed very pleased by this.

As I entered the church I saw many very comfortable-looking pews with cushions on them. I proceeded to the front row with Tall Paul at my side just trying to blend in. Soon after we arrived, the musicians took their places, and the church began to rock. There were drums and guitars and a bass and a woman on keyboard. A giant screen came down from the ceiling with the words to the songs plastered up for the whole congregation to see. Everyone stood and clapped and sang. I just tried to blend in and sang right along with them. I think I even did the Jewish two-step, I'm not sure. Anyway, this went on for almost thirty minutes, and I was beginning to believe that going to church was a giant party. Everyone was singing and clapping, and I was in the midst of it all.

Soon things quieted down, and the pastor came out. He was a short man with a booming voice, and he proceeded to walk back and forth waving a handkerchief and yelling "Amen!" I was even yelling "Amen" back with the crowd, though I did not know why. It was just fun. He spoke for thirty or forty minutes, and it was quite enjoyable. Then the service took a different turn. A woman came up from the audience and proceeded to quietly play the organ. The pastor moved to the center of the stage and asked, "Is there anyone out there who would like to receive Jesus as his personal Savior?" The place, once very noisy, had now come to dead silence. I turned around to see why everyone was so quiet, and then I saw that everyone was staring at me! I looked ahead and the pastor was standing in front of me. I gulped. Here I was in a church, and suddenly I was being gawked at and somewhat invited to stand.

I decided, why not? I was here. I might as well go all the way. So I stood up and, being in the front row anyway, did not have far to go. I approached the stage. The pastor leaned over and said, "Do you accept Jesus Christ as your Lord and Savior?"

"I certainly do", I replied.

"Do you ask Jesus to forgive you of your sins?"

"Yes, I do", I responded. Then the pastor leaned over and said, "Have you ever been baptized?" I wasn't expecting this. I didn't even have a change of clothes! "No", I replied. He paused and suddenly a curtain in the back opened to reveal a clear tank filled with water. I gulped again. "Do you want to be baptized?" I responded from somewhere in the pit of my stomach, "Sure, why not?"

Now I didn't know that you should make potato salad, bring a video camera, make tamales, none of that. He asked if I wanted to be baptized. That was it. I went to the back and was given a white robe to put on. I was then lowered into the tank and the pastor, with great glee, baptized me. When I came out of the water, I have to tell you, I felt changed. I felt like I had finally done something Christian. I had professed faith in Jesus publicly, and I felt as if I was literally dripping with the innocence of God.

Following the baptism some men approached the tank and said, "Have you ever received the Holy Ghost?" I didn't even know what the Holy Ghost was, but it sounded good. I shook my head. Immediately they all laid hands on me and began speaking in "tongues" over me. I had no idea what "tongues" were. I thought they simply forgot the words. Anyway, I was welcomed with open arms and a large towel and felt like a new creation. I had fire in my bones. While I was filled with the Spirit and still wet from the water, I did what every good Jewish boy should do. I called my mother!

Needless to say, she was less than enthused. I called her up and I said, "Mom, guess what I did tonight?"

"What's that, Honey?"

"I got baptized."

There was silence.

Then she spoke again. "What you have done is like taking a knife and stabbing me in the back."

Now it was my turn to be silent.

"How could you say that?" I began. "You are not even religious; you go to temple maybe once or twice a year—how could you say that to me?"

She paused. I could tell she was starting to cry. "You have broken with tradition. You are not my son!" She hung up the phone.

My Christian "high" soon left me. I was now hearing other things from my new Christian friends. Statements like,

"You know, Brother Bob, now that you're saved, your family has to get saved. You don't want to see them going to hell." I didn't. Their words tore my soul apart. I began to think of all my ancestors. All my grandparents and their parents, my aunts, uncles, and cousins who had never accepted Jesus. Were they doomed to hell? And why was I so lucky? This hurt my spirit very much.

After I was discharged from the navy I began attending the nondenominational churches. They are a lot like the Pentecostal church except toned down a little. My mother and I could talk about everything but religion. She would say, "You believe what you believe, and I believe what I believe, and I don't want to hear it in this house." This was tough for me. Many were the nights I cried out to God on my knees for my mom. In the nondenominational church you learn many things. How to quote Scripture, debate verses, and how to witness to your family. I soon began leaving tracts around my mom's house. I put them in the bathroom, the bedroom, in her drawers. I even got the tracts that resemble phony dollar bills and dropped them on the floor just in the hopes that she would pick one up and read it. This did not work. If anything it made the walls between us even higher.

Not long after, my mother was diagnosed with cancer. She had been a smoker for more than forty years, and her prognosis was not good. She was moved from a hospital to a Catholic hospice of all places! I walked in one day, and there above her bed was a giant crucifix.

"Doesn't that bother you?" I asked.

"Really," she said, "I don't care anymore." Her face was gray; she had begun to wither away. I could tell the effects of her treatments had taken their toll. "I just want it to be over. I am tired of being sick, I am tired of hurting, and I just want to die."

This hit me like a ton of bricks. I didn't know what to do. Now, I had been to many healing services and healing seminars. I had purchased the books and tapes, and I knew what went on. I decided to drive to my local Christian bookstore and buy a small vial of healing oil. My thinking was that if I prayed over her, God would heal her, and she would become a believer. I entered my mom's room and unscrewed the cap on the vial. Using my index finger, I put some on her head and began to pray for her. Nothing happened. I prayed harder. Nothing happened. Day after day, nothing. Finally, feeling fed up with God I cried out to Him and said, "I have seen You heal many people. You do it all the time with the televangelists and in the seminars; You heal people all over the world. Why won't You heal my mom! Is it because she's Jewish?"

I was angry with God, and once I calmed down I began to hear God whisper into my soul. I am not saying that the clouds opened and a voice rang down; God simply spoke to my heart of hearts. "Tell her who I am." I was perplexed. I didn't know what to say. So I asked, "Who are You, Lord, really?" The voice in my heart grew louder. "I am the God of the friendless. I am a God of the heartbroken. I am a God who will hold her hand. Tell her that."

The next day I went into my mom's room and told her what God had laid on my heart. To my amazement, she could accept that. See, my mom didn't know Genesis to Revelation, but she knew what it meant when God said He would hold her hand. It was beautiful to see the compassion and trust fill her eyes as tears flowed. She had been broken and wounded, and God was now telling her He would be there for her.

Not long after this event, I began to tell my mom stories from the Old Testament. Stories that were never made into movies. Stories of Elijah and Daniel. Tales of David and the prophets. Psalms and poetry from the Song of Songs. My mom loved this. Soon people who were also in the hospice would hear me coming in to tell Bible stories to my mom, and they would wheel in or use their canes and walkers to come in and listen. It was amazing. I can remember being at my office and getting excited over a story that I was going to share. This was a good time between my mother and me, and in many ways a time of healing and sharing.

One day I just had to ask her, "Mom, what is it you have against Jesus?" There it was, I had said it. I really wanted to know why she had such an aversion to our Lord.

"Really," she responded, "it's the name. You see ever since I was a little girl growing up in Brooklyn, New York, that name has been a curse word in my home. When I hear you say it, it sounds like the worst curse word there is. I just can't hear it coming from you. Do you understand?" There was silence. I saw tears in my mom's eyes, and I knew this was painful for her to explain to me.

"Yeah, I understand." I paused. "How about if I use Jesus' Hebrew name? It is *Yeshua*. It actually means Joshua. Do you have a problem with that?" I waited for her response, which came quicker than I was prepared for.

"No," she said, "I don't have a problem with *Yeshua*."

Upon hearing those words my heart leaped within me, and I could feel the Holy Spirit at work. I began telling her stories of *Yeshua*. Meeting a woman at the well, healing a blind man, healing a lame man, and finally rising from the dead. Shortly before my mom passed away, she asked *Yeshua* to forgive her of her sins. She accepted *Yeshua* as her Lord and Savior. And she passed away in her sleep resting in the blessed arms of our loving Savior. The reason I share this part of my conversion with you is because sometimes, the greatest prayer we can ever pray is simply to hold someone's hand and say, "God loves you. He really does."

As I shared earlier, I moved from the Pentecostal church to a nondenominational church. While there, I learned many things. I became proficient at quoting Scripture. I also became a very good debater. I began to wield the Bible like a sword; only I often used it to destroy a person's belief rather than to build him up. I knew all of the Scripture passages that people would use to try and justify their position. I had attacks and counterattacks for all of their various arguments. The problem was, with all this knowledge I began to lose my own faith. I didn't know what was true any more. I still believed in Jesus, but I had lost my faith in organized religions and in going to church. What was the point? I longed for holiness, not just a good band or an exciting pastor with a good youth group. I was tired of the same old routines. I wanted something holy, with roots, something that I knew was true. I began to feel a lot like Pilate, when he asked, "What is truth?"

During this time my job transferred me to California. I thought it was the land of dreams. When I arrived there, however, I met many people who were somewhat cold and wounded people, workaholics. I quickly became one of them. I would go to work, come home, click on the air conditioner, and veg out in front of the television. Occasionally someone would invite me to a church service. "Oh, you have to come. They have a great band, and the pastor is very dynamic", they would say. I would politely decline. I had been there, done that. I was no longer interested. My soul ached for real truth. I remember crying out to God and asking Him, "What should I do?" Again I heard the voice of God in my heart, and His response was, "I want you to study Judaism."

This took me aback. I had not expected this, yet an unknown hunger called me forth. I looked in the yellow pages for an Orthodox Rabbi. I wanted the guys with the beards and the ringlets, who dressed in black. I wanted the complete *Yentl*[2] experience. I soon met with an Orthodox Rabbi and told him of my desire to learn Judaism. I also told him that I believed Jesus is the Messiah. "I will teach you Judaism," he stated, "provided that you do not teach my congregation Christianity."

I quickly agreed. I could keep my mouth shut. Soon I began to learn beautiful things about Judaism. I learned about keeping kosher and reading the Torah. I especially loved learning about the "mystical" side of Judaism. I learned about the Kabbalah[3] and about Jewish saints and mystics. These great rabbis spoke of a love relationship with God that goes beyond words, beyond thought and reason, and ultimately into a love union with God. This was what I longed for. My soul grew excited as I learned many things.

During this time a friend of mine sent me a book about Saint Francis of Assisi. I had never heard of him, except in conjunction with birdbaths in the back yard. As I read about Saint Francis, I began to fall in love with his passion. Here was a guy who came from an upper-middle-class family, was a bit of a party boy, and who gave it all up to live like Christ. He actually lived it. I was blown away. Then another friend gave me a copy of *The Collected Works of Saint John of the Cross*. I absorbed it like a sponge. I began reading about intimacy with God that goes beyond words. It was at this time that I began comparing the words of Saint Francis and Saint John with those in my Jewish mystic books. To my

[2] The name of a popular 1983 movie set among Orthodox Jews.
[3] The Jewish mystical tradition.

amazement they were using the same phrases and words to describe this heavenly type of union, which could be attained through prayer. The hardest thing for me to accept was the fact that these saints were Catholic. This was the one church I had always been told to stay away from. Catholics were idol-worshippers, and the Catholic Church was the "whore of Babylon". How could these saints be Catholic? I decided that maybe I should check out the Catholic Church just to satisfy my curiosity and to prove once and for all that they were in error.

I went to my Rabbi, and I told him what I had learned. I said, "Rabbi, I have loved what you have taught me, but I cannot deny that Jesus is the Messiah, and I must continue my journey."

He looked up at me and said, "Bob, I hope you find what you are looking for. Go in peace, and may God keep you and watch over you."

I drove home that night feeling a sense of loss and a twinge of excitement. However, I knew nothing about the Catholic Faith, so I decided to call up a Catholic bookstore and ask if I could come in and ask some questions. The conversation went something like this:

"Hello, my name is Bob Fishman, and I am a Jewish, Pentecostal, nondenominational, anti-Catholic who is deeply confused."

"How can I help you?" came the voice at the other end.

"I have some questions about Catholics, and I would like some answers."

"Why don't you write down some of your concerns and bring them into the bookstore. We can meet at three o'clock, and no subject is off limits. Don't be afraid to ask the questions."

"Perfect", I responded.

Immediately my mind went into overdrive. I was going to prepare the toughest questions this guy ever heard. I came up with twenty. I called my list "Bob Fishman's Top Twenty". I had everything from "Why do Catholics worship Mary?" to "Why do you call a priest 'father'?" to "Why do you worship idols?" and right on down the line. I thought there was no way this guy would be able to answer these.

I arrived at the bookstore with list in hand, and the owner took me around the counter. There against the wall were two folding chairs.

"Have a seat, Bob", he said. "My name is Victor, and before we get started, I have to tell you up front that I am a Catholic apologist."

"That's very nice", I said. "The Catholic Church should apologize."

"No, no. An apologist is one who defends the Faith."

"Then let's defend", I said and produced my list.

With loving patience and Scripture, he went through all of my questions with me. He answered every one of them. We talked for over three hours, and I learned things I had never known. He showed me writings of the early Church fathers, people who were students of Paul and John, disciples who knew what they looked like, early Christians who wrote after the reign of the apostles. I had never learned anything about these guys. Most of the churches I had gone to used the Acts of the Apostles like a catechism. However no one had ever told me what happened to the Church after the book of Acts. Did the Church that Christ started fade away? Did the gates of Hell prevail?

I slowly began to learn that the Church Jesus had started over two thousand years ago is still around today, and it is the Roman Catholic Church! All other Christian denominations broke off from this Church. She was the original one, and she has survived. The Catholic Church is the only one that can actually trace her roots all the way back to Christ. If this was true, and I professed to believe in Christ, then I wanted to belong to His Church, not some church that wasn't even a hundred years old. I became tremendously excited. Finally I had found what I was looking for. At long last to be able to join the actual Church founded by Christ!

After months of private instruction, I decided to enter the RCIA—the Rite of Christian Initiation for Adults. I have to tell you honestly, there were times when I thought I could teach this class! I learned many things. I learned about tradition and apostolic succession. I saw all of the beauty of Judaism being fulfilled at Mass: we have a priesthood that comes from Judaism, we have incense and holy garments, we read the word to the congregation, we sing the psalms. All of this was Jewish. We have an altar and a tabernacle with candles burning before it. As I witnessed all of these things, I knew that I was experiencing the fulfillment of my Jewish heritage.

Then there was the lamb, and not just any lamb, but the Lamb of God. This to me was the most beautiful. I understood the connection to the Passover meal immediately. In the Passover story in the Old Testament, it is the blood of a lamb—a lamb provided by man—that covers over and protects God's people. It struck me like a thunderbolt that, when the priest holds up the sacred Host and says, "Behold the Lamb of God ...", these were the words of John the Baptist. I suddenly realized that the Lamb of God had to be slain so that His Blood could take away the sins of the whole world, not those of just one family, but of every family, all of creation. What a divine and profound mystery. The God of Abraham, Isaac, and Jacob humbled Himself to become a man, and then the Lamb of God, slain for the sins of the world. This was and is Jesus.

As if this weren't enough, this same God has now humbled Himself even further to veil Himself behind Bread and Wine. In the Old Testament, God always veiled Himself. In a burning bush, in a whispering wind, in a pillar of fire, even in a still small voice. Why? Because if He truly showed us His glory, the very molecules that make us up would burst forth into glory. We could not handle it. Our finite minds would unravel at the glory of the Infinite. So our God, in His loving compassion for the world and to reconcile us back to Himself, took on flesh and blood. He became not only the sacrificial Lamb, but also the High Priest intervening on our behalf. Now this same God veils Himself behind the appearances of simple Bread and Wine. Why? So that His flesh and blood could literally flow into us and that we could share our flesh and blood with Him in an act that is beyond all words or description. The intimate union I had so longed for was right here in the Blessed Eucharist. The Body, Blood, soul, and divinity of God Almighty would commune with me. This was an act far greater than even sexual intercourse, for now I could become His child, flesh and blood. So often we tell our children, "Johnny, I would do anything for you because you are my flesh and blood." Or "Susie I would lay down my life for you because you are my flesh and blood." Now I understood. Jesus loved me so much He wanted me to be His child, flesh and blood. He laid down His life for me because He loved me!

On Easter Vigil night 1992, I was received into the one, holy, catholic, and apostolic Church. I received my First Holy Communion and was confirmed into the Roman Catholic Church. I had come home at last.

Every once in a while, God will blow you a kiss. God blew me such a kiss with my wife, Karen. I met her after I became a Catholic. She had been a cradle Catholic who was reviving her lagging faith. We met on a retreat in Arkansas, and God kissed me. He gave her to me. God spoke to my heart and told me that He was giving me a jewel that was precious. I was to take care of that jewel and protect and nurture her. To this day I am still fascinated by the many facets of this jewel I lovingly call my wife. We were married in the Church on July 27, 1996. Together we have raised three children, Kara, Kayla, and Justin.[4] Recently I have become a grandpa. I am called Pappa, and Karen is called Nanna. Eight years ago, Karen and I joined a religious community called the Brothers and Sisters of Charity. This is a Franciscan community approved by the Church. We took our permanent vows as "domestics" in this community before the Bishop of Arkansas. We are allowed to live in our own homes and be married. It is similar to the Benedictine Oblates or the Third Order Carmelites.

What a long, strange trip I have taken. The path leading me to our Holy Mother Church has given my faith a vibrancy I deeply appreciate and am hungry to share. I desire and challenge you, the reader, to look into the truths and riches of the Roman Catholic Church and, perhaps after a long journey, you too will find your way home at last. May the God of Abraham, Isaac, and Jacob richly bless all of you.

---

[4] Karen had been in a previous marriage that had been annulled prior to her meeting Bob.

Surprised by Grace

Roy Schoeman

Roy Schoeman is the son of German Jewish Holocaust refugees. He grew up in a suburb of New York City, studying Judaism under some of the most prominent rabbis in contemporary American Jewry. After receiving a B.Sc. from M.I.T. and an M.B.A. from Harvard, he received an appointment to the faculty of Harvard Business School and began a career of teaching and consulting. A series of dramatic conversion experiences led him to embrace the Catholic Faith enthusiastically. In 2003 his first book, Salvation is from the Jews: The Role of Judaism in Salvation History from Abraham to the Second Coming, *was published. Since then he has become a popular speaker at conferences and on Catholic television and radio. He may be contacted by email at schoeman@catholic.org or via his website: www.salvationisfromthejews.com.*

I was born in the early 1950s, the son of German Jewish Holocaust refugees who met and married in this country. My father had fled Germany at the beginning of Hitler's reign, when it was still possible for Jews to leave; my mother had a more difficult time of it. Her family fled to France, but then got caught up in the Nazi occupation of France. She escaped from prison the night before the train was to take her to the concentration camp. She eventually made it to Cuba, and from there, after the war, to the United States.

My parents settled in a suburb of New York City. At the time they moved there, it was the one town in the area that permitted Jews—the neighboring towns were all "restricted", that is, no Jews allowed. Having grown up in religiously observant families in Germany, my parents became active in the local Conservative[1] Jewish synagogue, and soon became pillars of the local Jewish community. I was never unaware of my being Jewish—it was the basis of my identity from my earliest glimmerings of self-awareness, defining all aspects of my relationship to others and to the world around me. As soon as I was old enough to go to school, I went, in addition to ordinary secular school, to a twice-weekly after-school religious education program at my synagogue, known as Hebrew school. I had a naturally devout nature—I was always aware of God, desired to please Him, and I took great joy in being on (or so I thought) the "inside track" as a Jew, one of His own people. It was in Hebrew school and in the activities that revolved around the synagogue that I felt most in my own skin, in my Jewish identity.

This is not to say that I had no experience of, or even yearning for Christianity or, to be more precise, Jesus. It was a complicated interaction; perhaps a few memories of early experiences will best explain it. For instance, the first full sentence that anyone remembers me saying (it later became a sort of a family joke) was "I want a Christmas tree!" although in my inability to speak clearly yet, it came out "I wanna bibabee!" This I would ceaselessly repeat to the great annoyance of my parents and older sister. I remember clearly the motivation behind my monotonous insistence: I sensed the warmth, the love, the joy of Christmas, and the very real presence of the Baby Jesus at the center of

[1] See footnote 3, p. ix above.

it all and had a great yearning for all that, but most of all for the Christ Child.

Although I had no idea what the word "saint" meant, and certainly no idea who Saint Joseph was, whenever I felt particularly distressed, or that no one understood me, I would push a low stool over to the medicine cabinet in the kitchen, swing open its door, and silently talk through my anguish to the bottle of Saint Joseph's Orange-Flavored Aspirin for children, coming away feeling loved and consoled.

I don't think it is all that unusual for small children to sense the spiritual world viscerally and to have their own, childish, interaction with it on that basis. The fact that I found great natural consolation in my participation in my Jewish religious life, such as it was as a small child, did not in itself make me less aware—perhaps quite the contrary—of the Christian presence that I perceived in the spiritual world. It was precisely this yearning for the Christian presence that was later transmuted into animosity, hostility, to all things Christian—a sort of "sour grapes" reaction to being rejected, excluded, from what (actually Whom) I most deeply yearned for.

All this is not to say that I did not find a great deal of satisfaction, and even richness and depth in prayer, within Judaism. As I grew older, my religiosity continued to deepen; by high school I was one of only three or four who remained from the original thirty or so students in my Hebrew school class. The tendency was for Jewish children to drop out of religious education as soon as they were through with their Bar Mitzvah[2] at the age of thirteen, as though that rite of passage made further religious education unnecessary, somewhat as Catholic children often stop going to catechism class once they are confirmed.

[2] See footnote 1, p. 98 above.

I not only continued with Hebrew school, but it became an ever more important part of my life. I was particularly blessed by Providence in my Jewish education. My own hometown Rabbi was extraordinary—he came from a long line of Hasidic rabbis and was, at the time, the leading Rabbi in Conservative Jewry in America. I also had some truly extraordinary Hebrew school teachers. They were seminarians studying to be rabbis in nearby New York City. One in particular, who became my mentor for my high school and early college years, later became a leading Reconstructionist[3] Rabbi and the head of the largest rabbinical seminary in the United States.

Let me try to draw these strands together. I was quite gifted in school, always first in my class and usually in every subject, but I knew that that was not what really mattered—what really mattered was God. I knew, or so I thought, that it was only the Jews who really knew God, being His favorites not only by race, but also because they were the only ones who knew how to worship Him properly. I knew, or so I thought, that two thousand years ago a particularly misguided and deluded Jew had created a watered-down, mongrelized version of Judaism—Christianity—that was a sort of (excuse me) "idiot stepchild" of Judaism, yet, perhaps for that reason, became wildly popular. Yet, viscerally, internally, I still felt the presence of Jesus and felt drawn to Him. I saw the relaxed joy on the faces of "misguided" Christians and was frequently the recipient of their uncritical acceptance and love. I couldn't help wanting what they seemed to have. Although I felt contemptuous of, and

---

[3] Reconstructionism is a branch of Judaism that externally resembles Conservative Judaism; most Reconstructionist rabbis take positions in Conservative congregations.

superior to, Christianity, I couldn't help longing deeply for what I felt at the core of it. The deeper this contradiction, the stronger the simultaneous pulls in the opposite directions, the more bitter the antagonism I felt to all things Christian.

In the spring of my last year of high school a very charismatic Hasidic Rabbi came to our synagogue for the Purim[4] service, to lead an evening of music and worship. Raised in the heart of the Hasidic community, he had been appointed by his Hasidic master to leave their enclave and go out into the world, to bring back to Judaism the assimilated, fallen-away, sometimes "hippie" Jewish youth of America. I was immediately entranced and enthusiastically joined the number of his disciples. When the school year ended, I followed him to Israel as a member of his entourage, sitting at his feet to absorb his Hasidic wisdom and stories, and joyfully participating in his nightly "concerts", actually Hasidic worship services filled with music and dancing. While in Israel I considered abandoning my plans to go to M.I.T.[5] in order to stay in Israel and study at one of the Jerusalem *yeshivot* (which are schools where young men devote their time to prayer and religious study, the closest thing Judaism has to religious life). But I was turned off by a certain sterility and coldness I saw in them, which did not speak of real intimacy with God.

So I returned to the United States and started college. I felt very lost, because anything that did not have God at its

---

[4] Purim is a Jewish festival celebrated with great joy that commemorates the saving of the Jewish people from extermination under King Ahasuerus through the intervention of Queen Esther, as recounted in the Old Testament's Book of Esther.

[5] Massachusetts Institute of Technology in Cambridge, Massachusetts, more commonly known by its initials M.I.T.

center seemed to have no point or meaning, yet there was nothing I *could* do that did have God at its center. The former Hebrew school teacher who had been my mentor had become a Rabbi and moved to Boston, where he started a kind of counterculture, hippie-oriented Jewish seminary/commune. During my first few weeks at M.I.T., I considered dropping out to join it, but he encouraged me to stay where I was, and I did, but spent much of my free time at his seminary/commune.

Although I tried to maintain my religious orientation, there was a fatal flaw in it that soon led me astray. I had no understanding of the relationship between religion and morality, particularly sexual morality. As my religiosity became mixed up in the drug and "free love" culture that was rampant, my Jewish religious practice fell away, and my faith degenerated into the immoral, vague, hippie spirituality of the time. For a while my thirst for God was sated by the false consolations and delusional spirituality of that environment, but then, under the influence of the evolution-based, so-called scientific world view then prevalent at M.I.T.—one which condescendingly considered belief in God as either ignorant superstition or as a psychosis that evolution had hardwired into the human brain for its survival value—even that amorphous faith dissolved, to be replaced by a hedonistic agnosticism. For the next fifteen years, I lived in a state of tremendous inner tension. I had a yearning for transcendent meaning and a refusal to let go of that yearning for more than short periods, yet I had no knowledge of what that yearning was truly for, and hence no sense of a direction to go in. At M.I.T. I went through four or five majors, in part because I kept hoping to find a way to address what mattered most, the meaning of life. I finally settled on linguistics because, according to my professors there, human consciousness itself is as close as there is to real meaning in life, and language is the only way to get at thought.

Upon graduation I began a career working with computers. Since a conventional engineer's life in the United States seemed to me devoid of "meaning", I moved to Denmark. I sensed, in the deeper relationship that Danes had with life and family, a greater spiritual meaning, but I soon realized that that was not my real life and moved back. For a few years after my return, while continuing to work as an engineer, I lived for rock-climbing, with the excitement and sense of danger and accomplishment that it produced providing an anesthetic for my thirst for meaning.

Five years after finishing college I went back to school, to Harvard Business School for an M.B.A., but the momentary feelings of success that produced did not assuage my desperation for real meaning for long. Anything I tried, whether a career switch or a romantic relationship, only produced a momentary illusion of purpose that soon faded, leaving me with the desperate sense that there *must* be something more. That is why I never settled into a career or married.

At Harvard Business School I did extraordinarily well, winning most of the available awards in my class and graduating among the top few with "high distinction". Upon graduation I took a job at a management consulting firm, on the principle that if there was no real point to anything, I might as well sell myself to the highest bidder. But within a few months I was recruited by my former professors to return to Harvard to teach. Thus I found myself on the faculty of Harvard Business School, teaching marketing in the M.B.A. program, at the ripe old age of twenty-nine.

It is at that point that my conversion story per se begins. After my initial euphoria at the ego gratification of being a

Harvard professor and the adulation of the students wore off, I found myself in a deeper despair than ever. All my life I had been searching for the real meaning in life, for the essential, for God. As a child I felt that I knew God, and that although I didn't yet know how that would translate into how I should spend my life, it would become clear when I grew up. Well, before I "grew up" I fell into—actually not fell so much as raced headlong into—sin. Thus I lost the sense of living with God, but initially had not cared, distracted by the very fallen consolations of the path I had chosen. When that intoxication wore off, I was again pained by a hunger for real meaning in life, but was able to keep myself distracted by the challenges and gratifications of each new hope, each new ambition, each new accomplishment. But at this point in my life I had reached the end of that road. I had gotten into Harvard Business School; I had been a "star" there; I had taken one of the most prestigious and high-paying jobs upon graduation; and now I was back on the faculty well ensconced on a tenure-track career. Still nothing had any real meaning, and now there was no longer anything else out there on the horizon to strive for, to hope for, to hold the illusion that life would have real meaning when only the next milestone is finally reached.

It was around this time that I got involved with my last false consolation, my last false direction to provide meaning to my life. As a child I had been an enthusiastic downhill skier, but I gave it up when I went to college. I now took it up again with a vengeance, spending several months every winter skiing in the Alps. I became very good, and my skiing companions in the Alps were all professional skiers, "circuit" skiers, Olympic hopefuls, etc. For a few years I lived for skiing, finding enough consolation in the physical excitement, the speed, the aesthetics, the sense of accomplishment, and the camaraderie to dull the thirst for meaning in my life.

Of course, God was using everything in my life to bring me to Him, and it would soon bear fruit. It was when I was in the spectacular natural beauty of the Alps that I became aware of the existence of God for the first time in many years. I remember the scene—I was high up on the mountain, still well above tree line, shortly after sunset, with the sky glowing a soft red and the snow and granite cliffs glowing blue in the twilight. My heart opened with gratitude, and I knew that such beauty had been created by God. It is worth noting that the area of Austria that I was in was still deeply and piously Catholic, with beautiful crucifixes everywhere, both inside the houses, hotels, and restaurants as well as along the roads and even trails. Even in the ski town, the church was packed for Sunday Mass. (In fact, in the bed-and-breakfast where I was staying a carved wooden crucifix, with corpus, hung over my bed. Every evening when I returned to the room I would remove it and place it in a drawer—I had no desire to sleep under a cross!—and the following day I would find it had been rehung over the bed, without comment, by the devout, elderly woman in whose home I was staying).

After a few years of living for skiing, that too began to pale, and I became more and more despondent. My only solace in those days was solitary walks in nature, and it was on one of these that I received the greatest single grace of my life. I was walking in a nature preserve on Cape Cod early one morning, in the low pine brush just inland of the dunes, when I, for lack of a better term, "fell into Heaven". From one moment to the next I found myself very consciously aware that I was in the presence of God. It was

as though a veil had dropped, and for the first time in my
life I saw what had always been around me, unseen. I was
amazed, not only by what I saw, but also by the fact that I
could ever have been oblivious to it. One moment I was
just walking along lost in my thoughts; the next I found
myself in the presence of God, looking at my life as though
looking at it from after death, in His presence. I saw everything that I would be happy about, and everything that I
would wish I had done differently. I saw that everything I
had ever done was recorded, had a moral content that mattered for all eternity, and that for all eternity I would be
grateful for every right choice I had ever made. I saw that
everything that had ever happened to me, especially those
things that had seemed the worst disasters at the time—the
things that had caused the most suffering—had been the
most perfect things that could have been arranged for me
by the hand of an all-knowing, all-loving God. I saw that
my two greatest regrets when I died would be all the time
and energy I had wasted worrying about not being loved,
when every moment of my existence I was held in an ocean
of love greater than I could imagine coming from this all-
loving God (although unaware of it), and every hour that I
had wasted not doing anything of value in the eyes of
Heaven. And I knew, from one moment to the next, that
the meaning and purpose of my life was to worship and
serve this God, my Lord and Master, who was revealing
Himself to me.

I prayed on the spot to know His name so that I could
know what religion to follow. I remember praying, "Let
me know Your name, so I can worship and serve You properly. I don't mind if You're Buddha, and I have to become
Buddhist; I don't mind if You're Krishna, and I have to
become Hindu; I don't mind if You're Apollo, and I have

to become a Roman pagan; as long as You're not Christ, and I have to become Christian!" Well, He respected that prayer and did not reveal His name to me. But when I went back to Cambridge a few days later (the experience, the immediate state of consciousness, gradually faded over the next few hours, although the euphoria lasted for weeks), I was in some sense happy for the first time since childhood. I had been in agony over the meaninglessness of life, and now I knew that life had infinitely more meaning than I could have ever imagined or hoped for. Every hour, every moment has meaning, has a moral content, which matters for all eternity! Every moment we have the opportunity to do something, the benefits of which we will enjoy for all eternity! The slightest good action is noted, and infinitely appreciated, by the most loving God; pleasing Him alone would be more than enough to give infinite meaning to the action, even if we weren't to be rewarded for it, yet we are! And of course, we live forever, in literally unimaginable bliss, if we do things right here below. Of course I was happy!

I went back to my former routine, but now fundamentally happy and determined to find out more about this experience. I wanted to grow in my knowledge of God, to find out what His name is, what "religion" this was. Where could I start? Well, I thought, since this was a mystical experience, maybe I should get in touch with someone who knows something about mystical experiences. A dangerous thing to do in Cambridge in the early 1980s! The first person I spoke with was an old acquaintance whom I had vaguely known as a fellow student at M.I.T. I had recently run into him at a local venture capital firm where I was doing some consulting. There he was, barely eking out a living as a temp typist, while pursuing his "true" vocation as a mystic and kabbalist.[6] I gave him a call and arranged to drop by his place one evening, to see what he could tell me about my experience. What he had to say wasn't very useful, but something else of great import happened while I was at his apartment. While we were talking I noticed a large, heavily illustrated book on his coffee table, with a title something like *The Hundred Greatest Miracles of Modern Times*. In casually leafing through it I came across the story of the apparition of the Blessed Virgin Mary at Fatima, an event that I literally had never heard of before. It immediately caught my attention, and I asked my friend, "Is this really true?"

When he replied, "Yes", I excitedly asked, "Does anyone else know about it? Is it written about anywhere else?"

He assured me that I could find books on it in any public library. My immediate reaction was one of angry indignation. Here all my life I had been wishing that miracles still existed—my constant plaint in Hebrew school was why did God perform miracles in Old Testament times but no longer? And yet here an actual miracle had happened, the miracle of the sun, witnessed by almost a hundred thousand people, and no one had told me! I left his apartment with a number of useless books on mysticism to read, but with the story of Fatima indelibly etched in my mind.

I spent most of the following year reading New Age mystics, looking into various streams of occultism, and dabbling in one or two unhealthy meditation practices. More than ever I was spending my free time alone in nature, but now to read spiritual works and meditate there.

---

[6] Kabbalism, roughly speaking, refers to the mystical and occult tradition within Judaism.

I still wanted, more than anything else in life, to meet
again the God I had met that day on the beach. So every
night just before going to sleep, I would say a short prayer
to know the name of my Lord and Master who had revealed
Himself to me. A year to the day after the initial experience, I received the second great grace of my life, the second "half" of the conversion that brought me to Christianity.

I know that it was a year to the day because before going
to sleep I prayed fervently in gratitude, in awareness that it
was the anniversary. Then I went to sleep.

Now, I know that what happened next was a dream, and
that if there had been a video camera going in the room it
would have shown me asleep. But I can only describe it as I
experienced it. It seemed that I was wakened by a gentle hand
on my shoulder and taken to a room and left alone with the
most beautiful young woman that I could imagine. Just to be
in her presence, to be in the presence of the intensity and
purity of the love that flowed from her, was to be in a state
of ecstasy greater than I imagined could exist. I knew without being told that it was the Blessed Virgin Mary. She said
that she would answer any questions that I wanted to ask her.

The beauty of her voice was at least as intoxicating as
the beauty of her appearance, but most intoxicating of all
was the love itself flowing from her. My initial reaction was
to want to throw myself down at her feet and honor her; I
remember wishing that I knew at least the Hail Mary! In
fact, the first question I asked her came out of that desire
to honor her. I asked what her favorite prayer to her was.
Her initial reply was "I love all prayers to me!" I was a bit
pushy and pressed, "But you must love some prayers to you
more than others. . . ?"

She relented and recited a prayer in Portuguese. I knew
it was in Portuguese without being told. I know no

Portuguese so I couldn't understand the words. The best that I could do was to memorize phonetically the sound of the first few words and write them down the next morning when I awoke. Later I identified the prayer, to the best of my ability, as the Portuguese version of "O Mary, conceived without sin, pray for us who have recourse to you." At the time I knew that the prayer being in Portuguese reflected, in part, a particular childlike devotion to Mary still present among the Portuguese. Perhaps it was also an allusion to Fatima. It might also be significant that that prayer was first given by Mary at another apparition, the one in 1830 to Saint Catherine Labouré in Paris, that resulted in the miraculous medal.

I asked four or five more questions, and when I was finished, Mary said she had something she wanted to tell me. She spoke to me for about another ten minutes, and then the audience was ended. The next morning when I awoke I knew that it had been Christ on the beach; I was, thank God, hopelessly in love with the Blessed Virgin Mary; and I knew that I wanted nothing more than to be as complete and as good a Christian as I possibly could.

However, I still didn't know what a Protestant was, what a Catholic was, what the various Protestant sects were, what the difference was. There was little I could do but look in the local phonebook for a church. I started out going to a Protestant one, but as soon as I felt comfortable I asked the pastor, "What about the Blessed Virgin Mary?" When he answered disrespectfully, I knew it was no place for me.

With my newfound love for Mary, I began to spend all my free time at Marian shrines, out of a desire to commune with her, to sense her presence. Whenever I found myself at one while a Mass was going on, I would be overwhelmed with a desire to receive the Blessed Sacrament, although I did not even really know what it was.

It was these two things—my love for Mary and my desire to receive the Eucharist—that served as the compass that led me into the fullness of Christianity, into the Catholic Church. I will just touch briefly on some of the milestones along the way.

The Marian shrine to which I went most often was a shrine to Our Lady of La Salette, about forty minutes from my house. It commemorated the appearance of Mary to two poor children pasturing their cows high in the French Alps in 1846, in which she gave them a message about an upcoming famine and the need for the people to repent. The winter after I had the dream, I was on a ski trip in the French Alps, when after several days of dreary rain I decided to take a short trip in my rental car to the original La Salette apparition site. A snowstorm and a mishap with the car prevented me from leaving when I planned and forced me to spend the rest of the "ski" trip there, much of it in deep prayer. Someone I met there recommended that I make a visit to a Carthusian monastery, and I ended up doing so, spending a week there, on a kind of solitary "come and see" although I was still Jewish!

There, for the first time I became aware of how the Catholic Church was itself an outgrowth of Judaism. It was unavoidably obvious, given how the monks spent many hours a day chanting the Old Testament psalms, with their continual references to Israel, Zion, Jerusalem, the Jewish Patriarchs, and the Jewish people, visibly identifying with the Israel, and the Jews, of the psalms. A small illustration: one day when I was working alone in the fields, an elderly monk came out to speak with me. He approached and shyly asked, "Tell us, if you don't mind—we couldn't help noticing that you do not receive Communion, so you must not be Catholic. What then are you?" When I replied, "Jewish", he grinned and with a deep sigh said, "That's a relief! We were afraid you were Protestant!" At the time I had no understanding at all of the difference between Protestants and Catholics—they were still just meaningless words to me describing Christians—yet I was deeply struck by the fact that in some mysterious way this monk identified with Jews as opposed to Protestants. I later realized that in his eyes Jews were elder brothers in the Faith who had not yet received the grace to recognize that Jesus was, indeed, the Messiah they were waiting for, whereas Protestants had once had, but then rejected, the fullness of the truth.

At the Carthusian monastery I grew to feel Mary's central, penetrating presence in the Catholic Church. I also became even more distressed at not being able to receive Communion. It was my desire to receive Communion, more than anything else, that drew me to the baptismal font.

Soon after my return to the United States, I began to look for a priest to baptize me. The first one I approached was also Jewish. He had been a Jewish philosophy professor at the University of Chicago and then a Jewish psychiatrist in New York City, before entering the Church and becoming a Trappist monk. When I met with him, he asked me why I wanted to be baptized. At the time I could not truthfully say that it was because I believed in all of Catholic doctrine, so I just bluntly blurted out, "Because I want to receive Communion, and you guys won't let me unless I'm baptized!" I thought he would throw me out on my ear at such a disrespectful answer, but instead he nodded sagely and said "Ah, that's the Holy Spirit at work ..."

So in early 1992 I was baptized and confirmed, by a different priest, as it turned out, just in time for another more extended stay at the Carthusian monastery, to discern whether that was my vocation. I soon discerned that it wasn't, but still hoped, and prayed, for several more years that I might have some other form of religious or priestly vocation. When I came to the realization that I didn't, I felt adrift and worried that I had missed the boat and failed to respond to God's call. Then, to my great relief, out of the blue I felt like I was being given a book to write—it certainly felt like orders from above. The result was *Salvation Is from the Jews: The Role of Judaism in Salvation History from Abraham to the Second Coming*. It was written to give Christians a deeper understanding of Judaism as the religion that God created to bring about the Incarnation of God as man, and as the religion into which He incarnated, and to reveal to Jews the full glory and importance of Judaism, a glory that can only be recognized in the light of the truths of the Catholic Faith. My hope is that when Jewish readers see Judaism so illuminated, their pride in being Jewish, rather than being a stumbling block, will draw them toward the Catholic Church.

I will never know, this side of Heaven, whose prayers and sacrifices purchased the graces for my entirely unsought after and undeserved conversion, but I can only thank them profoundly and exhort others, too, to pray for the conversion of the Jews, so that the people to whom Jesus first made Himself known may come into the truth and into the fullness of their relationship with Him in the Catholic Church. How tragic that we to whom God first revealed Himself as man should be among the last to recognize Him! This sentiment was beautifully expressed in a petition circulated at the First Vatican Council, signed by almost all of the Council Fathers, and heartily endorsed by Pope Pius IX. It has become my constant prayer, and so I would like to close with it:

POSTULATUM PRO HEBRAEIS

The undersigned Fathers of the Council humbly yet urgently, beseechingly pray that the Holy Ecumenical Council of the Vatican deign to come to the aid of the unfortunate nation of Israel with an entirely paternal invitation; that is, that it express the wish that, finally exhausted by a wait no less futile than long, the Israelites hasten to recognize the Messiah, our Savior Jesus Christ, truly promised to Abraham and announced by Moses; thus completing and crowning, not changing, the Mosaic religion....

... [T]he undersigned Fathers have the very firm confidence that the holy Council will have compassion on the Israelites, because they are always very dear to God on account of their fathers, and because it is from them that the Christ was born according to the flesh....

Would that they then speedily acclaim the Christ, saying "Hosanna to the Son of David! Blessed be He who comes in the name of the Lord!"

Would that they hurl themselves into the arms of the Immaculate Virgin Mary, even now their sister according to the flesh, who wishes likewise to be their mother according to grace as she is ours!

Our Lady of Zion, pray for us!